An Intimate

Guyana

Journey

A Pomeroon Destiny Uncovered

An Intimate
Guyana
Journey

A Pomeroon Destiny Uncovered

JOSEPH MAHASE

ARPress
45 Dan Road Suite 5
Canton MA 02021

Hotline: 1(888) 821-0229
Fax: 1(508) 545-7580

Ordering Information:
Quantity sales. Special discounts are available on quantity purchases by corporations, associations, and others. For details, contact the publisher at the address above.

Printed in the United States of America.

ISBN-13:	Paperback	979-8-89356-401-3
	eBook	979-8-89356-400-6
	Harback	979-8-89356-402-0

Library of Congress Control Number: 2024902496

Contents

Dedication

This book is dedicated to my wife, Maria,
my daughter, Wenonah Rosa, and my son, José-María.

A NOTE FROM THE AUTHOR

The story is built on the experiences that I have shared or witnessed among families in a very unique part of the country. The names and characters are fictional and do not represent anyone living or dead. The story records the life of a family spanning roughly a hundred years, 1873–1972, covering four generations. It is set in the Pomeroon River District of Guyana, South America, starting with an affair around 1905 by Rafa de Melo, the great grandfather of Vernon Atkins, the story's protagonist. This triggered an unpredictable and emotional life's journey of the family that culminates in the 1972 marriage of Vernon to his childhood sweetheart.

PROLOGUE

His life as boatman and boatbuilder emerged out of his love for the different styles of boats he grew up seeing in the waterways of the northwest area of Guyana, his homeland. The rivers and creeks there traverse a landmass in what seems like a labyrinth carved out between the mighty Essequibo and Orinoco Rivers. His parents exposed him to the beauty and simplicity of life in the Pomeroon River, instilling in him the awe and appreciation for the elements that made life unique, livable, and sustainable. The wild coast was like a teacher ever releasing lessons and reasons for his own existence each day.

The agricultural and forested lands embraced and hosted all forms of intelligent and unintelligent life, which, he learned, were not their selfish possessions but fellow pilgrims accompanying them on a journey. The water of the many rivers, creeks, and lakes ran through the land like veins of blood cleansing and nourishing all forms of life.

The ever-blowing trade winds of clean air permeated the landscape, ventilating the settlers like the diaphragm of a pipe organ airing climatic music as its mood dictated. The incessant fire of the sun, whether or not veiled with clouds, shared a divine light and warmth for mind, matter, and spirit.

Not least of them, the open sky showed him how infinite this universe was, a firmament laden with countless planets and stars, reminding him of his smallness and the distance of the journey they had embarked upon families and generations ago reaching for the skies. They told him that he came from afar, a far away place and time. He had traveled long distances and stopped at hemispheric and cosmic ports of call. He had sailed through eons, acquainting with various types of knowledge and memories. And yet, the journey he had embarked upon continued, this time in a land as beautiful as any he would ever see—Guyana.

Vernon Atkins lived the life of a full-time boatbuilder and a part-time boatman, ferrying passengers along the Pomeroon River. He also ventured out across to the Moruka and the northwest settlements from time to time when he was called upon to do so and for the right price. The right price must always include a restating and rekindling of his desire to traverse once more the many waterways his family traveled in generations gone by. He had occasionally sped across the Atlantic stretch from the Pomeroon mouth to the Orinoco Delta, where the experience relived in him a union with the Great Spirit of his Warrao and Arawak ancestors there in Tucopita, in San Felix, in Ciudad Guayana and Ciudad Bolivar. His family traversed those waters out of necessity and the love for this part of the South American continent and that was what still drove him. They had left their remains in dust and their energy in the elements of these parts, enhancing the beauty of the flora and fauna. He had seen and felt them around him, and he had sensed the urge to coexist with them forever, through his journey in this life and at the reunion of spirits within the infinite spirit, where every individual rejoined the all-encompassing spirit of the universe.

INTRODUCTION

In the Pomeroon region of Guyana in the fifties, people were well disposed to insights and ideas of any sort if they made life easier. However, they would not easily accept any fleeting whim and fancy presented to them. A change occurred only after insights were intensely digested. This was a viable instrument in their perennial fight against isolation, both physical and political, and poverty fueled by meager returns from the drudgery of their hard and productive farm labor. This isolation bred in them a unique culture, only the keen eye seemed to recognize, of difference and indifference to the rest of the country. People in the Pomeroon were not bound together in village communities that dictated how they conventionally lived worked and played. Instead, a community for them was something they chose to construct out of convenience when and where it mattered. A tacit agreement of this principle of interaction was the bond that sealed a unity among them and gave them the license to be different, if they so chose to, without sanction.

There was exuberant nationalism expressed openly but only to mask the covert autonomous lifestyle and even independence from governance wielded by Georgetown, the national capital. A recipe of hard work on the farms, general honesty among friends and neighbors and liberal, uninhibited camaraderie, fun, and intercourse in both the public, private, and personal domains molded the way of life in the Pomeroon. This provided a recipe for unique innovative growth in a part of what was termed the hinterland of the county.

Life was centrally celebrated at Charity, the port of call for all the settlements and inhabitants of the Pomeroon River basin and for the neighboring coastal townships and villages that depended on the region for a large part of their food. It was the central hub in the northwest of the country, connecting that area with Georgetown and more unassumingly with the Venezuelan frontier towns. Charity, even in those days, showed signs of a natural pole for spherical influence.

The common liberal mindset of the people stayed unchallenged. They would listen to influential political leaders, whose seemingly hollow discourses hardly made a noticeable impact on how they lived their lives; they made decisions despite state influence. Not even the many established and less established churches could curb their kind of idiosyncratic way of reasoning and deciding. The sphere of church influence peeped out on Sunday but only for the few who cared to go to church services more out of tradition than need, duty, or profound conviction. As a result, the churches had an insignificant impact on the lives of the Pomeroon populace and barely survived on their monetary subscriptions. What did have some subtle and real influence on the people were the two main rum shops, the name used for pubs. One was found closely adjacent to the rustic *stelling* or port wharf, and the other at the crudely exotic edge of the seminal township of Charity, where the Amazon Creek meets the Pomeroon River. The latter's quiet seclusion attracted the younger set. It afforded a welcome rendezvous for fun-loving and secretive acquaintances.

The churches, pubs, retail marketplace stalls, grocery shops, and the produce sales and trading post at the stelling were the central points of attraction for households every weekend. Monday, however, was the highpoint of the week. The rum shops were always a hive of activities. Gathering at the larger one, men of all ages looked through lenses of alcohol-glazed eyes, adoring the women passers-by. Rum and Coca Cola or rum and ginger ale, along with a profusion of cold beer and *pak-pak,* a barreled Madeira wine, were a delight to look forward to on the market days after a hard week on the family farms. They injected a pungent dose of self-confidence into the usually taciturn farmer folks and awakened the ability for conversation, commentary on, and analysis of any subject matter. The women, for some reason, were rarely seen in the main pub and only a small number of younger women in the corner one. The male folks, however, would make a beeline to these watering holes, so to speak, as soon as they completed their farm and produce transactions. This certainly equipped them with the means to enjoy a break from a week-long, sun-burning or rain-drenched labor on the farms.

The women and other family members who accompanied them to do the household shopping enjoyed the pleasure of meeting up with family and friends and strangers, ready to catch up with the major events and news, and for a juicy gossip or a laugh. On those days, the women liberated themselves temporarily from the cooking chores in their homes and settled for feeding their families at one of the various cook-shops or casual eating joints. People in easy access to Charity extended the frequency to two or three times a week. Riverside grocery cafes spread throughout the region equally serviced those who lived farther upriver and downriver. These also provided beer parlors that served as cherished drinking rendezvous points. In this riverain region of Guyana, they were the de facto community centers.

The riverside parlors were the centers of recreation, political analysis, social commentary, economic decision-making, and, not least, family planning. A lot of the dating among youths and young adults happened at these places and then often prolonged romantically in canoes, called *corials* locally, and *ballahoos*, a unique Pomeroon built boat, drifting along the river. Many a union was initiated at those parlors, and similarly, many met their downfall there. Many a conception was triggered there, as were the many fistfights over accusations of betrayal among both friends and foes and their women. Moreover, many a household was brought to near bankruptcy by the magnetism of these parlors. Then it was time to return to the serious business of farming the land again—the main factor for survival in the routine cycle of Pomeroon River life.

The Essequibo public road was the mainland thoroughfare that ran from Supenaam on the left bank of the mighty Essequibo River to

Charity, the inland port on the Pomeroon River. This unpaved coastal road with its litters of potholes—many some three-feet deep—proved a brutal challenge for the few cars and busses that supplied a vital commercial and social link between Charity and the Essequibo Coast communities to Supenaam. Supenaam was a farming community up the river by that same name that ran into the Essequibo River. Less populated than the Pomeroon, with farming on a smaller scale, Supenaam was strategic because it was the beginning of the public road, a riverfront Essequibo River community, and served at that time as an emergency point of departure to Parika, some twenty miles across the river mouth on the other bank. Small launches and ballahoo boats propelled by outboard engines would sometimes make the trip to Parika for an escalated price when needed. Access was made easier from Parika to the capital city of Georgetown than farther away from the Essequibo Coast, and so, it became a strategic and pivotal port of call from the Essequibo Coast and Pomeroon communities, if only as a transit point.

Supenaam's importance was overtaken by the communities of Adventure, Suddie, and Anna Regina on the Essequibo Coast. Adventure was the major government Transport and Harbours port at the mouth of the Essequibo River, from where a publicly run passenger and car ferry plied twice daily to Parika. The ferry stopped in those days at the Wakenaam, Hogg, and Leguan Islands before ending its journey at Parika. Suddie was the local government headquarters for the Essequibo Coast, with the office of a commissioner representing the national government. It also accommodated the major public hospital that handled most serious cases across a wide swathe of coverage, from the Essequibo Islands and Coast to the Pomeroon and Moruca regions. Anna Regina housed a large-scale rice milling factory, said to be the largest in the hemisphere then, surrounded by expansive rice fields. It was the center of the largest population concentration on the Essequibo Coast and a must-stop point for most of the traffic plying the Essequibo Coast road to and from Adventure and Supenaam. It was a center with untold prospects for growth and development.

While the coastal communities on the Essequibo Coast struggled to endure the ordeals of using the Essequibo Coast road in its poor condition, those in the Pomeroon were considered to be lucky to have a pristine and naturally well-kept highway—the beautiful river. A deep and navigable tidal river, it accommodated boats from large ocean-going cargo vessels to the locally made wooden *bateau* and ballahoos and the humble but desirable dugout corial. The river and its various tributaries were the only transport channels that moved people and the ever-flowing farm produce yields from the fertile river basin plantations.

Coffee, coconuts, cacao, citrus, bananas and plantains, tropical roots and tubers, like cassava, sweet potatoes, yams, dasheen, and tania, cayenne peppers, vegetables, and a large variety of fruits were some of the produce the farmers would boat to the markets at Charity. Logs and cut lumber also formed a significant commodity brought to this port on rafts floated down the river. From there, the produce would be loaded onto seagoing vessels for the city and urban markets around the country and even to some of the Caribbean islands. On returning, the vessels brought back essential goods not produced locally to Charity and the Pomeroon. This, in turn, enabled this region to serve as a hub of activities for replenishing supplies in the northwest of the country. This factor largely accounted for the special place the Pomeroon played in the life of Guyana.

The unique position of the Pomeroon grew out of the progressive and liberal mindset and initiatives of its people. This region started to be an ethnic melting pot, as new farmers made their way there acquiring abandoned plantations and escalating farm production. Making an honest and practical living was as much the reason for attracting them as was the exotic nature of the terrain. The rolling river, the verdant coffee, and citrus groves, the constant swaying of coconut fronds caressed by the Atlantic trade winds, the untouched rainforest with the sweet smell of wildflowers all contributed to signaling a beckoning call to new aspirants to the region. The abundant river and sea fishing at the estuary of the river, as well as hunting for the *tapir* or bush cow as it was called, deer, *labba,* a pig-like rodent, *acouri or agouti*, wild hogs and turkeys and a host of other wildlife, provided another exotic mode of sustenance. So, remaining close to nature and the land was a heartening invitation to outsiders to a livelihood of peace and contentment. This perception was always what seemed to flash across the minds of visitors to the Pomeroon.

Newcomers appeared to have little trouble in fitting into a population, comprising native peoples of Carib, Arawak, and Warao tribes, descendants of Dutch planters, and African slaves, as well as early British, Portuguese, East Indians, and Chinese settlers. This composition was a true microcosm of the national population without the ethnic ghettos seen in largely single race villages and settlements across the country. Already mixed races were surfacing with beautiful children as beautiful as hybrid flowers. The racial divide rampant in the rest of the country seemed to be missing in the Pomeroon in those days. This was as noticeable as the unique, somewhat cool microclimate that fed the luscious flora and fauna. It was truly a microclimate for cosmopolitan growth in the country, genetically fusing the blood and the cultures of the region.

The growing population carried on this trait, changing those who might have entered with influences from their former backgrounds into a new breed. Pomeroon settlers were proud to uphold and exhibit this difference often through their physical toughness and their quiet sense of optimism and assurance even in the midst of their hardships. Their hardiness and resolute outlook seemed like a page torn from the book of life of the First Nations of the South American continent. The Dutch settlers met them when they first landed on the continent and built their first fort, Zealandia, at the mouth of the Pomeroon River. These native peoples were not only used to guide them in navigating the treacherous low-lying forest lands and network of waterways west, east, and south of the Orinoco River but also later to keep a tab on runaway slave workers on the newly established European plantations.

By the time this story begins, the separate colonies of Essequibo, Demerara, and Berbice each have already changed hands a few times between the Netherlands, France, and Britain. They were eventually ceded to the British and were molded into one territory called British Guiana comprised of three counties in the frame of British-styled administration. These previously separately administered territories carried over a tension between them that seemed to fester just beneath the surface. Demerara was the main satellite for metropolitan European domination and, in the new British-combined colony, retained that superior role. In turn, it became the new local metropolitan over its satellites, Berbice and Essequibo. The Dutch administrative headquarters of Stabroek was enlarged into the new capital, Georgetown. New Amsterdam, the last Dutch administrative center in Berbice, was relegated to a second-level capital town. Essequibo, with only several dispersed and relatively small concentrations of the population, was hardly seen to have a dedicated capital. Bartica, a town fifty miles up the Essequibo River at the confluence of three rivers, the Essequibo, Mazaruni, and Cuyuni, was designated the capital of Essequibo only in name. With nearly sixty percent of the land area of the new colony, Essequibo was in reality governed by a network of district commissioners responsible to the British governor in Georgetown.

The First Nations peoples or native tribes in the Pomeroon and North West Districts were made to live on so-called Indian reservations, where outsiders needed permits to enter. Yet the native peoples were free to go in and out or leave and settle elsewhere independent of the regulations of the reservations. Some did live outside of these reservations because of marriage to outsiders of various ethnic backgrounds or because of work and labor, particularly on Pomeroon farms, in the hinterland goldfields, and mineral mines. An urban drift that began to surface in the country was already having an impact on the First Nations as well.

Vernon Atkins looked back on the threads of information he had gleaned about his family's origins and tried to weave them into a mosaic in which to locate and track his own personal journey and that of four generations of his family. The past of a twenty-five-year-old boatman is not at all long in time, a mere chip from a block of manifestation from eons gone by and from generations in the northwestern area of this country. However, it placed him amidst a depth of knowledge to be grasped and understood. History has laid a foundation for him that he did not have a conscious hand in molding. It had been the springboard catapulting him into the present condition. Each of several high and low points in his life were contributing to his understanding of who he was, of what he was made, and to where he was trying to go. There never seemed to be answers for why some events happened, were happening, or would happen the way they did.

However, the legacy of his family's life, which he was carrying forward, was seen as a reliving of the memory and consciousness of fragments from the universal spirit of life and love. Those sparks of light within his family had continued to guide them back into harmony with the infinite light of the universal spirit. This, he thought, would only be fully understood in a reunion with that spirit of the universe, as his native heritage taught him. The journey started with the spirit sharing itself in individual beings and persons, a splintering of light and love, a self-giving of itself through the ages that would climax in its return to the togetherness of all in that spirit. This is the way he was inclined to see it.

His life had been intertwined with the waterways in the northwestern regions of the country where, from the age of three, he already fearlessly waded in the shallow parts of the mudflats of the Pomeroon banks. He was a natural swimmer and, at that tender age, never stressed himself with the lurking danger of the ravenous *pirai* or *piranha* that infested the rivers and their tributaries. No tree was too tall for him to climb like a young howler *baboon* or *sakiwinki* monkey in search of food. In his early years, he was handed a paddle to suit his small frame, and in no time, his hand and body coordination geared him to be a genuine part of the team that paddled their corial.

He had to wait though until the age of five before his mother trusted his ability to steer the slithering canoe on their way to the grocery or across the Pomeroon on his return from school. After the brief confusion and anxiety of not managing to control the circular rotation of the canoe one day turned into his eventual rapid mastery in navigating a straight course, his mother trusted him to cross the river on his own to bring his father home from the other bank as she watched from their jetty with great trepidation and expectation. The encouragement of his father bolstered his self-confidence not merely as a young boatman who could paddle his own canoe but more generally as a maturing Pomeroon native. This fortified his growing swiftly into an independent entity whose survival and wellbeing was primarily his own destiny, albeit nurtured by his elders and foreparents.

His first six years were spent in a home with his two parents, who adored each other and relied on each other for support to cope with the demanding life of farm work for a somewhat eccentric landowner. His parents were at the beck and call of Mrs. de Castro, whose reclusive life at a relatively young age pointed to an untold story hidden behind the walls of her aloofness. She was an enigma with a kindness masked only by her reticence and economic dialogue with his father on whom she depended to operate her estate and simultaneously work as a field hand, a laborer. She always appeared to have a softer outlook toward Vernon's mother but seemed slow to engage her in casual conversation. She regularly handed her a plate of cooked food and other commodities they could not afford, almost like displaying an embarrassment for herself having something that his family could not dream of acquiring. She never invited them to the inside of her house.

Over time and subsequent to life-changing circumstances in his family, Mrs. de Castro began to open up gradually to the young Atkins. She became the most charming persona in his life and a surrogate beacon on his sojourn for the truth about his past. She also became a valued sounding board and prop as he faced the unfolding of the present and future meanderings and groundings in his life's odyssey. Morsel by morsel, she fed him the secrets of his family's past over four generations, and this, in turn, provided him with a mirrored picture of his family's foundation. This provided a symbolic explanation, if not justification, for his own life experiences.

So, his story is told while he marvels at the beauty of nature revealed in the romantic setting of the Pomeroon and the northwest of his country, reeling in awe at the endless movement of the river—one time going north and another time going south, like ridiculing the boredom and monotony of a one-dimensional journey through life. Yet it stands mighty and unstoppable, treacherous and benevolent to the populace that uses it day and night, as if it were a prostitute only returning to it the useless excesses and remains of pleasure, they dispatch.

His story is told while he shivers in wonderment at the cool of the river nights as he listens to the swishing rains on the troolie palm thatch of their cabin *logie* and the pitter-patter on the galvanize roof and glass windows of the big house next door—a contrast that have been part and parcel of the culture of his family. His story is told while he marvels at the stately purpleheart, crabwood, and cabacalli trees in the verdant rainforest, standing proudly like ghosts of their ancestors, providing a shadow for their secrets and their survival, and while he listens to the cackling of the *marudi* bird joining the crowing cocks to awaken the working sinews of Pomeroon men and women at dawn. His story is told while he hears the songs of the pretty *kiskadee* and the blue *sackie* birds, reminding him of the beautiful people who had entered and left his life and those he longed to entertain again. He is awed at the noisily screeching but gorgeous parakeets and Amazonian macaws and parrots feeding on a *manicole* palm tree, highlighting the boasting of achievements and cries of burdens borne by his brothers and sisters in this beloved part of his native land.

Moreover, his story is told while he salutes the spectacular sunrises on the glistening Pomeroon, unashamedly exposing the hidden secrets of love and hate, of intimacy and passion, and a lack of leaders' concern for the less endowed and less privileged of the land, and his story is told while he watches the magnificent sunsets at the dying day, bringing the curtain down on his fulfilled and unfulfilled aspirations and those of his family.

CHAPTER 1

A MOTHER'S ABSENCE

Vernon's mother's absence was beginning to tell on his peace of mind. She was away for less than a week, but it felt like he had not seen her for an era. She was the guiding light in his life. He spent most of his days in her sweet, refreshing company. A boy, then, of age six could understand what true mother's love was. When her hugs enveloped his tiny frame, her warm presence spoke volumes of her joy of being his mother. He, in turn, believed that she was the greatest human being in his entire world, someone who would be by his side through thick and thin. Hers was a manner of calm and patience, never of rebuke but of tranquility, presenting options and alternatives, which, at his tender age, he was learning fast to discern. He missed her most acutely in the evening time when his father came from the citrus groves and coffee fields and joined them for dinner and their usual pre-bedtime family gathering. She would sit in a rattan-type *tibiciri* rocking chair with him in her lap, as if he was still the baby she rocked to sleep when he was tiny. She either hummed a country and western tune or told him interesting stories only she seemed to know until his eyelids were heavy with sleep. His mother's attention to his comfort was only interrupted by his father's pensive and affectionate interjections, which started a conversation between his parents. The tender joy of his parents being so close together filled him with warmth and security that began to nurture in his contentment and mental fortitude from those early years.

Most evenings, they sat in the soft dim light of a kerosene lantern, musing the thrill and adventure of a closely-knit family seeking out a livelihood in the heart of the Amazonian rainforest. He had never seen a grandparent and pictured that they had to be like his devoted parents. His mother spoke of her mother, who died of malaria when his mother was only ten. She never spoke of her father, and he wondered why but never questioned her. Perhaps he was too young for such an inquiry. It was his mother who told him how his father's parents drowned in the Moruka River when his dad was just a young bachelor. His father spoke very little of his family, and it was only later in life that he realized that his reticence was expressive of a heavy burden he bore in a noisy vacuum in his heart.

His mother's family were farm hands, who sought work as seasonal laborers tending the farms in the Pomeroon wherever they could find work and a *logie* for shelter during their contract. Theirs was a life of hard work and frugality. After a stay in the Pomeroon for a few months, they would pack their few belongings in their corial, and the long journey back to Kamwatta area in the Moruka River would begin. Their savings covered them until they needed to return, engendering their never-ending Gypsy-like existence. Her mother and relatives paddled their way to the mouth of the Pomeroon and hitched their boat to a mangrove tree there until the tide was low and the trip across the Atlantic stretch from Pomeroon to Moruka was safe to make. That patch of the ocean at the estuaries of the two rivers was known to be rather treacherous. Small engine-driven boats and paddling canoes must travel the shallow channel and ensure that they did not hit any of the hidden dead tree stump *takouba* and run the risk of capsizing. Venturing out further into the deep would only pit them against high choppy waves that would not guarantee a safe passage.

Once they entered the Moruka, they would stop at the beautiful landing of the trade store owned by a gentleman originally from the Essequibo Coast, who allowed travelers like his father's and mother's family to moor their boats without a fee or conditions as to time. The more passers-by who moored there and used the wharf as their camp for the time they spent there meant a constant flow of customers, a win-win situation for both the owner and the visitors.

Consequently, this post at the mouth of the Moruka, just a short distance from the mouth of the Manwarin Creek, was reputed for building friendships among many travelers in the region. The Manwarin Creek ironically runs back into a branch of the Pomeroon called Akawini, and while it is a possible route to the farms in the Pomeroon, it is hardly used for this purpose because of its narrow and winding nature. After a long and unhurried trip back to the Kamwatta area, stopping at the Anglican mission at Waramuri, the Catholic Mission of Santa Rosa, and the government post at Aquero, his mother's family would arrive at their remote hamlet of Parakese. The bitter cassava crop they planted months before they left for work in the Pomeroon would have matured enough for them to harvest. They would then begin the processing of this harvest into a sauce, called *casareep,* used for cooking and keeping the wild meat and fish they caught, into cassava bread, and into starch for textile. These would supplement their regular food consumption and provide surplus products for trading on their next trip to the Pomeroon. That was the pattern of the routine existence of many Arawak and Warrao people, especially those who did not benefit socially from living in a formal "Indian" reservation community.

That night, he did not feel the same wonderment he cherished being rocked to sleep in his mother's arms. His father was doing his best to replace his mother's natural way of caring. Denis Atkins was aware of the huge vacuum left in his son's heart by his mother's absence. His sensitivity to Vernon's sadness was noticeable as he tried to divert his son's attention from wandering into a dreamlike search for his mother's caress. His lack of success betrayed his own angst of missing the presence of his wife, Anita, every time they sat together before going to sleep.

Vernon vaguely recalled how, one night, his father broke into storytelling, recounting how a young man met a beautiful, shy girl at the Moruka mouth landing, where various families met on their way to and from the Pomeroon. He really believed his father was genuinely telling a bedtime story, coaxing him to turn into bed. Later in life, he was to hear that story again from his father in more realistic details. It was his parents' own story.

Then the inevitable happened. A swell of tears burst forth as Vernon quietly began to ask for his mother. "Where did you take her, Daddy? Why has she left me alone? I need my mom!"

Denis sullenly replied, "You are not left alone, son. Am I not here with you? You know how much your daddy loves you, as much as your mom does. I too want her back home with us very soon. I miss her so much!"

"Where is she, Daddy," Vernon asked through a broken-hearted whimper. "When will she return? Can't we go and bring her home tomorrow?"

His father responded unenthusiastically, "Your mom has gone away to see if she could bring you a little brother or sister. She is with your uncle and aunt, my family, at their home downriver. She needs their help to get a beautiful baby boy or girl for us. She is carrying that child in her tummy and must get help to take it out. Your auntie Winifred knows an old woman who delivers new babies. But that takes a bit of time. Tomorrow, while you are at school, I will go and see how they are doing and try to speed up this visit. If all is well, I will bring them back with me."

That explained the reason why his mother had become so heavy and round. She was unable to caress him at night in the last weeks in her rocking chair as she regularly did. However, for a moment, a ray of joy flashed across his mind as he thought of his mother's imminent return and the added expectation of having another one to play with. His query was answered, but the torment of his mother's absence was hardly attenuated. No one could ever fill or was filling her place at this moment in his reckoning. That his father would go and look her up the following day was promising for him, and bringing her home with a new baby would repair all the brokenness he was suffering since she had left last weekend. He was hoping for this to become a reality when he returned from school the next day.

Denis Atkins took his son in their corial to a short distance down the river on the other bank from their home across to the *koker*, at that end of the Charity township. From there, he daily joined other students and proceeded to the Charity Catholic Mission School. The koker was the sluice gate at the head of a drainage canal, the people colloquially called a trench, running into the river. Charity was protected by three such kokers that served to keep the low-lying settlement dry and above the water level of the river. A fair-weather dirt dam on the bank of the river doubled as a levee and as a walking thoroughfare from the Amazon Creek at Charity. This road passed through the cemetery and extended through private farms for over a mile downriver. It was only used publicly up to where the private farms began. The private lots of farms were called "grants." The term survived from the days when the Dutch and later British administration parceled out plots of virgin land and granted them without cost to eligible planters. Those were the early pioneers in the Pomeroon. Many of the sugar, coffee, and tobacco plantations were later bought by newcomers in an abandoned state and converted into new flourishing coconut, citrus, coffee, fruit, and food farms.

Vernon went to school that morning with a heart heavy with pain and a mind full of anxiety and expectation. His mother would return home later that day and that should give him a reason for excitement. But nothing before then was able to ease the sadness he was feeling. His teacher, Gloria, asked him why he was so grim all day. His friends Albert and Leander tried to engage him in a cricket session of "get-ball-bowl" cricket by giving him a handicap of batting first. But even his favorite pastime did not appeal to him. He had been merely picking at his meals since his mother left home and deep down was hungry. His classmate Adele van Sertima offered him some of the mouth-watering snacks she brought from their cake shop, the term commonly used for snack outlets. His parents took him sometimes to this venue when they visited Mrs. van Sertima. She was one of the few friends of Portuguese mixed-race origin with whom his mother always seemed to be so happy and comfortable. Adele's offering looked tempting. The red-colored grated coconut filled *salara* sweet bread, the meat patties, or the pineapple tarts on a different day would have been gladly accepted. Adele was always so generous to him. But today, her generosity did not feel so fantastic. The gap left by not having his mother home for three days was too big to be filled or to dispel from his worried mind, and this destroyed any appetite for food. He would find joy once more only when he felt the soft and warm kiss of his mother on his cheek and behold her radiant smile consuming his entire being. Then he would smile again.

He was impatient. The day seemed too long at school. He was eager to go home hoping to reunite with the love of his life, his mother. The group he followed to the koker trench landing were the children of his neighbors from the range of farms on the opposite bank of the river from Charity. A range referred to several functional farms between two densely forested expanses. Cora and Krishna were usually the leaders, walking faster ahead of the others. Valerie, Bernie, Savitri, and Kayla would bring up the rear, and Vernon would usually be in this group. However, that day, he lingered many paces behind the group. He felt that none of them or being in the company of the group could alleviate the pain of his aloneness. He thought that by the time he arrived at the landing, they would all be picked up by their respective families and his father would be left waiting for him. Only in his father was he able to find some companionship in this hour of sadness and forlorn. Denis understood how his son felt because he, too, was missing Anita and was grieving her absence.

He was surprised to find Valerie and her mother waiting in their *ballahoo* boat there, his father nowhere to be seen. He suddenly sank into a fit of deep depression with tears welling up in his eyes. He was being enshrouded in a depth of despair when Valerie's mother spoke to him in a gentle tone. "Come into our boat, Vernon. Your dad has asked me to collect you today and take you to your aunt Madeline. You will stay with her until he returns with your mother."

This was the first time he had heard of the widow in the big plush house next to theirs as his aunt. He was under the impression that they were merely a laborer family living and working on her farm. But his mother did on occasions refer to her as Aunty Madeline. But she more often spoke of her as Mrs. de Castro. His father always addressed her as "Missy" when she inspected the produce he harvested and loaded for the market and when he returned with the cash from the sales.

A strange emotion overcame Vernon. Never had he entered the house of Mrs. de Castro. The nearest to doing that was accompanying his father to the small kitchen room downstairs where Denis interacted with her and where he was paid weekly. She was always polite to his father and appeared to be a strange but kind-hearted woman. Most times, Vernon sat quietly and well behaved at the front door of that room on the lower of two steps outside. His mother seldom went next door or engaged with Mrs. de Castro in any deep conversation or long visits. She merely delivered some of the food supplies they bought each week at Persaud's grocery with a modicum of verbal interaction. Vernon was confused at the thought of staying with a woman he hardly knew and whom he was more inclined to look up to with reverent temerity and respect. He could not fathom the significance of staying with her in her house; its lavish look seemed incomparable to their humble thatched dwelling. This was surely very much out of the ordinary for him.

Valerie's mother, Mrs. Marjorie James, first took him to their home and served him a snack, which he reluctantly nibbled at, leaving most of it uneaten. She did not demand that he finish it. She was a kind and matter-of-fact woman, who always seemed to enjoy the company of her daughter. She and Valerie acted more like sisters than a mother and daughter. They lived without a husband and father. The story seldom told was that her Guyanese-Panamanian partner ditched her soon after Valerie was born and left with his family back to Central America. Marjorie James scarcely spoke of Valerie's father, and there was no certainty if she was ever married to him. She lived and brought up her daughter on her parents' neighboring farm a short distance downriver. She maintained a good neighborly relationship with everyone on the adjacent farms but spent more time with Mrs. de Castro and Denis Atkins. She and Mrs. de Castro were bosom friends. In later years, Vernon more clearly understood the affinity between Madeline de Castro and Marjorie James. They both had to bear the setback of losing a partner in their young adulthood.

She handed Vernon a small travel bag his father had packed with his belongings. "I will accompany you now to your aunt Madeline. I will pick you up for school in the morning at her landing. So be ready and wait for Valerie and me. We'll give you a shout from the landing."

Mrs. de Castro came down to the kitchen room to greet them when Valerie's mother knocked. She thanked her for bringing Vernon to her. As Valerie's mother left, Mrs. de Castro took his hand and said, "Come on, son, let's go upstairs. Let me show you to your room."

Her welcoming demeanor for a fleeting moment dispelled the fear and dread that arrested the young Atkins over the thought of coming to stay at her house. She did not at all seem to him now as that woman with the quiet but overpowering presence and personality his father dealt with each day. She was most endearing. Yet he wondered how real this was and what was behind it all, especially at a time when the preference of having his mother was more paramount in his tortured heart.

"I hope you like fried Banga Mary," Madeline invited Vernon. "We are going to have some 'boil and fry' plantain, cassava, and eddo." This dish of softly boiled ground provisions was fried in hot oil and mixed together seasoned with a generous amount of onions and garlic. "There is some leftover pepper pot and some freshly fried Banga Mary fish to go with that. If you prefer, you could have a little leftover cook-up rice with black-eyed peas also. You could have that with the Banga Mary."

Vernon's family frequently ate Banga Mary fish at home, especially cooked in casareep sauce as a pepperpot dish. From time to time, his father and a friend would travel to the river mouth with fish lines, a small trawling net, and pin seine packed into the large wooden boat used normally for transporting Mrs. de Castro's produce to the market. They spent a day and a night there securing a catch. They would then return towards Charity, sounding their conch shells, which echoed a long distance ahead of them, announcing to the neighborhoods they had fish for sale. Banga Mary, butterfish, queriman, gillbacker, shad, cuirass, mullet, snapper, and shrimps were some of the catch that they would sell along the way after they had put aside portions for their own home needs.

Often the catch was sold out before they reached Charity, and when they did have some for the demand at Charity, the crowds that assembled at the port to buy the fresh fish far outweighed what was available. Vernon's mother would spend many hours that day cleaning the batch of fish his father dropped off on his way to Charity. A large part of it was salted and dried on the open fire *babricut* Anita built at the riverside. This was an unassuming smoker built as a platform of green bush wood covered with coconut fronds and fired by a slow wood fire. The fruits of this tiring but effective labor of necessity lasted them until his father's next trip to the Atlantic. Part of it was given to Mrs. de Castro, presumably as the tariff for the use of her boat.

Mrs. de Castro placed two plates of food side by side on the table in her dining-room kitchen upstairs. The table pressed against the wall separating this room from the living room was used as both a dining table and a kitchen counter for preparing the food to be cooked. She pulled one of the two chairs at the table and ushered Vernon to sit there. She occupied the other and bade him with a smile to enjoy the meal.

"You will have a glass of Ovaltine later before you go to bed."

He had not had much to eat since his mother left and continued to have no appetite. His stomach was empty, but the anguish of missing his mother somehow restricted much of an intake. It was difficult to swallow anything. Soon he was finished, and at attempting to rise from the table, she disappointingly said in an apologetic tone, "You've eaten very little, my son. Don't be afraid of me, darling. We are family even though I have taken too long to acknowledge this. I wish I had a more intimate relationship with your mother and with your grandmother, God rest her soul." Then in a low tone, she mumbled, "She was my sister after all, and I, of all persons, should have judged her less before my father took her back to the Moruka. Anna Torrealba was the sister I detested, and her dreams were not to come true."

Her talk with him was more of a soliloquy as he listened and heard her but could not translate much of it into an experience he could understand. He was still too young, and he never knew any of his grandparents, paternal or maternal. His mother, however, spoke with joy and serenity of her own mother to him. She was sad that Vernon was not fortunate to experience the fountain of love and beauty his grandmother had to impart. The way his mother described his grandmother painted in his mind the image of a beautiful woman whose Portuguese father and Spanish-Arawak-Warrao laborer mother created an angel in this world. She was beautiful, patient with people and intelligent with the most vivacious personality, and much sought after by the desirous eyes of men folks everywhere she went. He curiously wondered in his not yet mature mind if the Anna Mrs. de Castro spoke of and the one his mother referred to as his grandmother were the same.

CHAPTER 2

REMEMBERING A LITTLE-KNOWN SISTER

Mrs. de Castro's revelation of Vernon's origins was to become more freely discussed between her and him as he grew in age, intelligence, curiosity, and confidence, and as the scenario at her estate changed. He was able to note in his memory a lot of her storytelling and later slowly fitted the pieces of the jigsaw into a more comprehensive picture. This is the basis on which he could recount the story of the journey of his ancestors:

Rafa de Melo loved Sonya, Anita's grandmother, the seasonal farmhand whose parents, Augustine and Verna Torrealba, were regular workers at the Rafa de Melo's farm. He lived with this secret weight in his heart. He overtly hid his feelings and urges toward the native maiden for as long as he could.

Madeline grew up believing that she was the only one apple of her father's eye. It was not until his beloved wife, Mona, passed on that Rafa de Melo's loneliness shocked his foundations. He consequently began to disclose the surprise to his growing daughter.

Madeline de Castro related how she later learned from chatting with her father in his later years how he adored Sonya but delayed revealing anything about her while Mona de Melo was still alive. She later understood that he could not entertain her in his home. He was forced to choose between, on the one hand, the wife he had newly married and their daughter, and on the other, the seasonal farmhand he loved and wanted, whose family worked at Grant Miriam's Delight. In the end, Mr. de Melo chose what a notable and distinguished member of the Catholic community would choose amidst the threat of social pressures. He chose his wife and daughter in the open and, very discreetly, the native maiden in the secret of his heart. Or perhaps more clearly in the given context, he chose both in his own inimitable way.

Throughout her later years, Madeline de Melo never ceased to acknowledge her guilt for not treating her half-sister, Anna Torrealba, with any real sisterly love after her father disclosed the truth to her. She held a quiet disdain for Rafa de Melo for betraying her mother, as she put it. She also felt that when Anna Torrealba later came to live in Rafa de Melo's household, she had reason to be confused. On the one hand, her father made it clear to her that Anna was her sister. Yet to the workers and the people he dealt with every day, her arrival was seen as a favor by the magnanimous Rafa de Melo to adopt and care for an orphan girl from an Amerindian reservation.

Vernon Atkins had pieced her story together and reflected on the strange collision of two different worlds.

* * *

It was the end of the coffee crop season, one year since Augu Torrealba and his family returned to the Akawini mission after a stint of farm labor. Rafa de Melo, whose family life appeared happy, was nevertheless incomplete in his mind. He was out of sorts regularly even though he lived and worked heart and soul for his wife and their daughter, Madeline. As soon as the time for recruiting new labor drew closer, he equipped his launch with a few days of supplies and set out downriver in the name of finding labor. This boat was a comfortable live-in vessel, in which he often spent time away from home. It was on one of these trips that he traveled up the Akawini Creek, looking for his illicit Spanish Arawak-Warrao love, Sonya, to fill the void he felt after her family's stint of work on his farm.

On arriving at the mission landing, he obtained permission from the Toshao (Chief) to moor his vessel there for a few days as he gathered a band of prospective workers as labor for his coffee plantation in the upcoming harvest season. Among the party that greeted the launch, he found the familiar face of the flower that lit up his life from the very first instance he saw her in her family corial as they called in at the de Melo's jetty a few seasons earlier, looking for work. She was a very attractive rustic teenager. She had matured after two moons into a breathtaking beauty.

After a while, the curiosity of the gathering at the landing dissipated and all left, save that haunting face that deep down inside his conscience truly led him there to the mission. As he peered at her through the corner of his eyes, he recalled how it was love at first sight for him, a young married man of thirty, and how so many doubts and longing intermingled in his heart ever since. She was merely sixteen at that time when she first set foot at Miriam's Delight and awesomely ravishing. Now two years later, her beauty was tauntingly overpowering.

He began to relive the memories of the moments she spent watching him in the coffee house as he pulped the newly picked coffee berries actually picked by her and her parents, and how he felt a mutual attraction growing between them. He remembered how he yearned to hold her body close to his but never did nor physically tried to because of the proximity of her family and his own young family on the farm, and the fear of a scandal that would break loose if word of this got out. He recalled how on several occasions she touched his arm, trying to get his attention, and how he melted like a ball of ice in the warmth of the sun's rays. He feared to respond lest it was later seen as an abuse of his authority to make advances on the young woman. For Rafa, he ostentatiously lived for his wife, Mona. But in the secret recesses of his heart, he was intoxicated with love for Sonya, the light of his dreams and the smoldering fire of his passion.

"How are your parents, Sonya? Are they enjoying being back in the Akawini? And are they looking forward to working in the Pomeroon next coffee season?"

"They have often talked of your kindness while we stayed at your grant and how you treated us like family." replied Sonya. "They have worked before with people vastly different from you. Those that treated us like stupid buckman[1]. I know if they came back to work in the Pomeroon, they would wish to find another grant owner just like you. And I long to come back to your place, Mr. Rafa!"

"Why so, my dear Sonya? Why do you wish to come back to Grant Miriam's Delight?"

She laughed and said, "I don't know!" She giggled again and said, "You should know why." She then blushed into a strange silence. They both listened to the melody of that silence through steadfastly fixed eyes on each other.

Rafa de Melo was pleasantly stunned by her reply, and after a gap of pensive reflection, with eyelids drooped in astonishment, he said, "It would honestly be my debt to have you and your family back. It would be a joy to see you around for a few weeks. I wish I could have you for longer than that. That would make me happy beyond doubt." Then in sudden silence again, he uttered a painful cry deep down in his soul, "It would heal the jagged rupture in my heart and quench the thirst for the effervescence of your spirit." His lips parted once more, and he quietly asked her to inform her parents of his eagerness and willingness to secure their choice to return to Grant Miriam's Delight for the upcoming coffee picking season in three months' time. "You and your parents would always get first preference in my selection of farmhands. Perhaps your family should come earlier to work on the pruning and weeding in the orange beds. The work is getting too much for me these days."

Dusk was overtaking the brilliance of the sun's radiance on the Coca-Cola-colored water of the Akawini, and the shadow of the launch was lengthening like a ghost in pursuit of a soul's shelter to haunt it.

---

1   A derogatory label for native peoples.

Sonya looked at Rafa with eyes as if beckoning him and began to leave the landing with a smile on her face brandishing two rows of pearly white teeth. "I have to go home before it is too dark," she said. "There are a few lads who make any excuse to pester me when they have the slightest opportunity, when I am alone and away from my family. My father gets anxious when I am out, knowing their ploy. I do not want him to come looking for me. I must go."

Rafa stared at her until she disappeared behind the coconut grove and, in his imagination, caressed every sinew of her body's erotic movement as she left. He felt that this vision of her smile and her grace would indeed haunt him as he lay down to sleep alone that night in the launch's cabin.

He was alarmed about twenty minutes later by a female voice calling out to him from the jetty. Thrusting his head out of a port window, he was overjoyed to see Sonya and, for a moment, thought it was just an apparition or a mere fantasy that had begun to taunt him— or more seriously, that she had returned to escape the harassment of the boys that fancied her.

She jumped onto the front deck of the vessel and asked if she could join him in the cabin. "My father has sent me to invite you to our house and to bring you back with me since you might not remember where our home is and would find it difficult to locate it in the dark."

A tsunami of joy overwhelmed Rafa. "Of course, I will accept your family's kind invitation. Sit and wait a while. Give me a few minutes to find the bottle of wine I brought with me. I will wrap it up in a sheet of newspaper for your parents. A guest should not come empty-handed."

As he busied himself frenziedly with the packaging of the gift, Sonya touched the back of his hand and told him that no gift was necessary to come as her family's guest. In a flash, he turned over his hand and took hold of her silky-smooth palm, which was damp with sweat. She responded by submitting to his responding touch and moved her body close to his. Their lips met hurriedly as if they were objects on the edge of a precipice that easily slipped off their footing by a soft whiff of wind. It was like the same fleeting wind that casually blew Augu(stine) Torrealba, his wife, and daughter, Sonya, to Grant Miriam's Delight a few seasons ago. That wind that ever since played beautiful music in orange and coffee leaf violins whenever Sonya was near him, soothing his tired eyes to adore her elegant and rustic beauty. It lit an unquenchable fire in his soul to follow her as a disciple follows his master.

His left arm circled around her trim body under her arms and pulled her forcedly but warmly to his bosom, groins rubbing against groins. His right hand explored her round and hardened breasts, whose pointed nipples rubbed madly against his chest. His right worked its way to her groin and capped her private area. With every motion, she whimpered and quivered within a heat of joyful pain. Her hand slipped into his pants and grabbed the firmness she encountered, which erupted a wild animal urge in him. Freeing himself, he took to his knees and, as in a hurry, licked her inner thighs and wherever his intense energy led him. He sucked at the sweetness he found as if he was trying to extract every drop from a honeycomb. She reeled with excitement and felt primed as an artesian well ready to gush forth its contents into the open. One-handedly, he lowered the boat's bench extension to create a double bed and lifting her naked body lay her flat on her back. In a moment, the two bodies rhythmically gyrated from a fast rate to a faster rate and then to a climactic Krakatao-like explosion. They held each other as one and breathed a heavy breath of relief and exhilaration.

The time together with Sonya in the cabin of Rafa de Melo's launch recreated the providential garden of Serendib where carnal love originally blossomed at the beginning of time. It consummated the drive of a master to become one with his slave on an equal basis, providing liberation to both shackled spirits. Two worlds collided as they floated on the currents of energy that tugged at two unlikely heartstrings since many moons before. Now, these worlds cemented themselves in a caress of giving and taking life from the very spirit each nurtured individually in quite different surroundings. Together they fused their throbbing hearts, like two chipped splinters bonding once more to the log of universal love. As children worshipping before the eternal altar of intimacy, these two individual spirits prostrated in submission before the great spirit of infinity and worshiped in a symphony of unison and harmony that sent the darkness of the Akawini night into oblivion. Together, they sailed amidst the myriad of stars in the Milky Way and fed each other with the sweet nectar of Amazonian rainforest wildflowers as they lingered in a flight of ecstasy in each other's arms. It was a transcendental journey of spirits bound together in the liberating chains of intimacy—a fire that consumed their bodies and formed their every passionate movement into a symphony of music until it was time to proceed to Augu's home.

Rafa de Melo was filled with satisfaction. Sonya was convinced that the man she lay with was truly a real man and wished she could have him as readily as she would like. But she also understood that their relationship had to be covert. He was a man with a wife whom he was committed to as his legal and settled family. She would be stupid to try to disrupt that dedication. Rafa showed no signs of remorse for engaging this young unmarried woman. His only regret was the covert nature of his love for Sonya Torrealba. He strenuously maintained the façade of being a faithful husband to a woman who would love him for whoever he was. She lived the solemn vow they took that wonderful day of their marriage at the parish church in front of family and friends with undying satisfaction. She was prepared to stand by him in better and worse times and in the seasons of strength and weakness. Diverting scrutiny over his newly married status to a good, forgiving, and faithful woman was vital.

Their caress continued through the pitch-black darkness of the uneven gravel bush track, and as they approached the dim light of a kerosene lamp, a dog began to bark. Almost simultaneously the voice of Augu Torrealba echoed through the mango trees loud enough to disturb a *labba* (lappe) feeding on the dried seeds under the trees. The labba ran towards the approaching couple and, in a sudden fit of awareness on encountering a moving hurdle, scampered off into the brushes at the side of the track.

"Is it you, Sonya?" Augu asked.

"It is me, Father, and Mr. Rafa is with me, she answered, as the couple created a space between them before entering the house.

"Come into our humble home, Mr. de Melo. It has not changed since you last came here two years ago. You are a welcomed guest, and I always want to return something for the kindness you bestowed on us when we worked for you in the Pomeroon. Now we can only share our modesty and respect and the food we struggle with honesty to acquire. I do not think you would have had dinner yet, and it is already close to eight o'clock. So, Verna, my wife, has prepared a meal for you to share with us. She made a nice pepperpot with a *haimara* fish I caught in the creek today. Hope you like fish and *casareep* food for a change," said Augu.

"I appreciate your kindness, Augu. You have always been a hard worker and an honest man, you and your family. People like you make the best of friends. I am honored to be welcomed in your home again, something I never ever reciprocated within the two years I have known you and since the first time we ate together right here. But good friends are those that eat together, and you have been more a friend to me than me to you," replied Rafa. "It is never too late for me to make amends, and one of these days, when you are back at my place, if you are willing to come and work again, I will make it up to you."

Augu went into his kitchen cupboard and, as he was returning with a bottle, said, "First we must have a drink of a bit of *casiri*."

This fermented cassava beverage, with a pungent alcoholic strength, was often used by native peoples to initiate friendship and generate self-confidence at *kayaps*, the communal functions, and gatherings for work and celebration. It was also enjoyed whenever it was available even outside of the kayap settings.

"I was keeping this bottle for a good time like this when a friend is visiting. The bottle of *piwari* I also had only finished today when we were out line fishing further upstream. Have you ever had piwari, Mr. de Melo? I wish I knew you were coming to the Akawini. I would have kept the bottle to drink with you. Piwari is a strong refreshing drink we make from sweet potato. It is as good as or even better than the casiri, which we make from bitter cassava. I will keep some for you when you visit us next time."

"I have tasted piwari once before and did like the taste. But I'm more familiar with casiri. So, I will enjoy your hospitality tonight over this bottle of casiri," Rafa replied.

Augu distributed the bottle of casiri into four large enamel cups and called his family together. "Verna and Sonya, come out here and join in a drink with Mr. de Melo. And let us eat before it gets too late. He must be starving like me," he jested.

The meal was good and so was the company. When the last drop of casiri was sipped from each cup, Rafa rose to take his leave, thanking his hosts for the evening. Augu offered him to stay over the night rather than risk the threat of wild animals going through the track again. In his deeper inner feeling, Rafa was eager to stay over but declined. Being under the same roof with the one he treasured so much would have been the pinnacle of his joy and satisfaction for a day. However, the thought that he would be under the same roof but unable to hold the one that mattered in the presence of her parents blunted any enthusiasm emerging.

"I must return to my boat, Augu. The Toshao only gave me permission to stay there, not on the reservation," he offered as a logical and dispassionate excuse, which was far from the true yearning within him.

"Then I will walk you to the boat, Mr. de Melo. That would be fine," Augu said.

"Thank you, Augu, but don't worry yourself with coming down with me," Rafa pleaded. "I have a small flashlight with me, and I think I can easily retrace the direction through the track to the launch. I'm a Pomeroon man, you know, and we are made tough."

Nevertheless, this reassurance could not prevent Augu from taking the walk. Sonya and her mother who were listening in the background decided that they too would accompany them. This would ensure that Augu was not alone on his return to the house. For Sonya, she too was fighting the urge and magnetism to be close to Rafa de Melo every moment she could secure, as the electricity of their bonding in the launch cabin earlier was still vibrating in her young breasts and in her soul. She too was very conscious of the forbidden nature of their love in the conventional etiquette of Pomeroon society. While she so desperately and compulsively desired his strong gentlemanliness, she wondered if and how such a forbidden future would ever materialize. She would be foolish not to acknowledge the prominent place Mona de Melo and Madeline had in his scheme of things. A shade of worry already began to rattle the climax of joy she felt that day as she wondered how she could face Mona de Melo again if her family ever went back to work at Miriam's Delight. After all, she was an intruder trespassing in a legally married wife's domain. She was quietly destabilizing the promise Rafa made solemnly and religiously some five years ago, to honor his wife professing to love her without reservation.

"Here we are at my motel for the night," de Melo joked. "It is still in one piece and is holding well against the tugging falling tide. Thanks again for the evening and do get back safely to your house. Sleep well and see you tomorrow sometime before I leave in the afternoon." He was offering good night wishes to the family but, in effect, really directing a call to the flower he had plucked and pinned to the lapel of his heart.

That night neither Rafa de Melo nor Sonya Torrealba slept. It seemed like the phantoms of the night kept reminding them that the warmth and promise of intimacy were already being nipped in the bud by a rude act of destiny. The chirping of the crickets and the croaking of the bullfrog sounded like heckles at the separation they so much did not wish for but had to tolerate for political correctness. The night air that seeped through the crevices of the latticed windows of the launch's cabin created a chilling ambiance for Rafa's recasting of the fiery affection he had only so recently entertained with the dream of life. He dreaded that by the next night, he would be relocated into the reality of the family he had no doubts about caring for and loving. Yet he was struggling to establish first in his own belief that there was nothing wrong with the capacity to share his spirit in the adoration of two beautiful women. If only the value set of the Catholic community, whose pedestal he occupied, could unpack the infinite nature of love and beauty of the Divine manifested so profusely in every fragment of creation.

Sunrise was heralded by the crowing of the many cockerels on the reservation, like jeering sirens clearing the way for a manifestation of a secret that two sleepless beings were covering safely. The new day dawned brightly over their mental bliss and turmoil. A number of onlookers had come to the jetty, admiring the launch, few of whose kind ever drove into the Akawini as far as the mission. The district commissioner came in sometimes on a powerful outboard engine propelled speedboat, which was also a spectacle. The police from the Charity outpost and from Aquero in the Moruka often visited the reservation in their flashy police boats. They were greeted more with fear and suspicion regarding their true motives for frequenting the mission. For many of the coastal men, the native girls carried an aura and general infamy of being merely good operators in bed. They were shunned as prospective life partners, except when their pregnancies were in the open. Nevertheless, those who could evade the need to obtain a permit under the pretext of authority made it a habit to spend nights there. Yet despite the sometimes frank or tacit protective reaction by young men from the reservation on behalf of their women, visits from the police and other government officers continued to take place. Any visit from the outside though, broke the insular monotony of work, loitering, illicit sleeping together, and rum drinking on the reservation.

After a strong cup of Pomeroon's essence rich liberica coffee that he brewed on the pump stove on the launch, Rafa de Melo visited the Toshao around noon and gifted him a small flagon of pak-pak wine. This was a custom he maintained to preserve their friendship and the ability to visit the reservation without too much red tape. The Toshao was pleased with his gift and, pulling down the neck of the paper bag, brandished a wide smile at the purplish red wine.

"Your visit calls for a drink, Mr. de Melo. Why not let us share a bit of this gift together."

He poured the inviting brew into two glasses and handed one to Rafa. "Here's to your health and to your family's and to all your endeavors, Mr. de Melo," wished Toshao Rudy Pearson.

"And to yours, Toshao Rudy," Rafa replied to the Warrao Chief, who was getting on in age, yet with a sharp mind and a naughty sense of humor.

"This bottle is too heavy for that table and would damage it if we don't do something about it," he quipped as he replenished the emptying glasses.

The conversation and jesting between the two men had waned considerably. However, the Toshao had become rather jovial and appeared as if he was just priming up for a party. "The damn bottle must have had a hole. I can't see anything left in it," he proffered laughingly.

"I will need to bring a bigger bottle of the stuff next time, Toshao Rudy," suggested Rafa. "But that won't be until the coffee crop is over, if that's not too long for you."

"You know you don't have to wait to hire labor to have to come to Akawini. You are a friend, and you can come anytime. It's nice to see people like you here from time to time to add some spice to my boring life here. I am the head of my people here with little authority of my own. When I speak to my people at gatherings, it is the voice of the commissioner directing them all the way from Suddie. I am just his mouthpiece. And when it is not him, I must simply endorse everything the Parson at the church requests. Do you think this is how it should be?" he questioned with an ironic giggle.

Rafa de Melo was not the kind to dabble in politics and less so in church policies. He evaded the searching criticism by the Toshao masked by a few shots of pak-pak by commending him. "You are a fine leader, Toshao Rudy. Your people think and speak highly of you. You are lucky to have such a wonderful community."

This successfully diverted any further discourse of criticizing the status quo of the power over the reservation system in the country, which appeared to be the direction the Toshao was embarking on.

"But don't worry about them, Mr. de Melo," Toshao Rudy added. "Here at Akawini, we live how we want to after we listen to what they want. Deep in our hearts, we listen to the spirits of our ancestors who roamed the whole place from the Orinoco to the Pomeroon from so many eons before. They are still celebrating life with us today. And even when I am placed back in the earth in our burial mound, my spirit will join with those ancestors within the great spirit of the sun wheel to continue to come and celebrate here. Every cassava harvest kayap and every gathering of the people to help build a dwelling or something like that, we would celebrate—the whole Akawini—those of the past and those of the present."

"I always admired the Akawini people, Toshao Rudy. They have kept their past and their loved ones sacred in their memory. That's why the Amerindian way of life would not die. It must not die. There is a lot the authorities should do to protect it—the wealth and wisdom and captivating beauty of the original peoples of this country," Rafa sincerely wished, deeply inspired by the vision and memory of the intimacy of his Sonya. "I must say goodbye to you now and go back to my boat. I should prepare to return to Charity this evening." He was referring imprecisely to his estate, which was close enough to the port.

"Why are you returning so soon, Mr. de Melo? You should not miss the celebration tonight. St. John's Night is important to the Spanish-Arawak people in this country. The big celebration is usually at Santa Rosa, but we also celebrate it here. This custom of having a festivity on this night has been preserved for many years now since it was brought by families who settled here from the missions in and around Santa Rosa. We have many Arawaks and Warraos from the Kamwatta area. You would be my honored guest tonight if you stayed over for another night," said the Toshao.

"Let me give it a thought. I am thinking of how worried my wife would be with me not returning home tonight. If I decide to honor your kind invitation, you will see me tonight at the community center. Please forgive me, though, if I do decide to travel back to Charity tonight," Rafa responded graciously and took his leave.

He made his way back to the boat, knowing full well that he could have left in the morning to catch the high tide and speed up his return trip to Grant Miriam's Delight. His lingering on was for the sole motive of seeing Sonya one last time until her family made it out again to Charity. That could easily be a gap of three months, which was far too long to temper the painful wait he must endure. His visit to the Toshao was necessary but was primarily an ulterior action to kill some waiting time and afford his Sonya an additional opportunity to venture to the jetty.

He had tidied up his launch and re-packed his belongings in the bag Mona had prepared for him on setting out on this trip. He gathered the few food items he had leftover into a thick paper bag and hoped that Sonya would come to meet him, and he would personally hand it to her rather than sending it to her family by some stranger. He cleaned and primed the Kelvin diesel inboard engine that powered his launch and started up the engine, ensuring that everything was ready for his now imminent departure. He was quite despondent when by six o'clock, he had not seen any appearance of Sonya, and instead of switching off the engine, he revved it a while, as if to build up momentum, but was not at all ready to release the hitches from the jetty and move off. Such a next step would deflate the secret urge within him to stay for another night and deny both his secret plan and the Toshao's invitation.

In the distance, up the track leading to the landing, Rafa could see a lone tired-looking man approaching him. He waited in anxiety for a message from his Sonya if only that could be the case. Hearing the launch's engine, Augu, with his hand in a heil Hitler manner, hoping that the boat would wait for him, yelled, "Mr. Rafa, you are leaving."

Rafa waited for him to reach the gunwale of his boat and answered, "Just getting ready to move off." There were no curious onlookers this time, as almost everyone was gathering at the community center for the night's celebration.

"I am glad then that I caught you just in time," Augu replied with an air of achievement. "Sonya and Verna hustled me out to catch up with you and bring you to the festival at the community center tonight. We forgot to tell you about it last night, and to invite you. I have personally talked with Toshao Rudy, who is happy for you to come. Please bless us with your presence."

An invitation from Augu was just what Rafa de Melo hoped for, to dispense him from spending the evening at the Toshao's side as his guest. Being a guest of Augu instead would ensure he was close to Sonya, the only reason for his staying on. That Verna Torrealba, along with her daughter, had asked Rafa to come to the festival was an invitation he could not refuse. This was a woman who had communicated largely non-verbally and merely by smiles in her reticent and shy manner. In turn, Rafa had usually spoken to her by speaking generally to her family. He now felt that he had gained an additional level of acceptance from the very mother who shared with her daughter a deep mutual adoration. This had ratified Rafa's decision to stay a night longer.

He, nevertheless, gave a response to indicate his eagerness to return home even though, deep inside him, he knew he had a done-made decision to stay the night. He wanted to dispel any impression he might have given of his hankering to stay on and that his extra night was merely an exception.

"I had planned to leave here in an hour, Augu, and be on my way back to my family. However, now that I can see the smoke of the bonfire rising into the night sky, how could I turn my back on it and the wonderful and beautiful people of Akawini? You and your family have made me so happy and I welcome these last days! You are as much my family as the others. I will enjoy this night in your company," Rafa replied and turned off the engine.

He shut the front deck door of the boat's cabin behind him and began the light uphill trek towards the sounds of entertainment buzzing at the community center. The "mari-mari" rhythms from the twanging strings of quatros and guitars, a scratcher, a shack-shack, and a bongo drum permeated the atmosphere with revelry and frolic. A bevy of colorfully dressed young female singers, swaying in their white armless tops and wide flowing flower-patterned skirts singing along with the musicians, would have conjured up sentiments of an exotic Mexican night as seen in the films. However, Rafa was carried away in a mist of excitement as he wondered at and pondered the living reality before his eyes. He was bursting with pride at knowing that this was not the fantasy of an orchestrated film show but a spontaneous celebration of joy, beauty, and togetherness right there in his country. The strumming of the instruments, the melodies exuding from the voices of native young women, and the soft light of the crescent moon glistening on the creek water told him that there was so much to love about his country. Guyana was indeed a beautiful place to live in despite the pervasive poverty, corruption, and the wanton greed of those with any kind of power and authority.

"Oh, beautiful Guyana. Oh, my lovely native land!" he whispered under his breath with gratitude. "Dearer to me than all the world and more so because of the radiant jewel with which she has illuminated my life!"

Rafa de Melo could not help but admire the work of the Toshao and his organizing group for the program that was unfolding. The singing, the dancing, the jokes, the stories, and the walking of young men and women on live embers, as well as various group performances and recounting of tribal lore and memories from different sections of the community, showcased a performance he had not experienced before.

It was a world his Portuguese heritage was not too familiar with, scarcely daring to venture out of their narrow Madeiran influenced customs, which was subsumed into their local Catholic traditions. Sonya had made this native heritage all become a part of him—just a short distance away apart from the core of his everyday Portuguese existence—but truly a vivid outpouring of a tiny part his bloodline that had become forgotten. His first foreparent lived with or might have been formally married to an Amerindian girl in the absence of Madeiran girls when the Portuguese first came to Guyana. Madeiran girls, who would have been preferable among the Portuguese migrants to the colony, were in short supply at that time.

The new generation emerging from those early unions downplayed that native part of their heritage in their ethnic community for reasons that tried to separate them from what they considered an inferior and backward race. They prided themselves as true sons and daughters of Portugal and, as soon as the opportunity came again, married largely within their own ethnic group. Later, because of the cessation of immigrants from Portugal and its territories, the so-called Portuguese community further dispersed into mixed family unions. The outcome of this was to gift the northwest of the country with a new generation as beautiful as the different and exotic shades of flowers in the Amazon basin. But a small group still strove to preserve their Europeanness and ignored the other ethnic traces of their past.

As the festivities continued into the night, there was a profusion of local indigenous alcoholic beverages, whose influence was soon noticed when the program of the evening transformed into a revelry of spontaneous entertainment. Shyness and fear to act and perform in any way whatsoever were vanquished by shot after shot of various drinks, resulting in the outpouring of a zest for life and living under the canopy of the South American rainforest.

Augu had had his fair share of imbibing as bottles of various spirits were passed around. Each recipient leaned his head backward and released a measured quantity down his throat. Later, a bottle of rainwater was used in the same way to chase down and dilute the fiery sensation in their throats. He turned and quietly whispered in Rafa de Melo's ear, "Do you want to try a bit of 'bushy'?"—the label commonly used in the area for illegally distilled spirits.

"I have tried the thing before, and for some reason, it did not like me, although I quite liked it," Rafa replied likewise in Augu's ear as Verna looked and wondered what was being said. "I'd prefer not to indulge this time and keep my head clear for an early start in the morning," continued Rafa.

Then out of nowhere, the beautiful smile of Sonya appeared before them, like an apparition of an angel coming to announce a mysterious message. "Are you having fun, Mr. Rafa? I wish I had more time with you and my parents. I had to stay with the musicians all day today rehearsing and, tonight, singing with them. It is fun to have these celebrations. The people in Akawini look forward to them." She moved closer between her mother and Rafa so that she could whisper in his ear. "I so much wanted to visit you in the launch today, Mr. Rafa, so that I could feel your body close to mine one more time before you left. I was deep in thought of you all day today, which prompted the members of our singing group to ask me several times if I was ill. I missed you so much. What will I do without you, Mr. Rafa?" she sobbed.

Rafa leaned over her ear and replied, "I am missing you so much, Sonya, that every sinew in my body hurts and my mind is in turmoil over the beauty you have brought into my life." Only a strong will power prevented him from hugging her and wrapping her within his bosom even for a fleeting moment.

"I must leave early in the morning, and so I should return to the boat and have a rest before I do. It is long past midnight, and I can hear the paddles on the gunwales of the corials. People are leaving. I must go too," Rafa reiterated.

The moonglow was fast disappearing, and the flambeaus were all but one out of fuel. The lone flambeau light and the pale glow of the embers of the bonfire created an ambiance, which a few young lovers were treasuring. Every celebration like this was an opportunity to share romantic time together without the scrutiny and gossip of the small reservation community in the everyday run of activities. There were joy and freedom resulting from the flow of alcohol largely across the board engaging male and female, young and old. It bridled the wandering eyes and chained the garrulous lips at least for a while and allowed a spatial corridor for hearts to explore one another.

Rafa and Sonya, however, could not help but see themselves as prisoners incarcerated in a dungeon of love that was hidden away that moment when even eyes around them were blind to the secret lovers' serenade that had begun to swallow them. Augu and Verna tried to communicate with their daughter their eagerness to retire to their house, which was only a short way from the center. Like a Gypsy reading from her crystal ball, Sonya seemed to read their minds and spoke to them, "Father, I will stay a little longer with Mr. Rafa and join you shortly. Mr. Rafa will walk me home, okay?" she said in a rhetorical question.

Augu, who was quite happy and without inhibition after a night of revelry with his friends, turned and hugged Rafa de Melo. Verna

Torrealba was similarly relieved of her taciturn nature if only for the night. She also turned to Rafa, hugged him, and pressed a loud kiss on his cheek. In no time, they were out of sight, and Sonya did not spare to clasp Rafa's hand in hers and caress it. Instantly a large voltage of electric energy bolted through them and thrust them into a hunger for another taste of intimacy like the evening before.

Sonya quietly spoke as if she had a message for the creek, "Let's walk to the landing and watch the never-ending flow of the Akawini. Tomorrow it will take you away from me, back to Mrs. de Melo and your daughter, and leave me in an abyss of longing for you, Mr. Rafa. And I am not sure if it will bring you back again too soon. She is a lucky woman. I respect her, and without any venom, I envy her. I wish I were in her place to have and to hold you not for what you have but for who you are. Love has brought us together, while fate wants to keep us apart."

They were only steps away from the jetty and the launch, none of whose lights were on. Rafa led her into the cabin without lighting his flashlight and closed the door behind them. Both were speechless and engrossed in an embrace of wild silence. They were as intoxicated as the revelers at the festivity that night, although only with the nectar of passion and deep intimacy. In a moment, they sailed off on a cloud of intense pleasure, giving each other a fullness and completeness that drained the very life in their limbs. Rafa could hear the pounding of Sonya's heart as loudly as she could the throbbing of his. Every time he feigned to withdraw from her consuming clutches, she drew him back into her bosom, entreating him to stay firmly within the sacred cavity of her being. They traversed the paths of paradise and ate all the forbidden fruit they found, feeding each other with gay abandon. His exploration into the very core of his angel's soul rushed them into the climax of a journey that had just begun.

Benumbed, an anguished, Rafa opened ajar a side window of the cabin and stared and marveled at the stars as Sonya lay in silence on his shoulder. Aware of the shortness of night, with dawn lurking just around the corner, he gently tried to awaken the sleeping Sonya drunk from the fountain of their intimacy. In Rafa's mind, a covenant was made with this his messenger of love even without a party from the church or state witnessing it as they did when his union with Mona was solemnized. He was convinced that the divine spirit had witnessed and sealed their covenant, repealing any semblance of detachment between them with a call to begin an odyssey of love. He believed that he must walk the avenues of life hand in hand with two sparks of beauty that had detached from the great spirit of love and came into his life. He must stand up to the forces of convention and seek his spirit's liberation within those chains. He was prepared to do this.

They walked through the dark night, which was getting tired of maintaining a cover over so many secrets unfolding from the night's festivities. A glimmer of the new day was already forcing its way out of night's shadowed womb. They embraced and kissed goodbye some distance from the doorsteps under a somber sapodilla tree. This was surely the last farewell until destiny would lead them together again. Until then, their spirits had vowed to bind each to the other in a secret, forbidden to the world, but blessed in eyes of the spirit of love, if only the world around them could understand and feel this affection.

* * *

At close to six o'clock in the morning, Rafa de Melo hitched his launch against a mangrove tree at the mouth of the Akawini. He had left the jetty at the mission that morning and struggled through the foggy winding creek before any hungover early riser appeared at the water's edge. He felt he deserved a cup of coffee as he marveled at the spectacular sunrise at the junction of the Pomeroon. The rising sun glistened on the glassy water and portrayed itself like an oil painted canvas, with the shadows of the forested banks overhanging as a curtained edge. For Rafa, this was a majestic manifestation of the beauty of the infinite. He had found a radiant spark of it in Sonya Torrealba. He could not understand why his adoration of infinite beauty manifested in his Sonya should be forbidden if this Pomeroon sunrise was so admirable and acceptable to everyone.

Esperanza, Rafa's launch, was moving fast at full throttle despite going against the strong currents of the falling tide rushing to the Atlantic Ocean. He stopped a few times on the way back home towards Charity. As was the custom while traveling on the river, every passer-by waved to him and he reciprocated. Outsiders were usually rather confused with this, as it gave the impression that people were closely familiar with each other, and this was not the case. Yet most of them knew who Rafa de Melo was, a notable and respected person from a prominent Portuguese family native to the Pomeroon for some generations since. The traffic on the river was quite active. Many paddled canoes and ballahoos laden with produce for the market weekend at Charity were making their way there. A tired-looking man and his wife struggling against the tide and moving pathetically slowly waved to the *Esperanza* and sought a tow from Rafa. He brought the vessel to a stop and waited for the couple to paddle to the side of the launch sandwiched between it and the mangrove bush at the river's edge.

"We are drained, sir. We have been traveling since last night from St. John's, at the river mouth. We have some copra, casareep, and cassava bread to sell at Charity. We are begging you to give us a tow. Up to anywhere would help us out and give us a chance to take a rest," they pleaded.

Rafa was immediately sympathetic as was his nature. "Chuck the boat rope to me, and I will hitch you to the back, and you just do the steering to ensure you do not run into my boat's stern when I need to slow down or stop," he relented. "I am letting you out to the length of your boat's rope so that you are a good distance behind me. This will save your boat from taking in water from the swell of the launch once we start moving fast."

The couple were so overjoyed and showed their appreciation with a grateful smile and by patting the palm of their hands against their chests.

A short distance farther, the occupants of another boat requested the same favor, and Rafa applied the same generosity and kindness to the Afro-Amerindian couple. Others he passed on the way might have asked the favor also but for the embarrassment to do so when two boats were already being towed behind the launch one on each side.

As they pulled towards the jetty at Grant Miriam's Delight, Rafa placed the launch's engine at the neutral idle setting and began to dislodge the tether and free the boats. "You have a short distance more to Charity. I hope you don't mind. I must join my family now. I have been away from them for several days. They are anxiously waiting for me."

"Not at all, sir! We are truly thankful for your kindness. You have saved us a lot of sweat and tiredness." Both couples paddled up closer to the launch and offered bottles of casareep and mammy apples. "This is the least we can do to thank you. Please accept this humble token."

"I would never take from your produce for the market. That would undermine my willingness to tow you and take away from the very way you labor for an honest living. Just reserve your thanks in silence and do something for someone in need when you have another opportunity to do so. That would be the best thanks for me," Rafa replied and moored his launch against the stelling at the riverside of his estate.

There to meet him with much patience and satisfaction was his beautiful wife, Mona, who locked him in her firm embrace and kissed him as a lover starved of romance would. Five-year-old Madeline tugged at her father's trousers and demanded that he lift her and share his love, which he gladly conceded to do.

"Did you find some people to work for you, Rafa, dear? We missed you. I find it so difficult in my lonely bed when you are away. Maddie tries to fill the gap, but her sweet lovableness is not the same as a husband that cares," Mona reassured her husband.

"Everything went to plan in the Akawini, and I had the most rewarding pleasure of celebrating the St. John's festivities," Rafa said. "The Toshao invited me to stay for it, and I could not refuse." On realizing how cryptically and unintentionally he was expressing his true ulterior motive for going there and the wonderful time he had just had with Sonya, he repeated in a matter-of-fact way, "Yes everything went well. I may have to make a follow-up trip again to firm up things there." He feigned a yawn and asked for something to eat to change the topic. "Hope you have some lovely home-cooked food for me. I miss your cooking even if it's just a few meals of yours that I miss. You could imagine what it is eating dried and canned foods and salt biscuits crackers for nearly a week. What saved me was the good Pomeroon coffee."

"We waited to have dinner with you last evening and gave up hope, waiting, thinking that something of importance must have delayed you, love," Mona uttered. "Let's not waste time now. Get ready and let's have an early dinner. Then we can go to bed early and let you catch up on some rest. You may have been sleepless as I was. It's always the case when you are not around. I need you more than anyone in this whole wide world and love you the same or even more than I did six years ago when we first met at that Easter Monday night dance at the school."

That night in bed, Mona was craving her husband's intimate warmth. She felt that something in his response was unusual and out of character with the physical revelry he usually had, losing himself in her nakedness without inhibition and restraint when making love to her. This time she accepted his excuse of tiredness and sleepiness. Yet Rafa felt it extremely difficult to sleep as the vision of his Sonya haunted his soul. He was convinced that a part of him was left behind.

Mona de Melo seemed to have accepted her husband's quiet retreat into what Rafa termed falling back into the routine of work and the business of running the estate. He was very sweet and polite to his wife and bowed to her every wish. However, he lost the zest to initiate anything that would leave an opening for Mona to question his new reticence. He began to devote more time to working in the fields alongside the handful of permanent workers he maintained and filled the rest of his day in the company of Mona and Madeline. He displayed a deep sense of satisfaction in and diligence to the duty of attending to their social and familial needs. He thought he was also fully satisfying his marital duties and did not for a moment want Mona to feel that he did not love her like before. She was still the special woman he knew over the years who would overlook all his weaknesses and focus on his goodness and strength. She was the mother of the apple of his eye, his innocent and loveable daughter, Madeline. He wanted to do nothing that would interfere with the bond between Madeline and himself.

He knew that Mona's equilibrium in a loving relationship with him would sustain that bond. Any sense of friction between them would negatively affect his daughter.

* * *

The church bells at the mission at Charity had rung the first eighteen strokes and then the second set of eighteen. Sunday Mass would begin after the bells pealed their last abbreviated three strokes, not to beckon worshippers to hurry on to the church but to inform them that they were late and that proceedings would begin without them. Rafa was elegantly dressed in his Sunday best attire with his wavy hair neatly parted in the middle of his head. Mona wore her longish-sleeved black and white plaid dress with her beautiful, curled locks covered by a lace veil. She never liked jewelry and did not wear any this time even though Rafa asked her to wear the gold necklace he gave her their first year together on her birthday. She did not require any additional adornments to enhance the natural and unassuming beauty she possessed. Heads turned in the pews to catch a rapid and admiring glance of her as the family made to their seats a minute before the priest and the altar servers arrived in the sanctuary. Madeline, festively dressed in a white and crimson floral-patterned dress and a large white ribbon bow in her curly hair, sat in between her parents.

The sermon that Sunday was a reflection on fidelity in love between husband and wife, which should inspire sound parental love in which children flourish and grow. Rafa listened attentively and vowed never to cease to love Mona, the person that had instilled in him a love and self-confidence that enabled him to love his family unyieldingly. Loving Mona as his wife was not in question in his mind. It was genuine love and his duty. Moreover, amid affirming in his mind the depth of his love for Mona, he wandered into staring as in a trance to the vision of Sonya smiling into his eyes and leading him into the cabin of his launch. The ringing of the altar bells after the consecration of the bread and wine by the celebrant snapped him out of the hypnosis he involuntarily drifted into. He hugged his daughter and then his wife and imparted a kiss of peace to them before sharing in the bread with the rest of the congregation.

As he sat and waited for the final blessing, he pledged to be faithful and loyal to Mona, but fidelity not in the terms of what he had just heard in the sermon. He would love Mona forever but felt he would explode if he did not share the love he had beyond her. He had too much of it and enough for Sonya as well. He just could not wrap his head and heart around understanding fidelity as the love between one man and one woman only. For him, real love could not be straight-jacketed nor made to become limited. Love was the manifestation of the true spirit of the universe that was eternally infinite. Society's limited nature had created finite boundaries and prevented the liberation of the spirit of love in the world. Rafa de Melo, the Christian gentleman, was now beginning to believe that his own religion, like all the others, had crassly propagated the denial of love without limits. In doing so, they had perpetuated a culture of selfish discrimination of convenience, which had extended into the many faces of hate in the country and the world.

He had begun to doubt some of the core tenets of what he thought he always accepted without question since his early upbringing. He was certain that this was not a justification for what the church would call his errant and sinful diversion from the straight and narrow. But he never expressed vocally his growing cynicism of the faith. He simply placed a lid on that and other tenets and lived, as if he had no quarrel with religion. He never ceased to pledge his untiring love and dedication to Mona and their daughter as fully as he could. Similarly, he felt no remorse for yearning for Sonya the other light of his life in the Akawini.

CHAPTER 3

THE HOSPITALIZATION OF ANITA

Vernon could hear the faint humming of an outboard engine in the distance. His restless sleep that Friday night at Mrs. de Castro's big house was constantly disturbed by the phantoms of the night reminding him of his aloneness away from both his parents. Mrs. de Castro decided to leave him in bed to have an uninterrupted sleep-in. She thought of a nice breakfast to make him since he had little of an appetite the night before. She was in the middle of preparing scrambled eggs with salted codfish when the motorboat she lent his father to attend to his mother's, Anita's condition down river pulled up at the waterside.

Vernon looked through the window and gleamed with insurmountable joy to see his parents. A torrent of glee flooded his heart as he watched his mother getting up to disembark the boat. However, equally in a flash, his joy drooped like a sagging branch as he saw his father quickly reach out to prevent her from collapsing against the gunwale of the boat. Vernon ran out to the kitchen and alerted Mrs. de Castro that his parents had arrived. He expressed his joy to Mrs. de Castro by repeating to her, "My mom is here, Aunty Maddie. My mom is here, Auntie Maddie." This pleased her immensely since she had asked him since he arrived two nights ago to call her "Aunt Maddie" claiming that his grandmother, Anna, was her only sister, the one she never accepted in her short lifetime.

Madeline and Vernon made their way down to the jetty only to see the pain Anita Atkins was enduring. She was weak and sore from the laceration, which the traditional birth attendant made to help deliver her baby. The little girl struggled to see the light of day and succumbed minutes after her birth. Anita was still oozing blood from the failed delivery. She languished at the home of Vibert Atkins, Vernon's uncle, as the despairing birth attendant tried to make her better. The herbal treatment together with Whizz and Phensic pills, aspirin-based medications, were having no remedial effect on what turned out to be a serious case of septicemia. This was explained by the dispensary aid, who was visiting a healthcare post on the lower Pomeroon between the estuaries of the Wakapao and Akawini creeks. Fortunately, Uncle Vibert and his wife had taken it in their own hands to terminate the treatment by the birth attendant and carried Anita to the healthcare post aware of the monthly schedule of the government service providers. Denis Atkins, on arriving to get his wife, saw her sitting in the sun on the built-in bench at the jetty and, panic-stricken, hastened to intervene. At the advice of the healthcare aid, he left with his wife for home at Grant Miriam's Delight and to eventual treatment at Charity.

"You are in terrible pain, my dear Nita, I can see it. You need to come in for a moment. Let me help to clean you up and get you ready for the hospital where you need to be," Mrs. de Castro offered in a motherly tone. "You are the only portrait I have left of my sister, Anna—a wonderful, strong, and proud human being, the one we failed when your grandmother, Sonya, and her parents succumbed in that dreadful boat accident. I understood later why my dad went to the Akawini for the funeral and brought her back to live with us. But I was a different person then. I need to make it up to her and look after her daughter now. I am starting too late and under difficult circumstances. Nevertheless, it is better late than never, my child."

Denis struggled to fully understand the meaning of Mrs. de Castro's utterings. Anita had occasionally spoke with her husband of ties she had with a plantation owner in the Pomeroon. She, however, in her reticence, preferred not to delve into the details of information that was handed down from her mother and her maternal family in Parakese. Both Anita and Denis had shared a common bond of family demise through boat accidents and found no comfort in trudging those pathways of memory again. Hence, there was limited discussion on such issues. Anita knew of her blood relations with the father of Madeline de Castro, and based on this, Denis generally felt some affinity to his employer but was not clearly cognizant of the infidelity that initiated this.

Denis lay aside his curiosity regarding Madeline de Castro's rambling about her sister and simply obeyed her command to carry his wife up the stairs to her bedroom. It was the first time he and his wife entered that far inside Mrs. de Castro's dwelling. The older woman quickly set about wiping her down with a warm, damp cloth. Denis left them alone and stayed with Vernon, just outside the room in front of the closed door. Mrs. de Castro was shocked to see the state of the vaginal wound she bore to free her baby. She wasted no time to get her a hot drink, which she scarcely sipped. Mrs. de Castro ordered Denis Atkins to take her immediately to the government dispensary at Charity for treatment.

Young Vernon was distressed to be away for so long without his mother and was getting peeved to hear that she was to be taken away again before he even had the opportunity to feel her presence and love once more. He could not withhold his tears and burst in loud weeping. He threw his arms around her neck and kissed her incessantly on her cheeks until he was dragged away from her painful joy of holding him. He saw the tears streaming from the corner of her eyes as she said, "I love you, son. I will be back to look over you forever. Don't you cry anymore! Be strong for your mother's sake, and for your dad's."

At that moment, he saw his father cry for the first time, and he knew something was really wrong.

His dad fetched Anita to the boat and told his son to go with him. The resident dispenser at Charity, who acted as a doctor, nurse, and dispenser of drugs, was not comfortable with Anita's condition and recommended that she be taken as fast as possible to the Suddie

General Hospital. He prepared a referral slip, gave it to Denis, and suggested that he should go to the stelling area right away and find a hire car to expedite the trip to Suddie. He did not want him to wait for the afternoon bus, by which time it would be too late. In his kindness, he loaned Denis the money to pay for the hire of the car, which was beyond what he could afford.

Vernon traveled the three-hour ride with his father and his sick mother to the hospital, stopping many times for the car to be pushed or pulled out of deep cavernous potholes where it had stuck.

By the time his mother was admitted to the hospital, she was so frail and weak that she was unable to stand on her own. The doctor indicated that she was inflicted with a severe case of tetanus. His tone told them that the outcome was not very promising.

Denis, who hardly spoke throughout the trip but rested his cheek against his wife's throughout the journey, whispered on several occasions to the doctor, as if to convince himself and his son, "She will beat this illness, Doc. She will get over this, Doc. Please help her." His trembling voice betrayed the strong front he tried to display to the physician.

When he turned to face his son, his sad eyes inadvertently allowed a tear to fall down his cheek. He hugged his head, held his Anita's hand, and said, "We shall always be the family we love. Don't leave us, Nita. Please come around and stay with us, my love. I am here for you as I have always been and will be."

With one hand, Anita squeezed the hand of her husband and beckoned their son with the other. Then with both her hands, she simultaneously again squeezed the hands of the two men in her life.

A nurse with attendants arrived and affixed a low partition around Anita's bed cordoning her off and isolating her from the other beds in the ward. The nurse told Denis to go home and rest for the night while the hospital staff took care of his wife. Denis explained and queried at the same time, "Where could we go and sleep? We left our home in the Pomeroon and have no family here. We would be better off staying with her here and return to the Pomeroon tomorrow."

"Only the doctor can decide that. I will have to get his permission," the nurse replied.

That night, they both slept on the floor next to Anita's bed in the hospital and woke with every tortured cry of pain reverberating from her weak body. In the morning, they were preparing to leave the hospital back to the Pomeroon. Vernon was for one moment happy and optimistic when his mother grasped him, weakly pulled him to her bosom, kissed his cheek with a prolonged kiss, and said, "I love you, son. Your grandmother would have been proud of you, as I am. I wish you had known her and my mother's wonderful father, my grandfather, Rafa. Ask your Auntie Maddie to tell you about him. You will love him. You have his eyes and his nose, I think, and that wavy head of hair is what he has left in you to keep his memory alive. You always remind me of my mother and your great grandfather. He was a great man, full of love for his Sonya and for her daughter, Anna."

This parting exchange from his mother stirred up a tumultuous mixture in him of wonder, joy, pathos, sadness, questioning, quest, and a journey he would indulge in all through his life. Since that day, he had travelled back again to discover the path that had led to the present time. That journey was his family's for four generations.

There was very little verbal communication between father and son on the early morning bus on the route home. Yet the speech of their eyes and silence in their hearts etched a painful tale of both uncertainty and hope in the sands of the Essequibo road until they reached Charity. Mrs. de Castro was perturbed and saddened to hear of his Anita's deteriorating condition and, out of despair, began to cast blame on the traditional birth attendant who brought this on her. "What a dreadful midwife to deal out such a blow to the only family I have left on this earth. Shame on her!"

Denis spoke unapologetically in her defense, "She is a good person, Missy, who has delivered most of the people in my family and many of them on the reservation and up the creeks in that area. She always tries her best and uses her gift and knowledge as best she can. What she did was a work of love for life, not for the pittance she received in return. If only she was given some training to update her methods and skills and ensure safe hygienic practices. If only the government recognized the vital role traditional birth attendants play in so many communities and equipped them with clean implements. She tries to manage with the same old knife and razor blades she can put her hand on and any cloth and string she feels is clean enough for the deliveries she performs. I do not want to blame her, Missy. All I want at this time is for my Nita to return home healthy."

Madeline so much wanted Anita to come back home healthy also. "I owe so much to her—an apology, an open acknowledgment as my niece and my father's granddaughter from a mother he adored as much as he adored my own mother," she again reiterated. "No, he worshipped Sonya Torrealba as his deity on earth, confounding the very faith that placed him on a pedestal. I want her back here at my father's Miriam's Delight, her mother's estate as much as mine. It's hers as much as mine. I owe it to her. I will start over when she returns. I will make up to her all the wrongs I've made to her mother, who left our home only because of the estrangement I generated. It is not too late to start over. You and Anita have been my family, although I have not spoken at will about it until now. It was my false embarrassment and defense of Mona de Melo, my mother, which made me see her through a set of self-righteous lenses. Oh God . . . please bring her back safely." Madeline de Castro trembled with a look of grievous hurt, as if she was trying to drain the pent-up anguish from her troubled mind.

That night, Vernon stayed with his father in their small two-roomed cabin. It struck him as undoubtedly vastly different from the big house of Mrs. de Castro, where he lived the last days. But it was home for them, not so sweet at this time with the illness of his mother hanging over them and her not being with them, completing the threesome they cherished together. This cast a heavy and damp shroud over them. That night he slept in his father's bed where often he would lie in between his parents and absorb their contagious devotion. That night there was little conversation. Instead, his father hugged him repeatedly and instructed him that he would be staying with Mrs. de Castro for a while. He pleaded with him to forgive him for leaving him behind while he went to the Suddie Hospital to keep his mother's company.

"Once she is beginning to feel better, I will come and take you to visit her, son. There is no place for you to stay there. I could rough it out on the floor there next to her, but it's not a place for you, my son. You keep Mrs. de Castro company while I am away. She needs someone like you to fill my place on this estate, not to run it but just to be around her," his father affirmed.

* * *

Early the next morning, Denis dropped Vernon off at Mrs. de Castro's and headed to Charity to board the early bus bound for the Adventure Stelling. By about nine o'clock, he would reach the Suddie Hospital and be with Anita. Denis worried about how lonely she must be without them since they never seemed to be away from each other before. Vernon knew, in her pain, there was no one more important than his father to ease her suffering with his always supportive love and care. On this basis, Vernon quietly submitted to his father leaving him behind.

"Hug and kiss my mama for me, Papa, and tell her that I love her. And miss her! And she must get better fast and come back home!" he uttered softly with a flood of tears welling up in his swollen eyes. When his father was out of sight on the other bank of the river, the floodgates burst opened, and he could not control his feelings of despair and brokenness.

Valerie and her mom picked him up for school. They tried to make a conversation with him, but they could not encourage any interest in him to respond. "He is going through a hard time, Valerie. It is tough to know that his mom is so ill," Mrs. Marjorie James advised her daughter, then she turned to the young Atkins, "She will be better, Vern. Just trust. We will celebrate when she returns, promise."

The next three days at school were as miserable as it could get. He was inattentive in all the lessons and his teacher, Gloria, seemed to overlook this knowing his predicament. When he dozed off, demonstrating the period of starved sleep he was experiencing since his mother left home, his classmate Adele van Sertima held his hand and gently brought him out of the subconscious state he had fallen in and out of recently. She, more than anyone else, spent a lot of time with Vernon in and out of class reflecting a show of friendship learned from her mother's relationship with his parents. He liked her and trusted her concern, but was always conscious of their affluent lifestyle so different from his.

CHAPTER 4

MADELINE'S RECOUNT

In Mrs. de Castro's care over the next days, Vernon was pampered amidst his pining for his parents and for wanting to be in the modest home he was accustomed to. Her persistent kindness did help to cheer him up in her sort of a way. He spoke with her more freely, albeit with a modicum of words. She responded to this with her ready smiles, showing a deep satisfaction for having him in her company.

"You have so much in common with my father—your looks and that slight swagger of a walk, which marked his uniqueness. I can see it so vividly, Vern," she said with a nervous grin. "He was your mom's grandfather, you know. If only he lived long enough to love her as he loved Sonya and Anna!"

The constant mention of Anna by Mrs. de Castro began to engrain a note in Vernon's mind. It corresponded more vividly with his mother recall of her mother, his grandmother, Anna. He now more assuredly knew that Mrs. de Castro was speaking of the same person and asked in inquisitive irony, "Who really was Anna, Auntie Maddie? Was she the same person my mama talks about?" He needed that endorsement.

With that, she exuded another outpouring of guilt and remorse. "The same beautiful person I loved as a real friend of mine and, at the same time, hated in jealousy in my teenage years. I never appreciated, nor was certain, nor wanted to believe that she was my sister," she replied. "In a way, I doubted that my father who adored my mother so unquestionably could have had another child besides me with another person. I treated her as an adopted sister in our home for a short while after my mother passed away and never accepted her rightful heritage. Only later in my father's last years, I became more open to the fact. It was too late, dear Vern. That was your grandmother for sure," she reiterated.

Those days with Mrs. de Castro filled in a major and integral chapter in Vernon's family's story and in his journey to find some answers for his existence at Grant Miriam's Delight. It also provided an opening for the widow to release a lot of her pent-up guilt and free some of the skeletons in her family's closet. What he learned then, still with limited understanding, nevertheless, engraved a lasting mark on his young consciousness. From that base, he launched his journey to re-visit the milestones in the family history and write the story of his family's sojourn in the Northwest and Pomeroon Districts of Guyana. It was a due confirmation from her that endorsed the affectionate memory Anita kept of his grandmother, Anna.

* * *

Reminiscing, Mrs. de Castro recalled, "During a new coffee harvesting season, my father showed a chronic sadness that my mother and I could not decipher. He often attributed it to being too tired to concentrate on running the estate when my mother inquired. My mother showed real empathy for the feelings of a husband she honored for his devotion to our wellbeing. She even asked if he wanted to take a break from farm work and go somewhere else, and he didn't."

Mrs. de Castro reflected that although Grant Miriam's Delight had its full complement of labor that year, the Torrealba family was not part of it. A farmhand from the Kamwatta area revealed to Rafa de Melo the reason why they did not make the trip to the Pomeroon that year. Sonya Torrealba, Augu's and Verna's daughter, was expecting a baby. She was having some complications and was put on bed rest until she gave birth. The farmhand told him that no one knew who the father was. All the young men who pestered her and wanted her friendship denied responsibility.

The farmhand explained to Rafa, "Her father, Augu, gave up trying to get answers from her as to who made her pregnant. He was happy only to see that his daughter was happy about having the baby. He gave up any attempt further to extract this information from her. The man just said that he was too glad that his daughter was giving him a grandchild he so much desired, and from that time, he closed his eyes and his mind to any of the gossips and judgmental comments about his daughter's promiscuous behavior that brought this upon her family. The man is happy, sir, and his wife looks like she is glad too. So that is why they did not travel down this time."

Rafa heard this news and queried in his mind whether one of the boys she avoided eventually made it out with her. He felt a jolt that his Sonya had moved on and left him by the wayside. In another breath of pondering, he told himself that their love was too intertwined to leave any crevice of a chance to let this happen. Their spirits were bound eternally, journeying hand in hand like children of the wind destined for eternal union within the all-embracing spirit of the universe. His thoughts wandered to the timing of when he was last with her and how he was waiting to entertain her and her parents in the next season, which would have been some eight or nine months thence. Then, for a fleeting a moment, it dawned on him that the timespan seemed somehow to correspond with his visit and when first they worshipped together under the dim light of the moon on that magnificent Akawini night; Venus must have smiled upon them and placed them into the arms of the fertility goddesses of her South American heritage, Coatlicue and Teteo Inan. He understood why she was reluctant to disclose the source of her love and joy to her parents. Perhaps she was simply waiting expectantly for the fruit of her joy from that consummation to emerge for the world to see. Perhaps she was also waiting on him to behold that fruit as the yield of their everlasting oneness. He wanted very much for this to be true—that she did not channel her love elsewhere.

Augu and Verna's message to Rafa came when a large ballahoo pulled up at the jetty of Miriam's Delight one Saturday morning, two months into the current harvest season. The Torrealba family was inviting him and his wife to the christening of Sonya's baby. They had arranged for it to be done at his former parish of Santa Rosa in two weeks' time. They were seeking his favor and approval to become the godfather and his wife, the godmother of the beautiful infant, Anna. Augu had asked them to make sure that they brought back a reply from Rafa de Melo.

That night Rafa broke the news to his wife. "They want us to join them in Santa Rosa for the christening ceremony and want us to be the godparents. This would be a terrific opportunity for you and me to take a break from the farm. We haven't had a holiday for many years now and I need the rest." He hoped by suggesting an acceptance of the invitation, he would mask his deep longing to see Sonya again. "We could prepare *Esperanza* for the trip, and we could live on the boat for a few days away. Old Mother de Freitas could look after Madeline for us until we return. That would avoid her missing school and not push us to hurry the trip."

He sent a message back to Augu and his wife that they would be honored to go to the Moruka for the baptismal ceremony. Their launch, *Esperanza*, would travel first to the Akawini to arrive early morning on the day of the afternoon ceremony. There, the de Melos would collect the Torrealbas, and together, they would all make the trip to Santa Rosa. The following week another message came from Augu. He was delighted with the kindness of Rafa de Melo's offer to pick them up and take them to Santa Rosa. Verna was particularly pleased that Mona de Melo would join them since she has never visited the Akawini and Moruka before.

Rafa and his wife arranged for Madeline to stay with his mother-in-law, Mother de Freitas. No return date was fixed. "We shall be back soon, Maddie," he said to his daughter, then to Mother de Freitas, he said, "You will see us when you see us. We need a holiday. Mona has been cooped up at home for too long, and I am feeling tired these days."

The Friday night before the event saw Rafa fitting his launch with everything he thought his wife and guests would need for the trip. He stacked a wide range of food and drinks under the stern deck, an amount enough for a celebration. He also placed there a bag with presents for each of the Torrealba family. There was a special gift for the newest member of that family. Without revealing his feeling, he intended to treat Sonya and her family on this great occasion. He recalled the celebration he once shared with that family in the Akawini and how that night changed his life so radically. He would commemorate it on this trip.

Mona was overjoyed to be traveling with her husband to the Akawini and the Moruka. That she was to accompany him further confirmed in her mind the trust she always maintained about Rafa's focus on farm priorities on his previous traversing of the area in search of needed labor. She never had questions about him secretly hiding things from her. Their going as a couple to the Akawini and the Moruka was indicative of this.

"We shall make an early start before sunrise tomorrow, Mona. It's far more pleasant to travel in the cool of the morning before the sun's heat begins," he spoke warmly to his wife. "I am so happy to have you with me on the boat to break the usual monotony I have endured traveling alone in the past."

Excited as a child counting down the hours, she slept only in spurts throughout the night. She rose early the next morning, tugging at her husband's arm at about three to get him out of his sound sleep. "Time to rise and shine, darling! We must get moving. There is a long day ahead of us."

By five, they were approaching the mission school at Marlborough. Rafa pulled the launch in and hitched it to the stelling there. They used the school's latrine facilities and took a break in the launch, drinking coffee and munching on sandwiches Mona lovingly made that early morning in anticipation. A splendid Pomeroon sunrise was surfacing, cleaning away the remnants of fog over the waters. The couple peered through a window in the launch's cabin and marveled at the beauty of nature. The sun's new rays brandished before them like bars of glittering gold reflecting on the glassy waters of the Pomeroon.

"This is what makes this part of the country so rich, Mona," Rafa uttered to deflate the awe they had submitted themselves to in silence.

Mona just smiled serenely and petted his thigh, her way of expressing to her husband the magic of his presence in her life. In an instant, it also rekindled the spark that six years ago welded them together as an inseparable pair. He threw his arm around her neck and kissed her as passionately as if they were dating again. Mona began to affirm in her mind that this was indeed turning out to be the break from work that her husband needed to ease away the tiredness that had been bothering him lately.

The estuary of the Akawini was in sight. They had made the trip much faster than expected even though Rafa kept the engine's throttle at little above half speed, enjoying the freedom from the cares, demands, and daily routine of farm life and maintaining his inheritance of Miriam's Delight. The falling tide had helped them to accelerate. They tied up against a mangrove tree for a while as Rafa had done repeatedly entering and exiting that tributary of the Pomeroon. It became a ritual of contemplation since Sonya ratified her place in his heart as one-half of his overflowing love. It was no different this time even in the company with the other half. Anxiety and impatience were triggered by this ritual, and he now wanted to arrive at the mission as quickly as possible to behold the vision of that countenance for which he never stopped longing.

The launch was pulling in at the Akawini mission landing, and in no time, a welcoming party gathered. The curious onlookers were by now familiar with the *Esperanza* and with the captain of that vessel. Nevertheless, that did not limit the usual curiosity stirred up by such a visit to the reservation. After boarding up and ensuring that appropriate fastening of the launch was completed, the couple stepped ashore and made their way to the Toshao's house to find Rudy Pearson, a welcoming friend. Rafa introduced his wife and handed the Toshao a bottle of pak-pak. He was incredibly grateful for the flagon of wine and insisted they come into his home.

"It is the first time I'm meeting your Missus, Mr. de Melo. I must pay her my tribute. You are welcome in the Akawini anytime, ma'am.

You have a nice wife Mr. de Melo," the Toshao observed, a statement that seemed to dispel in his mind some of the gossips on the reservation over Sonya's new addition to the populace. "Hope you are spending some time with us."

"This is just a pit stop, Toshao Rudy. We have stopped to pick up the Torrealba family on our way to Santa Rosa," Rafa replied. "We are going to take up that invitation from you in the future, though. I am sure my wife would enjoy a St. John's festivity, as I did the last one. I told her all about it." Then in a fit of guilt, he felt he did not really tell her all about it. Yet there was no remorse for sharing in the divinity of love with a goddess such as Sonya.

They walked up the track leading to Augu's thatched hut. A dog barked and then licked Rafa's trousers, as if it was fully aware that he was no stranger. Augu and his wife came out to meet them. Verna made a beeline to Mona and embraced her as if there was a mutual acquaintance for many moons even though at Miriam's Delight their role as farmhands had classified her at a lower level of interaction. As their host now, she presented a footing of equality in their home to Rafa and Mona de Melo. They were very gracious and willing to accept this since their status in society marginalized them from the common people's living, something they never found a way to change. Their kindness, open attitude, and generosity, nevertheless, differentiated them from the economically fortunate cream of the Pomeroon, whose preoccupation with becoming and keeping rich locked them in a cocoon of admiration and respect but devoid of affection.

"You are welcome in our home as a dear friend, Mrs. Mona. You all, come in, drink some coffee, and eat something. You must be starving after such an early start to get here now." She beckoned them in with a warm unfolding of cordiality.

With a smile stretching from ear to ear, Augu endorsed his wife's reception and ushered them in. "Make yourself at home. You are more than friends to us after all your kindness in the Pomeroon."

Rafa was eager with impatience to see his Sonya and her little one. "Where is the one for whom we have come to celebrate?" he asked, looking at his wife.

"Yes, we are dying to meet your grandchild and Sonya," Mona added.

Verna, whose delight could not be mistaken, replied, "Sonya is breastfeeding the little one. She is such a fussy mom. That baby is promptly attended to if she but scarcely whimpers. She adores her."

A strange feeling of desire overcame Rafa as his mind drifted away into nostalgic memory. He remembered how those firm breasts cushioned his frame as he dissolved in the heat of her intimacy. He felt an inkling of jealousy and simultaneous satisfaction over the infant's rightful place at the bosom of her mother. Then he beamed a response to avoid any betrayal of what was going through his mind. "What a lucky child! She has a good mother and wonderful grandparents to love and protect her through life."

"She has brought light over our home, just like that star over the manger at Bethlehem," Augu chipped in. "And now you come to our humble abode, just like the magis. I am glad we have you to celebrate with us. That's what Sonya and the two of us wanted. How can we thank you enough?"

Backing the bedroom doorway and not seeing Sonya's appearance, Rafa was alerted by his wife's beaming exaltation. "There is the beautiful angel, with a full head of dark hair, just like her mother's. Congratulations, Sonya," she said as she lifted herself from the *tibiciri* stool she sat on and embraced mother and child.

Rafa also stood up to see the grand entrance. For a second, he was blinded by what seemed a haloed apparition of a goddess before him. For him, she was his deity. He gently caressed the head of baby Anna while staring with his drooping eyelids into the beautiful eyes of Sonya Torrealba. Her radiance lit up his life with the always alluring smile he knew.

"Sit down with the baby, Sonya, and rest your feet," Rafa said, mainly to divert attention from and hide any revelation of the seething ferment in his inner core. He stared at her sitting next to Mona and thought how marvelous it was to look at both parts of his love so complete before his very eyes.

No one broached the issue of the father of the child, as each seemed to agree that neither the time nor place was right. Augu began to lay out the plans for the ceremony at Santa Rosa the next day. "The priest is expecting to start the baptism at one p.m. It will be a private ceremony after all the Sunday Masses are over."

Rafa added his concern, "We should leave Akawini at least by eight in the morning and take our time to the mission. We can cross the ocean to Moruka mouth early when the tide is high. The launch needs high tide to avoid the shallow mudflat and the risk of grounding." Rafa de Melo continued, "Waiting until one o'clock—if we arrive too early, it is not a problem because we have the launch to stay in, and the baby will be protected and can sleep."

Mona had packed two soft blankets and extra sheets with baby care in mind. "We could make a nice little bed for her in the cabin while we wait," she assured. "There are three women to look after her tomorrow."

Verna still could not contain her joy of having Mona and her husband under her roof, a dream she thought would never come true, but which in her humility, she wanted to happen. She argued in her thought that if this woman and her family could entertain them on their property at Miriam's Delight without reservation even though they lived there as laborers, she reckoned she had a duty to repay their kindness.

"Augu and I want the two of you to eat dinner with us tonight. I am slowly cooking the pepperpot on the fire outside. Augu trapped a good size labba two nights ago, and we have put it in casareep to keep some for your visit. I am also cooking some rice, and there is bread for soaking up the sauce. Hope you like our kind of food, Mrs. Mona," she said to everyone there but addressing Mona.

"You should not have troubled yourself with preparing food for us, Verna. When we travel on the river, we always carry enough supplies. However, how could we turn down your kind invitation? Something like this does not occur every day. Rafa and I will be thrilled to share a meal with you tonight. True friends eat together," she said.

Sonya spoke little and only participated with a yes, a no, or a contented smile to questions and agreements to the praise for her infant. When Anna woke from her peaceful slumber in the arms of her mother and started to whimper, Mona quickly reached out and took her into her arms. She was delighted to kiss the velvet smooth cheeks of the infant.

"It is six years or so since I last held such an adorable child. She reminds me so much of our Maddie, who would surely love a sister like this. She has asked for this repeatedly."

"So why don't you satisfy her wish, Mrs. Mona?" asked Verna almost sheepishly with a giggle.

"We wish we could, Verna. My master, Rafa, wants this so badly, but the Master above seems to have other plans. We have little choice but to accept the Master's way," she replied.

"Maddie must live with a lot of hope and disappointment then. I'm sorry for her," Verna added.

"She has to learn to deal with the disappointment, I think. You know, one of these days when you and your family come to Miriam's Delight, Maddie would enjoy Sonya's beautiful child as her own sister."

"We will have to try and make it out for the next season, God and Augu willing," replied Verna while the two husbands sat in silence and listened to the conversation.

Sonya leaned over Mona, took Anna in her arms, and excused themselves from the company. "I can see she is getting sleepy, Mrs. de Melo, and I must put her to bed now," she said and left the sitting room.

Rafa also got up and excused himself and his wife until they met again in the evening. "We are going to take a slow walk back to the boat and give Mona a chance to see a little bit of the mission," he explained, as he clasped his arm around Mona's waist. They left like two lovers who were going out on their first date. They were a young couple and never for a moment allowed the tensions of farm business and farm work to push them to be rigid, mutually selfish, and eccentric.

"That man really loves his wife," remarked Augu. "He hates it when he is not with her. He lives for her and her alone," he continued once they were out of earshot.

"And Mrs. Mona adores her husband also; it is so easy to see that. She is so comfortable in his company," Verna observed

A few hours later, the de Melos joined the Torrealbas again. A mouth-watering array of foods lay spread out on a small table. Around an aluminum dish containing a generous amount of pepperpot of cooked labba meat were dishes of sweet potato, eddo, sweet cassava and fried slices of ripe plantain and breadfruit, an enamel dish of boiled white rice, and a plate of sliced bread alongside pieces of cassava bread. Only a remnant of light from dusk remained, and a canopy of darkness was beginning to enshroud the settlement. Augu cleaned a kerosene lantern, lit it, and placed it over the middle of the room on a firm wire hook hung from a rafter in the roof. Its light shed a soft and romantic glow in the room and created an ambiance that matched a five-starred restaurant. It provided no real competition to the full moon that was appearing stealthily in the sky.

Rafa and his wife handed over the gifts they had packed for the family. Verna was first given a neat leather handbag, which she graciously accepted, giving Mona a tight and grateful hug. Rafa handed a flagon of wine and a bag with several bottles of Banks beer that cheered Augu immensely. Mona then opened her own handbag and took out two small, wrapped articles and spoke to Sonya.

"One of these is for you, Sonya, dear, and the other for the beautiful Anna. I had these ordered myself from Nazirudeen, the goldsmith from Huist-e-Dieren on the Essequibo Coast, after Rafa and I decided on them. I hope you like them and hope they remind you and your child of this blessed time in your life," she said in a caring manner. "Hope it reminds of our close friendship. We love you and this special child."

With that, she handed over the two sachets and asked Sonya to open them and see how they fit. She was thrilled to discover the two identically designed gold necklaces and heart-shaped lockets. The names "Sonya" on one of them and "Anna" on the other were engraved on the hearts. Sonya and her parents were happy and moved with emotions.

"This is the most precious gift I have ever received in my life, Mrs. de Melo. How could I ever thank you enough? We will always remember the two of you," said Sonya, shedding a tear in the process.

"We both decided on the gift, but it was my husband who chose the design," Mona clarified. "You need to thank him more than me. He always thought highly of this family and is always eager to show his care and concern."

"That calls for a drink before we eat, my friends. I got a small "cutty," Augu said, referring to a four-ounce container bottle of Demerara rum. "Would you break the seal with me, Mr. Rafa?"

"For sure, Augu, that spirit would raise some spirits, I think," he answered in jest.

"The women can have a wee bit, too, if they so desire," Augu added.

Verna, in her quiet unassuming way, quickly rejected with a wicked grin. "Like you, men, are ready for a good go tonight. We, women, have to make sure that we are on our way early morning without miss, so we are going to have a bit of 'lime swank' Sonya and I made this afternoon," she proposed as an alternative.

By the end of sipping through two rums with Coca-Cola, both Rafa and Augu had unloosed their minds from the baggage and inhibitions they carried and were laughing and chatting as close friends from early bygone years. It seemed as though they chatted about everything, including the crops, the cricket matches played between the various sides in the Pomeroon and the Moruka, and the sloops that were plying between the Pomeroon and Georgetown, with their powerful engines and tall masts. They even talked about the new and larger schooners that had begun to trade directly with the Caribbean islands, traveling straight from Charity with massive loads of plantains, ground provisions, and vegetables.

They enumerated all the families that have now acquired bigger and more modern outboard engines, with forward, neutral, and reverse gear shifts. These were a big improvement on the Seagull, Penta, Britannia, and Archimedes motors with fixed forward gears. They still served as workhorses for moving heavy loads of produce, albeit with slow patience and extreme effort. Rafa acquiescently conceded that his twenty-five horsepower Mercury outboard engine on his small flat-bottomed ballahoo was not the fastest boat in the river anymore. But he assured Augu that it could still give the newer bigger Elto, Johnson, Evinrude, and Yamaha motors a run for their money. Rafa liked engines, boats, and speed. He confessed that he inherited that trait from his father and his father's close drinking mate, Juan Camacho, an immigrant from Madeira.

Augu listened with keen attention and chatted with his guest as if he was himself an outboard enthusiast. Yet the fastest speed in a boat he had experienced to date above his efficient paddling of their canoe were the times he was lucky to get a tow behind a launch or sloop on the way to or from Charity. However, he was rather knowledgeable of the innovations taking place in the river, particularly regarding faster boats. The increasing numbers of speedboats and high-powered ballahoos were a phenomenon at which most of the people of the Pomeroon marveled. It was a poor indicator of wealth improvement and class mobility among the populace, but which was flagrantly exhibited as such.

"You men must come and eat now. The dinner is getting cold and lonely on the table and is begging for some company," joked Verna.

This gave the two men a knee jerk and got them off their seats, hurriedly apologizing for their insensitivity to the women. Sonya handed Mona a new-looking enamel plate reserved for guests and another to her husband.

"You have to help yourself at that table with the food," she explained. "The pepperpot is not hot, although my mom cooked it with five hot bullnose and tiger teeth peppers and hot cayenne peppers. She knows the secret to not creating a hot dish that only a few people would enjoy," Sonya chipped in.

"So, what is the secret, Verna? I want to know because I am so afraid to add any hot pepper to my cooking," pleaded Mona.

"Sonya is as good as me. Let her tell you," Verna replied.

Then Sonya took the tag from her mother and explained, "It is quite simple. We let the food cook slowly and absorb all the good juices from the peppers but not the heat. But you don't ever break the peppers in the dish. You remove them from the pot and keep them separately in a plate," she insisted dramatically, "and only then you stir the pot, not before this, never. Later if anybody wants their food hotter and spicier, they can partake of the cooked unbroken cayenne peppers."

"So interesting and clever, my dear," Mona commended. "It's so simple, you know, but how often we forget and overlook the simple things that can make life so much better."

"You all must help yourself to a lot of the casareep sauce," exhorted Verna. "That has all the sweetness of the meat. The bread and the cassava bread are what you use to soak it up and enjoy. Hope you like it."

The guests partook of all that was laid out before them and felt like royalties being entertained. Then Augu presented a bottle of pinkish colored contents.

"This is our piwari, Mr. Rafa, which I told you about sometime before. I kept this bottle especially for when you came, and now you are both my guest and my 'compere,' the godfather of my grandchild and Missy Mona, the godmother. I am forever indebted to your kindness.

Let us drink to yours and your wife's health and happiness, and long life," he said as he poured the whole bottle out into five cups. They sipped it to the bottom until it was time for each of the families to retire and rest before the next morning's early start and long trip on the waters.

Rafa and Mona bade goodnight individually to each of the Torrealba family members. Rafa's kiss on the cheek of Sonya sent a voltage of electricity up his spine and a shiver in his heart that cross-circuited to the one he quietly admired and longed for beneath all his revelry the whole evening.

"We shall be waiting in the boat for you tomorrow and continue the company, and then you give us the chance to be your host on the launch if only for the few hours of travel," Rafa said as the couple took their leave.

They slowly and casually meandered in the walk back to their launch. They strolled together clutched in a neck embrace, reliving their earlier years when he was absolutely bewitched by his Mona. They stopped at different points and kissed like young lovers on a date, grasping every opportunity to satisfy the impulse generated by skin against skin and the tongues of two people in love. They eventually settled in the boat's cabin and sipped at a rum and coke that Rafa mixed for the two of them. He drew her against his vibrating body and passionately kissed her in a prolonged manner as she responded with the fire of that love he remembered in the first week and years of their romance. That eventful night about a decade ago during a dance party at Charity initiated a dream companionship that gave him strength and endearment ever since.

Loving his Mona at this moment was again fulfilling all for which he remained humbly grateful. In a flight of exceptional exploration of her body again, after repeatedly doing so for many years, he felt her firm, velvet presence fused against him as if it was the very first time he had discovered the nectar of her love. She tasted so sweet and pleasing to him that he consumed every drop of her intoxicating love. Her soft fingertips caressed his face and then his strong body, releasing every bit of the sensuous magic that had controlled his world and bonded him to a devotion he never regretted. She was as much overcome by the heatwave of passion that was captivating his soul and his spirit. She wanted his warm and vibrating body as much as she ever wanted him before and sobbed in submission to his firm embrace. His strong and loving hold of her was another playback of the song of fusion they had enjoyed in each other's company, wherein every sung line filled their life with an inexplicable bliss.

That night though was different. It was more than what she grew to expect in their union that exuded energy from body mind and spirit. She completely surrendered her body and her life to him in that moment of fiery exultation as their fused flesh extracted every bit of energy from the other's exalted profusion of ecstasy. This rapture seethed with a fierce intensity within her core, as boiling magma peaked in a climactic flow of hot lava, as his strength drained from within him. Then two lifeless bodies lay in silence, breathing deeply as if contentedly awed by the aftershocks of a potent earthquake. Rafa could not help but relive the moments he shared with Sonya in this very launch moored at this very same jetty. His wife's body was but a surrogate for what he was longing for all day and since he had begun to plan for this trip. Yet while he could not devalue even an iota of the usual sensuous love from a very beautiful woman, that night, he felt that he was with two persons: one when they sipped drinks on entering the launch's cabin, and another in the heat of the personal and erotic encounter. He lay still and dazed at his unfolding collision with destiny. His love for Mona was undeniable and so was it for Sonya. He had regretted neither and quietly questioned in his mind how love's infinite nature, bestowed in its entirety to the universe, should be limited in human life.

Mona's satisfaction was so evident that she unavoidably had to acknowledge her husband's revival after what seemed like a mild trough in their partnership over the last weeks. He had complained of his tiredness and had been quite sedate in their relationship.

"Rafa, love, you are back to your old self, I could sense tonight. The man I first fell in love with and continue to love without reservation showed up again tonight after a worrying lull and made me feel like the real woman I am. You really needed to take a break from the farm. This is truly a blessing in disguise, coming out to the christening of Sonya's baby," she assured him.

"I am glad to be on the river, Mona. The river is in me, you know, and gives me life every day. The Pomeroon is the lifeblood that flows within the veins of this region and within my veins and yours, and that is why we both had so much sweet inspiration to adore each other tonight. I love you," Rafa replied, trying not to divulge the inner discourse with which he grappled.

That night, the couple fell asleep soundly in each other's arms, only to be awakened by the early light of dawn that seemed to have slipped through night's dark shield unnoticed. In a while, they were greeting three adults and a beautifully attired baby on the trip to Santa Rosa in the Moruka River.

"It's a gorgeous morning, friends," shouted Rafa to the Torrealba family. "I hope you had a great night like Mona and I had. So cool and pleasant on the Akawini!"

"Good morning, good morning, Mr. Rafa and Missy Mona," replied Augu, as if speaking for the whole family.

"It is just rightly timed to leave now. We should make it to the mouth in good time to get the rising high tide to cross the Atlantic from the Pomeroon mouth to the Moruka mouth. Then it is plain cruising to the mission," Rafa said, and Mona smiled and, along with Verna and Sonya Torrealba, nodded in agreement.

At the river mouth, Rafa steered the launch towards the deeper channel to ensure that the vessel did not encounter any hidden submerged objects that could interfere with a safe and undeterred passage. The *Esperanza* made it across the choppy waters to Moruka with ease, and as most travelers do, they stopped at the trading post and store just inside the river. The unwritten purpose of this stop was primarily to exchange good wishes and cheers, a tradition that appeared often like a thanksgiving for crossing that patch of the Atlantic victoriously.

"Let's drink something and have a snack," invited Mona.

"Yes. We could find a proper meal at da Silva's at Kumaka after the Baptism. Then we can drive more casually to Kamwatta and Parakese," added Rafa.

The two families had earlier planned to head to the hamlet of Parakese to celebrate with family and friends there, the place from where the Torrealbas originated. There was a good landing and a safe spot for the launch to moor and overnight. Both Rafa and Mona were looking forward to that trip since it was a first to that part of the Moruka for both. For Augu and his family, it was a welcomed visit to a place they cherished and missed. They had not visited too often since settling in the Akawini. However, they had kept in communication by messaging through people going in and coming out for work and commerce.

A brief rest stop at Waramuri was a welcomed one for the Torrealbas, who had relatives there, and a quick meet and greet was hurried through to make it on time to Santa Rosa.

The old Catholic priest was waiting at the entrance of the church and was very relieved when he saw *Esperanza* pulling up. He expressed his delight to see the family and the little child and greeted them with a broad smile.

"My hope has materialized. I prayed and anticipated that you would have a good trip and arrive safely and not too late, given the dependency on the tide at sea. Then I saw the *Esperanza* mooring. It has lived up to its name. Now that you are here, let's proceed with the baptism, my friends," he said, leading them to the baptismal font.

"What a beautiful infant, my dear! You are the mother, I guess," the priest remarked in a rhetorical question to Sonya. He did not ask for the father; something priests were sensitive about in the region. Too often, there were unmarried mothers carrying the children of fathers who had been visitors to the reservations and hamlets in the region and who had never acknowledged their offspring.

"Yes, Father. My name is Sonya; this is my father, Augustine Torrealba, and my mother, Verna. This couple here will be the godparents, Mr. and Mrs. de Melo, from the Pomeroon," Sonya said, pointing to Rafa and Mona de Melo.

"You have made a long trip from the Pomeroon and must be tired. I am so glad that you came back to this parish for such an important event in the life of your family," the priest said to everyone.

Augu looked at the priest and responded with a sincere conviction and nostalgia. "This is the home of my foreparents when they first fled the Orinoco during Bolivar's fight for Venezuela's independence from Spain, not very long ago. That's how the story goes. This mission and parish remain the home of the Spanish Arawaks and the Delta Warraos. It would forever be etched in our hearts and memory and be the umbilical magnet that pulls her children back to the home of our early days in this land."

The baptismal ceremony was brief and highly informative for Rafa and Mona. The priest took the opportunity to explain some of the symbolic actions that were taking place. The little Anna was in the arms of Mona throughout the ceremony. She had chosen to hold the infant. For some reason, she felt a strong affinity to the child and was very proud that she was privileged to become the godmother of an innocent one in a parish so far away from her own.

Anna slept in the arms of Mona most of the time during the ceremony. She sprang to consciousness when the chilly water from the font was poured on her forehead. She refused to end her displeasure by crying through to the end.

"Now she is washed of original sin. We are all born with it, inherited from Adam and Eve in the Garden of Eden when they disobeyed God," the priest explained.

Rafa de Melo heard what was said and in his mind began to question. *Why did this innocent, beautiful baby girl have to be cleansed of the sin the first couple on this earth committed? Was that a sin at all they committed if they loved each other and expressed that spiritual bond affectionately, emotionally, intimately, and carnally? How was that a sin?*

Why did this innocent infant have to bear the brunt of their so-called blunder? Moreover, this great and so-called merciful God of the world has ever since held this against them and their offspring up to the present? What kind of God was that? He was lost for a moment in his dreaming inquiry when the priest's voice was heard again.

"We are proud to welcome her in our community of believers. In time, she will be confirmed as a full-fledged member of this Christian community. You, her family, and godparents have a duty to guide her in the faith, care for her, and protect her into adulthood. I exhort you to keep her best interests at heart at all times," he continued.

Anna's crying only ended when Sonya caressed her in her bosom and, with no inhibition, fed the teat of her breast to her mouth. Both the priest and Rafa looked on with quiet approval. Rafa further remembered how beautiful and alluring every bit of Sonya's body was and recalled how he had at one time been in the same position as little Anna satisfied and in a moment of ecstasy as if sustained from those breasts.

The priest began to explain the role of godparents. They were not to replace the parents but to be role models and personal support in her development and maturity. "Would you support this child and her parents throughout her life with us?" the priest asked of Rafa and Mona during the ritual.

Mona smiled and joined her husband in replying in the affirmative, "Yes, we would!"

Rafa was overjoyed to be pledging his support for a part of Sonya and continued to wonder if this child could be a fruit of his romance with her mother. On the other hand, was this the child of someone else? Such a thought elicited a feeling of jealousy and a misgiving he preferred not to encourage. He did not want to conjure up suspicions regarding Sonya's love for him and any possibility that Anna's arrival marked the end of it. He would rather accept if it was a further sign of their love's continuation. He would have no worry in his heart if

Anna was his child, but he would have to keep such a secret locked away within him and Sonya's secure space, just as he had done of their intense intimacy.

When the baptismal ritual ended, the priest led them all into the sacristy behind the main altar where he opened a register and set about crosschecking the information he had earlier inputted. He seemed to have ticked off everything until he pointed his pen at one point in the baptismal register and asked, "Father's last name?"

Augu did not hesitate to respond promptly and instantaneously, "Torrealba!"

The priest filled this into the register and did not ask for any further explanation. Augu's matter of fact response was enough to reassure him and end any further questions, which that obviously begged. On Augu's part, he wanted to preclude any embarrassment for his daughter and, in his humble and sincere nature, open the way for his granddaughter to begin life in a positive and approved manner. He was telling the world that this little girl was truly welcomed among them without any tag or reservation. He was intent on bringing her up in that spirit and on not forcing his Sonya to identify the child's father. He felt that no such verification was important or necessary.

They were on their way to Kamwatta after a hearty lunch in Kumaka. Mona continued to act as a nanny in the launch's cabin. Her love for the child was growing from minute to minute.

"She reminds me so much of our Madeline when she was born," she uttered with a contented smile. "She will grow up to be a fine lady one day, I can see. You must be a happy mother as I was, Sonya." She turned her head towards the child's mother.

Sonya looked sheepishly and replied, "She is truly my life and my love. I must thank you, Missy Mona, for agreeing to be her godmother and for coming out to her christening. I will remember this day, and you and Mr. Rafa. You have made us feel important and as special as my little angel."

The river narrowed as they approached the Kamwatta area. Rafa held on carefully to the steering wheel of the launch, having throttled down the engine to just about a quarter of its power. Augu stood on the left side of the launch's front deck and kept a close lookout from his vantage point to ensure that the boat did not run aground on a takouba or some submerged obstacle. He was ready to shout a warning to Rafa de Melo should he spot a danger ahead. The two of them coordinated their roles in purposeful teamwork, knowledgeable of the boatmen plying the rivers and streams in the northwest of the country. As they drew closer to Parakese, villagers soon noticed and admired the vessel trying to moor, and in a short while, a party of about fifteen people gathered to greet them. A few young men volunteered their services to help to moor the vessel at the landing and secure and lash it up against poles in the water and on land.

One of them shouted to the boat, "Uncle Augu, Uncle Augu, good to have you home. Ma and Dad are awaiting you at the house."

The Torrealbas disembarked the boat. However, the de Melos stayed put in the launch, trying not to impose on the welcome and hospitality awaiting Anna and her family. They were soon hastened by Augu to join them to go to his brother's home.

"My brother and his family will be insulted for us to arrive at their home and leave you alone in the boat, Mr. Rafa. And so, I will be also," Augu said in a tone somewhat like a retort. "If you are worried about the boat, don't worry. It is safe. No one will enter it or take anything from it. This is a small community, and everyone knows and trusts each other. But just in case, my nephew, Rolf, will keep an eye on it."

"It is gracious to invite Mona and me, Augu, and we will come for sure. Just let me get a gift for your relatives," Rafa replied. He went to the cupboard in the stern deck and came back with a flagon of pak-pak wine. "We will have something to help us celebrate tonight."

After a short walk, they reached a small ground-level thatched house with its front boarded up halfway. The front door led to a long, opened living room hall used by the family for entertainment. It also served as a dormitory to accommodate about ten hammocks hung there at nights after an entertainment was over. Two private bedrooms and a kitchen comprised the rest of the house. A latrine and a bathroom occupied individual rooms outside the house. The bathroom was usually used by females in the household and guests. The male occupants of the house washed and swam in the river every day.

"Augu, my brother! I am so happy to see you and your family. Come on in, Verna and Sonya. We are anxious to see the new addition to the family," Nathan, Augu's younger brother, said. He bent over Anna and kissed her on her forehead. "What a darling little one! And she looks so much like a Torrealba."

"This is Mr. Rafa and his wife, Missy Mona, Anna's godparents," Augu replied to his brother, introducing his guests. "They are from the Pomeroon near Charity. Mr. Rafa and his wife are the ones at whose estate we always work and stay when we go to the Pomeroon. We are so privileged to have them agree to come for the christening. They are truly kind people."

"If you are kind to my brother and his family, you are kind to me and mine also. So, stay with us as long as you want. My wife, Margie, has prepared a room for you. Stay as long as you want with us. This is your home while you are here," Nathan welcomed them.

"We are so humbled by your gracious kindness to us strangers in your home. Nevertheless, we are going to turn your offer down. Please forgive us. The launch is our home when we are traveling on the river. We bunk in its cabin. Please don't mind. We shall retire there in the night," Rafa informed Nathan and his wife.

There was a stir of activities in the kitchen, an independent structure attached to the main house by only a narrow, covered corridor. Margie was in and out of it with two helpers, preparing a feast for the evening in honor of Anna's big day and the visit of the elder Torrealba's family.

The food was eventually laid out on a table in the middle of the living room and a party of some thirty persons began to participate in the festivities. A mari-mari string band made up of a quatro, a rhythm guitar, a guitar playing bass, and a mandolin serenaded the gathering with a list of local songs and music. They stopped playing only for a break to partake of the delicious spread of pepperpot labba, steamed and roasted fish, and an assortment of ground provisions, including cassava, dasheen, breadfruit, sweet potato, and yam, cassava bread, and boiled rice. Then they were back to the music again, filling the open hall with rhythms that mingled with the soft moon glow and the dim light of a lantern, blessing the party. As the midnight hour drew closer, the band sang and played some slow Latin rhythms that erupted into the frolic of dance. Five couples jammed the floor and enjoyed an atmosphere full of love and warmth.

Mona de Melo could not help but express her joy to her husband as she erotically danced the rumba with him reminiscent of the days when they were dating. "This is probably the most romantic setting I have experienced for any party, Rafa, love. Who said you have to be wealthy to enjoy a fete?" she remarked in Rafa de Melo's ear. "I am so happy to be here, Rafa. We are going to enjoy this as Anna's night and remember it for a long time."

"We surely will," he replied.

The couples changed partners and enjoyed the company without inhibitions after the fermented alcoholic casiri and piwari were finished, and the party started on the flagon of pak-pak wine, the gift from Rafa de Melo. Augu asked for a dance with Mona, who was looking resplendently dressed, and began on a slow beat. Rafa took the opportunity to use this as an opening to invite Sonya to dance with him. He was itching all night to hold her in his arms as he had done on occasions in the past. He wanted to feel her tender hands, press against her breasts, and transmit once more his deep love for her. This was his chance. He led her with the rumba rhythm to the dark edge of the room and together, their two bodies welded in dance to each other, cheek against cheek, and palms sweating in fear and wonderment. He was reassured that he was still part of her life, and she felt the reciprocity. This time their close togetherness was short, as short as the length of a song from the band. The short tune on the floor was insufficient, but it continued in his mind and heart, even when they returned to the launch that night, like an unending symphony.

Again, that night in the launch, Mona was swept away by physically ravishing lovemaking with her husband. She was more than ever before convinced that Rafa was the same intimate human being she fell for and married. They explored each other's body from head to toe until the light of dawn began to show its face on the creek's mirror-like water. He had loved his wife all night in a spell of bodily frenzy in the same manner he had done with Sonya before, and this night was again a repeat of the previous night with Mona in the Akawini. He felt he had little control of his body as it engaged with Mona while his heart and spirit dwelled in the caress of Sonya. He wondered if something was wrong with him and drifted away into rationalizing it.

Mona was still recuperating from another grueling night of pleasure with Rafa and felt like shouting about her satisfaction from the rooftops. "We need to get away together more often, Rafa, love. I was too worried for you when you were so tired at Miriam's Delight—work, work, and more work. I could sense we were losing that sting that brought us together in marriage when this happened recently," Mona observed.

"Whatever happens, you will always be special to me, Mona," Rafa quietly replied. "Yes, it is always so much pleasure and fun when we are together, not bogged down by everyday cares."

Augu and his family stayed on with his relatives in the Kamwatta area as was planned. Rafa and his wife left the landing at Parakese at about noon and headed to the Moruka mouth repeating the route stops they made on their trip in. They had to tie up at the Moruka mouth trading post and wait for the high tide. By the time they reached the Pomeroon mouth, it was already five in the afternoon. The river current towards Charity was peaking fast, and this helped to accelerate their trip to Grant Miriam's Delight. That night they both were glad to be back in their own home and longed to reunite with their Madeline. Nevertheless, they did not collect her from her grandmother that evening, mutually agreeing to spend a night alone together in their own bed. Mona was intent on re-living the two recent special nights they had spent together before their fond preoccupation with their daughter restarted the next day.

* * *

Mona suffered quietly for several years with an asymptomatic form of pancreatic cancer. She never paid much attention to the abdominal pains she felt periodically and ascribed them to minor indigestion. By the time her illness was diagnosed for what it really was, cancer had become metastasized and spread to her vital organs. She died when Madeline de Melo was just seventeen years old. Rafa de Melo was a broken man.

When Madeline de Melo at nineteen met and married James de Castro, she felt she was the most fortunate woman in the world. He was tall and handsome, Georgetown schooled, and a promising schoolteacher at Siriki. Her greatest misfortune, though, was that her adoring mother, Mona, had departed too early. James de Castro's advancement in education was rapid. He graduated from Teachers' college with commendation and was given a scholarship to study for his Bachelor of Education at the University College of the West Indies in Jamaica. Both Rafa and Madeline (now de Castro) were supportive of his break.

They saw him off at the Atkinson Airport at Soesdyke that fateful morning at five and waited until the propelled Caravelle airplane vanished out of sight into the dark Demerara clouds before they left on their long trip back to Charity and to de Melo's Miriam's Delight. Madeline de Castro saw her husband no more after only four years of marriage. She had since spoken very little about her marriage and her husband. All she learned was that James settled in Montego Bay and had two children with a sweetheart he studied with at the University of the West Indies.

Madeline bore her agony and emptiness in a seeming monastic silence and lived all her life alone after Rafa passed away. Her greatest regret was that she was very annoyed with her father for accommodating Anna at Miriam's Delight, when Sonya and her parents died in a tragic boat accident on the Moruka River. Anna was a forlorn orphan left with her uncle in Parakese. Madeline found it difficult to accept her as her sister as Rafa wanted her to. In her mind, she took offense at her father for being unfaithful to her mother if, in truth, Anna was her sister.

In the end, Rafa was forced to return Anna to Parakese where she was an important part of her uncle Nathan Torrealba's family. This family continued the tradition of seeking seasonal labor in the Pomeroon and eked out a contented living despite the hardships and uncertainties. On two occasions, they stayed and worked at Miriam's Delight under the aging Rafa and his businesslike but sad daughter, Madeline. While in her youth, Anna stayed with the de Melos in the big house and was ill-accepted by her half-sister. On returning with Nathan Torrealba's family, she was a mere laborer in Madeline's eyes. Over time, she listened to the stories of the poetic sojourn of her father and his weakness for Anna's mother. The plantation needed the Torrealba's labor, but she just could not hide her anger towards that family of seasonal laborers. She apportioned most blame on them for making her father unfaithful to her mother.

She tried her best to suppress the thought of Rafa's infidelity. She maintained in her mind that Mona was the sole pinnacle of her father's romance, and her, the only and rightful heiress in a love-filled family. Rafa, on the other hand, grieved deeply inside, remembering his Sonya and her little baby they christened at Santa Rosa. She was nothing less than his baby angel, living in the hospitality and kindness of Augu's brother. He treated them as very special guest workers who worked for Miriam's Delight. But this tore his soul, and he never got over that grief until his passing.

Anna returned to the Pomeroon one coffee harvesting season with the Torrealbas. This time with her little girl, Anita, who was three years old. She was eager to go with the Torrealbas that season with only one thing on her mind, to show off her sweet Anita to her father, Anita's grandfather, Rafa. This was not to be. She was broken-hearted on arriving at Miriam's Delight to discover that Rafa had been buried only months before. Her orphaned status was indelibly confirmed. Her ties and Anita's with Miriam's Delight seemed severed for good, and she just had to accept her fate. Her mother was tragically killed, her father died, and her sister disowned her. She was alone.

It was strange that on this occasion, Madeline de Castro showed greater openness to the presence of Anna Torrealba at Miriam's Delight. It was nevertheless an uncomfortable relationship. Madeline was sympathetic to the plight of baby Anita more than to rebuild a rapport with the sister she rejected in previous years. She had no tools to build a personal connection of any sort if she had wished to but secretly yearned for a mother-daughter relationship with Anita. She felt she tossed that opportunity when in the early years, she had Anna returned to Parakese. She bottled-up that longing and patiently waited for the right opportunity to arise.

CHAPTER 5

FROM A GRAIN OF GLEE TO LAMENT

A message came from Denis Atkins to Mrs. de Castro. Anita was in good spirits, although still intensely stricken by the illness. She had partially recovered from a paralysis and locked jaws, and while she was unable to move in her bed, she could speak a little. She was hankering to see her son, Vernon. As a result, Denis would return to Miriam's Delight in the evening and head back to the Suddie Hospital the next morning accompanied by Vernon. Then he will bring him back later that day and return to the hospital the next morning to stay with his wife.

Vernon was utterly delighted to learn from Mrs. de Castro that his father was coming home and would take him to see his mother in the hospital. He had eaten truly little the whole day at school and had been in a state of stupor since his mother's departure to the hospital. The food that Mrs. de Castro placed before him had no glamour for him. His only appetite was to be with his mother.

"Your father will have something to eat here with me, son. I could not let him go and cook for himself as soon as he gets home," Mrs. de

Castro informed Vernon. "Maybe you would put some food in your stomach when he arrives. You need to eat, my boy, or else you too will get ill."

When his father arrived, Vernon was delighted to see him and quickly wanted to excuse himself from Mrs. de Castro's to go to their own small house.

"Sit with your daddy, Vern, and let him have dinner, and you must have dinner also to be strong for your trip up the coast tomorrow," she coaxed the boy.

She was somewhat relieved to see that he ate a portion of the food on his plate as she listened to Denis's update on Anita's condition.

"I am praying for my wife to continue to recover. She has made a little progress, and this is a good sign. I know how strong a spirit she possesses, and this will bring her through to health once more," he surmised to Mrs. de Castro.

The widow concurred in her wish for Anita's recovery and encouraged the Atkinses to think positively and leave the rest to God. Vernon and his father left the big house and spent the night in their thatched dwelling next door. It felt more comfortable to the young man. He slept in his father's bed that night. He missed his mother and could not stop imagining that she was close to his father and him because, as he revealed to his father, "I can smell Mother's smell in the bed."

The night was a restless one with only occasional spurts of catnaps for both of them. They were anxious to begin the trip back to the hospital. They left mid-morning by bus and were at Anita's bedside just after noon time. She was awake and smiled happily to see Vernon, who immediately leaned over her and hugged her. He kept kissing her cheek with sobs of both joy and sorrow. There was exuberant glee of uniting with his mother if only for this brief moment. To him, the last days with her away had been nothing less than sheer torture. He was already dreading the thought of returning to Miriam's Delight in the evening without her.

This was how it looked. She was still extremely ill because she could not move and spoke so softly that it was nearly unintelligible. What he did hear from her was that he should look after his dad for her. He must get to know Mrs. de Castro better and treat her like a real family because she was her aunt, her mother's only sister, and so she was actually his great aunt. He must let Mrs. de Castro tell him about his grandmother, Anna, and his wonderful great grandfather, Rafa, whom Anna loved so much. All this registered more profoundly in his mind, and while it still raised many questions as to who he really was and was destined to be, it did contribute to unravelling the state of puzzlement he found himself in with the related pieces of information he was hearing.

Tears began to flow from the sides of his mother's eyes and run down her cheeks. It triggered a tearful sadness in him once more.

"Why are you crying, Mama? Why, Mama? I am waiting for you to come home. Please get better and come back home. I love you, Mama," he uttered, wiping the tears from his mother's face with the palms of his hands.

"Your grandmother, Anna, and your great grandparents, Sonya and Rafa, are here admiring you, my son. They are proud of you. If only you knew them, son," Anita said very quietly.

"Where, Mama? Where? I can't see them," he asked bewildered.

"You can't see them, son, but they are here with me. They have been with me all these last days. That is why I wanted you to come and be with us for at least this one day," she replied,

Vernon's father, who stood there and listened to the exchange between mother and son, held Anita's hand, caressed it, and interrupted her asking, "What are you telling us, Anita? You are scaring the boy, love."

"They have come to see me, my love. This is true," she insisted in her frail voice and lowered her eyelids as if to fall asleep.

A nurse entered the cordoned off cubicle and replenished the intravenous drip hanging above her. "She probably needs to have a rest, sir," she said to Vernon's father. "Maybe you and your son should go and get something to eat and let her sleep for an hour or so. Then you will be able to be with her again when she had rested."

The father and son took their leave and went outside the hospital to find an affordable snack kiosk. They shared a pineapple tart and an aerated soft drink, which was more than enough for two dwindled appetites during this period of challenge.

The time was moving too fast for their liking. They needed to plan the remaining time to spend an hour with his mother and make it on time to catch the bus for Charity at five o'clock.

At her bedside, both of them held Anita's hands. Vernon felt her firm squeeze of his and showered her cheeks with kisses of love, hope, and sadness. Then it was time for them to leave.

"I love you, Mama, and I am suffering without you. I will count each day and wait for you to return to us. I miss your stories at night and the songs you sing to me. Get well soon, Mama, and come home to Papa and me," he pleaded to her and felt even worse when an anticipated response of an assurance that she would be was not forthcoming.

"Be strong, my son. I will always love you," was all she said, and they left for the bus, their souls overflowing with sadness and mental torment.

Denis and Vernon Atkins spoke little during the trip back to the Pomeroon. The conductor called out the names of every village they approached to alert disembarking passengers of their upcoming stop. Theirs was the last stop at the end of the Essequibo Road at Charity. Vernon's heart and spirit were still with his mother in the hospital. She was all that he could think of and imagine during the long and rough trip on the potholed and unpaved road. He could vividly picture how thin and gaunt she looked at the hospital, so completely transformed from the last time she told him stories, laughed, and sang at nights rocking in her tibiciri rattan chair until he was falling asleep. She was so different now, and he could not bear to think of her in this state and in pain. She did not deserve any of this because she was the best human being in the world and his adorable mother.

In his helplessness and a desperate hope to reverse her condition, Vernon turned to God as they were always told at school and at church. "Please God be kind to my mother. You have seen how good she is with me and my papa. She is never angry with anyone. She is always a happy and helpful person with her friends and with strangers. Why is this happening to her? I beg you, please let her be well again and let her come home to us. We need her. You are our good and merciful God. Please do this for her and for my papa and me, I beg you, God."

He was hopeful that God would listen to the prayer of a child like him because he was told that God loved children and He eased the pain of those who trusted in Him. Now Vernon was putting all his trust in his hands. By the time they were coming off the bus at Charity, there was a positive feeling in him that his prayer would be heard. He kept this eager hope and expectation a quiet secret and convinced himself of the goodness of God. He would not disappoint him, and so, Vernon began counting the days until his mother rejoined their family.

Gwendolyn da Silva who was returning to the Pomeroon with her daughter, Kayla, offered the Atkinses a passage from Charity to Grant Miriam's Delight when they disembarked the bus. Kayla had been hospitalized with malaria at the Suddie Hospital. She had now recovered. They sat on the seats next to the Atkinses on the bus and occasionally Mrs. da Silva chatted with Vernon's father. His parents knew them before they came to Grant Miriam's Delight when they lived in the area of the Akawini mouth with Denis's brother. The da Silvas were a large family, based at St. John's at the Pomeroon mouth but with relatives throughout the Pomeroon and Moruka Rivers. Aside from whispering to her mother from time to time, Kayla seldom chatted with anyone on the bus trip to Charity. She was about the same age as Vernon, and in better times, he would have liked the opportunity to talk with her like when they were good friends. She had schooled a short time at Charity and was always his pleasant friend. This time, though, his mind was preoccupied with the thought of his mother. Their friendship was to later grow again as they both became teenagers.

At Grant Miriam's Delight, Mrs. de Castro was eagerly awaiting their return sitting at her jetty and greeted them. "I hope you both had a good trip. I have dinner on my table for you. Come in and tell me all about, my child Anita," she beckoned.

On entering the big house, she handed a glass of swank, a local lemonade, to each of them and showed them to her dining table. She uncovered the dishes and waited for them to eat and talk about Vernon's mother. She deliberately referred without diffidence to his mother as her niece, Anita. "Tell me about Anita, my darling niece's condition, Denis. How is she doing?" she inquired.

His father's seeming acceptance of Mrs. Castro labeling his mother as her niece surprised Vernon to a certain extent. This is because, in actual fact, he still did not regard her as a real relative. To him, she was merely the wealthy woman in the big house for whom his father worked and for whom he called "Auntie" to please her. She kept her distance from them previously and only the illness of his mother seemed to have brought her closer. Vernon thought until now that she only agreed to keep him these days when his father was away out of good neighborliness, like the way Valerie and her mother tried to help. The stories she recounted to him of the family did not make sense so suddenly in Vernon's young mind. They were still interesting stories that did not yet touch down as reality at the time. His perception of this sudden closeness as relatives was that it was simply the customary respect between older people and children. The Pomeroon culture taught people that children should call and treat every elder as an uncle or an aunt, or a grandfather or a grandmother depending on seniority and age, and elders referred to the young as "son" or "daughter" or "my child" or "my grandchild."

She dished a plate of food for Vernon and asked his father to do his own. He took a small portion enough for a small child and slowly picked at it, admitting he was under a lot of stress.

"Anita was in good spirits today and was overjoyed to have Vernon visit her. They spent so much time holding hands and talking about family. She expects you to tell her son everything you know about her family so that he would pass it on to the future. So, I am sure you are going to be very busy with Vernon in the days ahead until she comes home; and then the both of you can teach him of the past of which Anita only seldom spoke in much detail. I did feel strange sometimes how she curiously began a soliloquy about her grandfather and her grandmother but hardly pursued it to any length. The fact that she attempted to recall their memory told me that there was something deep within her, crying out to unravel a web of secrets."

Vernon slept with his father in their own comfortable house that night. He was less lonely there than in Mrs. de Castro's big house but still not as comfortable as when his mother was at home with them. There was a big, sad hole left in his family since his mother fell ill, and he longed for her to be back with them to complete out their little nucleus of joy.

His father returned to the hospital the next day and stayed there with his mother while they patiently awaited her recovery. Almost every day, there was a message to Mrs. de Castro from him on the condition of Anita. Vernon and Mrs. de Castro would sit at the jetty over the riverbank at Grant Miriam's Delight and ritually wait each evening for someone, a passer-by, to stop and deliver his father's message. Each day, they anticipated that it would be good news, that Anita felt good enough to be dismissed from the hospital. This would send a rush of elation into their hearts and prompt a preparation to celebrate her welcome home. It would also erase and obliterate all the anxiety and pain they have had to endure over this period and start a new chapter in Vernon's family's life.

* * *

Two days passed and no one stopped by while they sat and waited at the river's edge until nightfall. Each day, they reluctantly lifted themselves from the bench at the jetty and slowly and speechlessly returned to a lonely house. It felt like a gloomy cavern, staid and silent, without the presence of Vernon's parents. To him, it lacked life, light and any feelings of joy.

Then on the third mid-morning, that Thursday that indelibly imprinted itself in Vernon's psyche, a visitor wrapped on Mrs. de

Castro's door. She hesitated to answer promptly since she was not expecting anyone that day. After about four or five repeated knocks on the door, she eventually opened it to be greeted by Abel Mingra's father, whose farm was a mile downriver from Miriam's Delight. Abel was a big, burly classmate of Vernon, who seemed to quietly like him and protected him from other bullying and aggressive boys. He was with his father and peered at Mrs. de Castro and him as his father began to speak. "Good day, Missy Castro," he said and continued, "Could I talk with you alone? The boys can stay together for a while."

Mrs. de Castro told them to come in and sent Abel and Vernon into the living room while she spent a short while with Mr. Mingra. Minutes later, the Mingra's were in their canoe paddling away, leaving a tearful Madeline Castro, who hugged Vernon against her bosom and remained speechless. She only began to speak sobbingly in a staccatoed manner when, frightened, Vernon demanded to know why she was crying. "She has left us, son. She has gone. She has joined my parents and her mother somewhere I wished I was myself. We are so unlucky to lose her, and she is so lucky to be with our family, yours and mine, son."

"What are you talking about, Granny?" he asked her, referring to her as a grandma for the first time. Vernon could not remember if he ever referred to her so freely as family without weighing the gravity of this in his mind.

"Your mother has chosen to go ahead of us to the family reunion. She has joined them and will not return to us here at Miriam's Delight. She has left us, son. She has surrendered to her illness. She died peacefully naming you, dear Vernon, as she left with my dear sister Anna, Anna's mother, Sonya, and her father, Rafa. That's what she said last to your father. She was happy to go to the other side from where she will continue to love you and be with you and us all in a special way."

Vernon was too shocked to really understand what all that meant. He was crying primarily because seeing Madeline de Castro in tears was too heart-rending for a young boy not even seven. He reckoned something must have truly hurt her to generate this state of sadness and brokenness in her. As he began to ponder what she said of his mother's leaving, there was a sneaking doubt on his part that this could not be true. He wondered if his mother would leave him without coming back to Miriam's Delight if only to say goodbye. He knew the oneness they felt between them and that was telling him that his mother would never leave him alone. He could not verbalize his thoughts and emotions at this time and settled for burying himself in sad remorse and perplexity. Nevertheless, he dreaded that some, if not all, might be possible, and if this was the case, his world was about to crumble into what seemed like irreparable fragments.

Mrs. de Castro reached for a small towel and, after drying her tear-filled face, rested it on her shoulder. She continued to express her regret that her closest remaining family was not going to live with her anymore at Miriam's Delight. It was also her way of categorically declaring to Vernon that his mother was indeed dead and had departed from this life for good. As this news sank into his young mind, he drifted into despair and broke into a loud painful, heart-aching cry of helplessness. He quickly moved into his bedroom and buried his face into his pillow, using it to mop the gushing of tears, loss, and anguish.

Within a matter of an hour, the jetty at Miriam's Delight had become a busy port of call for friends and acquaintances of his parents and of Mrs. de Castro. Every passerby stopped in to acknowledge his mother's death. Others made it a point to formally drop in to offer sympathy and recall the goodness of Anita Atkins. Vernon did not need any of this to testify what a wonderful human being and mother she was.

He had mustered enough courage and will power to venture out of the fortress of his room where he was sheltered from reminders that his mother was not returning alive. Upon entering the living room, it was devastating to see Mrs. de Castro slumped in a chair at the table with her face all red and wet in her hands. He was surprised to realize that his courage had him reach out to her with a firm embrace in which he assumed the role of appeasing her sadness. She responded by caressing his cheeks and said, "You have inherited the kind-heartedness of Anita, your mother, and of my sister, Anna. I wish now I had treated both of them differently—Anna, when she came to live at Miriam's Delight at the death of her mother, and Anita, whose family ties I shunned even though I knew full well that she was my niece. She lived and worked here with her husband as a mere laborer.

"She was my father's granddaughter, whom he would have loved to death like I think he is doing at this very moment. I wish I knew Anna better, and her mother, Sonya, whom I vengefully despised in my younger years. At that time," she repeated again, "I could not accept her role in my father's infidelity to my mother. For me, his infidelity was wrong even though there was no doubt that he loved both my mother and me as deeply and as long as he did, to the end of his life on this earth." She paused. "But he also truly loved my sister and her mother with true passion as a genuine family, albeit in a forbidden manner, I think."

Madeline continued, "Only now do I cherish my father's struggle in his thoughts with human limitations in the expression of the fullness and wholeness of love in life as in death. So often he used to comment on how human conventions incarcerated the expressive splinters of universal love and barred them from every step of reunion towards wholeness. My father grappled in his mind, heart, and spirit throughout his life and often spoke with me of this in my teenage years. I used to listen to him but never understood or tried to understand. Today, I am beginning to think that there was meaning then and Anita's family's life and her death have shown me that dimension of togetherness and love's gathering of its pieces towards wholeness."

That evening, a group of Denis Atkins's friends and family arrived at Miriam's Delight. Mrs. de Castro allowed them to stay in Denis's thatched hut, and they soon had six hammocks hung everywhere in his house. They had come to make preparations for the funeral. By late evening, a group of local young men had joined them. Under the light of Tilley and Petromax kerosene gas lamps, they had already constructed a temporary frame for a large tent. Tarpaulins were put on it the next day as the roof, and they hurried for it to be finished and ready for the arrival of the body of Anita later that day.

News had spread quickly about the passing of Vernon's mother. Both on the night of her passing and the following night, an announcement was made on Radio Demerara on the program "Death Announcements." Denis Atkins arranged for this in a timely way so that family and friends back in the Akawini and in the Moruca could be notified. A "wake" or vigil began with the tent builders the very first night of her death. Under a starlit night and a tent without a roof, two guitars strummed away as an accompaniment to a wide variety of English songs, Spanish and mari-mari music, and a spattering of hymns. After finishing a few "cutties" of "high-wine" rum, provided by the tent builders, the gathering agreed that alcoholic beverages would be put on hold. They then turned to Pomeroon coffee and salt biscuit crackers. Card games of "troupe," the local name for whist, and dominoes kept teams of people awake and active in conversation as the vigil lasted until six the next morning when the last groups left.

On Friday, at about three-thirty in the afternoon, a canter truck pulled up at the Charity Wharf with the coffin accompanied by Vernon's father and a few men, who served to fetch it as necessary. Several family boats waited with their passengers at the wharf in anticipation of creating a convoy on the river on the way to Miriam's Delight. One large batteau was reserved for the coffin and that lead the way at slow speed to the nervous waiting of Mrs. Castro, relatives, and the young Atkins.

As the bearers carried the coffin to its overnight resting place in the middle of the tent, it was greeted by a cacophony of weeping, wails, and lament. Mrs. Castro could not control her emotions and had a problem keeping herself on her feet. She had to be helped to the tent by the mothers of Valerie and Kayla, who had arrived early to be with her.

By that time, Vernon felt his own tears had mysteriously dried up and he remained as if shell-shocked. His father took him in his arms and hugged him tightly, kissing him on the forehead. He said nothing and he had no power in his voice to utter anything also. The lid of the coffin was kept shut as was instructed by the undertakers, with a timeline to have the burial by nine-thirty the next morning. There was no luxury of a funeral home in the region, and funerals and burials had to be organized and carried out in a timely manner to avoid too much deterioration of the remains by the time religious or other rituals were completed.

Close to a short viewing that evening, a group of women followed the coffin to a room in Mrs. de Castro's home where they prepared the body and had it presented at a short prayer service that followed. Vernon and his father were the first to view his mother as the coffin was opened for the service and for a brief presentation to the people who had gathered.

Denis did not shed a tear but looked solemnly at Anita's face, kissed her, and uttered a deep groan of anguish that expressed multi-dimensional pain, grief, and loss. In his sadness, Vernon was still so happy to see the face of his mother, one with which he was so familiar and which was always so pleasant and agreeable to him. Somehow this time that living feeling of love and endearment was missing as she lay there motionless. He held her hand, caressed it, and kissed it, but this time, there was no reciprocity like there was in the hospital. He was sad and forlorn. An engulfing emptiness overtook his whole being and sent him into unbearable grief, wonderment, and pain. Suddenly everything had changed and there was nothing he could encompass that could return his family to the former normalcy they enjoyed. He was lost with no path back to where they were only weeks before that. In his abyss of loneliness, his spirit bade goodnight to his mother as they let the crowd of mourners pass by the coffin and offer their last farewell.

The coffin was shut tight and draped that night while a vigil kept the night awake. The moon and stars came out in splendor, as if to celebrate the beauty and charm Anita Atkins, in her simple and hard-working ways, brought to the Pomeroon community. The river flowed on in its eternal and patient meanderings, ebbing to the Atlantic Ocean at its estuary and swelling to the rolling jungle hills at its head. On its way, it continued even at this trying time to cleanse and refurbish the lifeblood of the tributaries and creeks and the various reservations and settlements. Its unending passage throughout the region, more so on this eventful night, was another reminder to those who were listening that the odysseys of life will go on like the age-old Pomeroon River despite everything.

The morning had broken with a dense fog enshrouding the Pomeroon River, gradually revealing its flat and glassy face of still water as if removing the veil from the face of a bride. The motorboats managed their routes on the river by the mere sound of the engines until some visibility appeared at a close-up distance from each other. The boatmen accustomed to this regular feature on the river at certain times of year ensured that their vigilance was never compromised. This resulted in minimizing accidents, which nevertheless still occurred from time to time.

At the jetty at Miriam's Delight, at five in the morning, several persons were having a wash and readying themselves for an early start to the proceedings of the day, the funeral of Anita Atkins. Vernon's father stayed with him in his room at Mrs. de Castro's home that night after he left the wake. His and his wife's family from the reservations spent the night in Denis's thatched house together with an addition of others who had decided to spend the night. Vernon had a minimum of sleep in about two stints of catnaps, feeling too anxious about saying a final goodbye to his mother the next day. He had attended a funeral with her once before, at the Charity cemetery, and the memory of that event filled his mind and imagination most of the night, restricting his sleep. For him, transposing his mother in the place of the person who was buried in that hole then placed a heavy and disturbing weight on his chest. He just could not bear to think that his loving mother, his best friend, would be put away permanently and so crudely. The pain was too much for his young mind, and the thought of the vacuum that would be left in his life generated the worst of fears in him. This was the most difficult time in his life.

He and his father joined Mrs. de Castro and a group of others in her living room the next morning. Each was sipping a cup of coffee. Not a sound was heard and not a word was spoken until Mrs. de Castro addressed his father and told him that there was food on the dining table and that they should serve themselves. Denis gave his son a cup of freshly squeezed orange juice and took a cup of black aromatic coffee for himself. He handed him a piece of bread with butter and homemade jam and nibbled on a piece himself, not because they were hungry but because of what he whispered to his son. "Vern, my son, today is a very tough day particularly for you and me, and we must have some energy to endure it. Your mom would be very pleased to see you eat something before we join people in the tent, in the church, and at the burial ground."

A group of women who had assumed the task of preparing his mother's body for presentable viewing to all who came to pay their respect was at it again. The coffin was just returning to its place in the center of the tent when the father and son arrived with Mrs. de Castro and the group that stayed and supported her since the news of his mother's death broke. Denis and his brother serenely opened the coffin and invited people to view Anita for the last time since it was important to proceed to the church in an hour's time. That announcement raised a sense of urgency and generated a long queue that orderly walked by, from the foot end of the coffin, as if to say "goodbye" as they came face to face with her lifeless body just for a brief moment. The mourners looked at her and lamented but had no response from her—something that would never have been the case a few weeks before. She was always pleasant and most agreeable with everyone with whom she came into contact. That was the gist and flavor of the comments made generally by those who came to pay their last respects, that she would be missed widely for the genuine concern and unassuming love she had for her family, friends, and strangers.

At exactly nine o'clock that morning, the group of men and his father made their way to the center of the tent and explained to the people gathered there that according to the instructions from the hospital, burial had to take place soon. They closed the coffin for viewing, and by that time, most of the crowd had moved to and boarded several boats moored at the stelling of Miriam's Delight. A convoy of about twenty motorboats had untied from the jetty and waited on the coffin to be loaded onto the main boat with immediate family accompanying her. The hum of outboard engines created a sad symphony accompanying the hymn singing of a group of church women who were close friends of Anita. Then the slow cortege of boats followed Mrs. de Castro's large farm boat on which Anita was taking her last ride. She and Denis had used this boat almost every weekend to transport produce to the market. This time it was transporting her in the last farewell.

Mrs. de Castro did not join the funeral procession to the port of Charity and from there by road to the Catholic church where Anita worshipped most Sundays. She and a few of her friends remained at the jetty, observing all with a grim air of devastation and sadness. She did not feel that she could endure seeing the once ever energetic and active Anita being carried away in such a helpless and surrendering way to become absent in this life onward in an irreversible manner. The thought of not openly accepting Anna as her true sister and Anita, her daughter, as her niece during her life continued to haunt Madeline's soul. Her mind sailed away as if in deep contemplative transcendence. She wished she could relive the past when Anna came to live at Miriam's Delight, that time when both Mona, her own mother, and Sonya, Anna's mother, had already departed.

* * *

Her father, Rafa de Melo, cherished both these two daughters without inhibition and needed them most at that time to fill the newly created vacuum in his life. But Madeline was far too reluctant then to curb the disdain she had for her father's secret unfaithfulness to her mother. She proved difficult to Anna for every reason she could conjure up. She was uncomfortable to have a sister who was a native, indigenous Amerindian. Anna's ethnic mixture was evident with her long dark hair and slightly slanting eyes, but her looks and complexion were closer to that of the de Melos, and no one would doubt the fact that they were sisters judging by that.

Madeline's months of an unreceptive mind-set then towards Anna that blamed her for her father's actions was intensely compulsive and ever reverberated in her conscience. Now she had received a late enlightenment that this should not have been the case. Anna was not responsible for Rafa's expression of his life and love. She was merely the fruit of something her father knew was forbidden in the eyes of the world around him, but something that he did not feel guilty about. He was enchanted with that side of his life and weighed it well in the larger scheme of things. All the logic and conventions made no sense to him that the love for both Sonya and Anna was anathema. In the recesses of his heart, they were special gems in the glorious but reserved life he lived. Madeline's attitude towards her sister in the de Melo's home that eventually pushed Anna to return to live with her family in Akawini and Parakese had grieved Rafa no ends. Subsequently, being alone with her father after that transformed Madeline's life into one of chronic regret. She had forfeited an integral part of her family and could find no courage or deliberate way to reunite. It left a deep hollowness in her existence. She became an almost recluse.

When Denis Atkins and his wife, Anita, arrived at Grant Miriam's Delight in search of employment, little did she know that the means to bridge the rift she had created with Anna was about to be addressed. She was in the early days not totally certain of the connection between Anna and Anita, who was a pretty and charming young woman with a young baby and a self-effacing, if not shy, husband. Yet without hesitation, she was attracted to the family. A polite husband and a young attractive woman reminded her of her own young days with her lover, James de Castro, whom she married after a rather short courtship. Her father had a lot of respect for him and depended on him to maintain the legacy of Miriam's Delight. This was not to be because in just three years, she was to become a widow of sorts at the tender age of thirty, only a matter of two years after she saw him off to studies in the Caribbean.

From that moment, Madeline's life was turned inwards. She exuded an air of independence, aloofness, and toughness. But within that shell, she was vulnerable and empty, with a feeling of sorrow and regret that she made no one notice. Hers became a withdrawn existence at Miriam's Delight, with only a handful of relatives and friends being let into her seemingly serene yet tumultuous inner being. The arrival of the Atkins family and her easy acceptance of Denis, Anita, and their baby gave her new strength and a new dimension in coping with her secluded day to day survival at Miriam's Delight. She quickly opted to retreat from her role as hands-on manager of the estate and found in Denis Atkins someone she could trust with decision making to effectively maintain the successful family farming operation Rafa de Melo built.

She never formally appointed him, an Amerindian, as the manager, which she thought would not have been easily understood and accepted. The sons and daughters of First Nations peoples were still tacitly placed at the lowest social class in the colonial milieu of the time. However, she grew to rely on him and his wife as irreplaceable props for her continuation in the Pomeroon. Then she magnanimously decided to improve one of the logies, laborer's house, especially for the family. She voluntarily and proactively, out of good-heartedness, invested a fair amount of money to lift it from its basic shelter style for hammocks to one of a two bed-roomed cabin for more comfortable living, albeit still far below the standard of the big house her father had built for his family next door and the average dwellings of small farmers in the area. The thatched roof was patched and renewed but not changed for a more permanent fixture. So, in the eyes of seasonal laborers and the Pomeroon community, there was hardly any noticeable promotion in the status of the Atkins family. Yet in the eyes and heart of Madeline de Castro, they had virtually become part of her household and what met the public eye merely belied the actual status quo.

Denis managed all aspects of the farm, from planting to the sale of produce, as its supervisor. He did all the necessary procurement and the proportioning of labor to workers, with Madeline no more than receiving the proceeds of sales, verifying the accounts presented to her by Denis, and disbursing the appropriate payments.

Anita worked part and parcel with her husband at farm jobs and served as the face and proxy of Madeline de Castro for all her shopping and day to day errands. Her support for Mrs. de Castro allowed the latter more space and ability to cope with her cloistered existence. Madeline never remarried out of choice, fearing that she could never find another man as lenient, trusting, loving, patient, and adorable as the two men she lost, her father and her husband. The Atkins family provided her the only alternative to those qualities and that was enough for her. She was satisfied.

In the peak of the next coffee picking season, after the arrival of the Atkins family, an unexpected bombshell exploded at Miriam's Delight. One of the current batch of laborers, Marcello, from the lower Moruka who came to work at Miriam's Delight seemed very friendly with Denis and his wife after various bouts of conversation. Marcello Torrealba discovered that Anita was formerly of the Torrealba family and that her great grandfather, Augu Torrealba, and his grandfather were brothers. They were related by blood and were of the same family line. They were proud Kamwatta and Parakese people who eventually settled in the Barama before moving to the Manwarin Creek. His father had married a woman from the Waramuri mission and settled in the estuary region of the Pomeroon and Moruka Rivers, eking out a livelihood from fishing and crabbing when no farm work was available. That was enough reason for the Atkins family to delight in the fact that they now had relatives nearby in a cultural world where they were mere strangers.

Madeline's curiosity was aroused when she saw Anita on several occasions with Marcello's wife, Evelyn. She congratulated her on her newfound friendship and ventured to query why they spent so much time together. Anita tried to explain to her that there might be a family connection even though she was not too familiar with all her relatives in the Akawini and the Moruka. She confessed to Mrs. de Castro that she would like to know more of her family and regretted that she learned only a little from her mother. The prying from Mrs. de Castro over a short time dramatically revealed to her that Anita's mother was no other than the very Anna she had turned her back on when they were teenagers, the sister who actually lived at Miriam's Delight with the de Melo family in the last years of her father's life. She was the same sister that Madeline harassed in her inimitable way when she came to realize her father's divided love between her mother, Mona, and Anna's mother, Sonya, and by extension between the two daughters, her and her sister, Anna. It was not jealousy towards Anna but disappointment with the hero image she had created of her father and his un-broken love for his family that shattered when she learned that Anna was her sister. Months of indifference to Anna followed and this eventually pushed her back to her maternal relatives.

A long gap with no contact between them had ensued since Anna left Miriam's Delight at age fourteen. She was now learning that, only after a handful of years after her departure, the sister she had forsaken had mothered a beautiful child and grew her into a beautiful young woman, one that she fell for almost instantaneously and instinctively. She was convinced that someone, and most probably her deceased father, was trying to bridge the divide between the sisters in a very mysterious way. At that moment, a deep love for her niece enveloped her whole being, but she could not bring herself to expressing it in any overt manner.

She simply said, "You could very well be related to my family, Anita, but we cannot be sure, you know," and made it look like a cloud of uncertainty hanging over the notion. However, in her deepest feeling, she was convinced that this was Anna's daughter. The looks could not hide it; the mannerisms and traits of modesty, gentleness, and kindness were relived in everything Anita did and said. Despite this, she intentionally chose to love her without explicitly intertwining her once more into the de Melo family.

In Anita's mind, there was no doubt that her grandmother, a Torrealba, was both a relative of Marcello and must have lived in the Pomeroon in the early days when the old Augu Torrealba traversed the region in search of farm work. Her mother had told her of the charm of Sonya Torrealba, her grandmother, and her strong and haunting alliance to the Pomeroon. What her mother, Anna, did not tell her was that she had continued that alliance as a teenager when Sonya died and that she was very close to the man who fathered her and loved her mother. Anna was not certain of the real reasons why her mother, Sonya, never tried to expound on her connections with the de Melo family. Surrounded by various gossips about her mother's life, Anna seemed to intentionally put a lid on the little she knew. She preferred to forget the many heartaches she endured in her childhood and youth and the basic early upbringing with her grandparents, Augu and Verna.

To make matters worse, Anna struggled with the many unanswered questions she could not deal with concerning her own father, Rafa, and her daughter's father, who ran away to Venezuela disowning that he fathered Anita. Both Anna and her mother were unmarried single mothers, and the rumors were many. Often her ethnic background was blatantly denigrated as compulsively promiscuous, and this label stressed her immensely. So, while she was aware of the rumor of her mother's romantic ties on a Pomeroon plantation many moons ago, she was never to divulge anything about her own affairs out of which her beautiful daughter, Anita, was born. Much of that chapter in the family's life was missing.

When Rafa went out of his way to seek out Anna and bring her back to the Pomeroon, he initially made it out to be under the guise of doing a humane Christian deed of caring for a poor orphaned native. The general information peddled in the Pomeroon and in the Moruka was that the almost mythic Rafa de Melo had adopted an orphan of a farm laborer family that served Miriam's Delight diligently many years ago. This is what he wanted Madeline to believe and courageously gave Anna a home alongside his legitimate daughter. He never expected new rumors would escalate. Subtle discussions arose if only among his own circle of friends who knew his love for sojourning the waterways of the region. Suspicion was rife, but no one could provide the burden of proof to confirm their suspicion. Yet many folks in the Moruka, the Akawini, and the Pomeroon secretly preferred to see it as Rafa's true motive for accepting responsibility for his outside daughter and a magnanimous act.

That was when it did not take too long for Madeline to process the news of her father's infidelity and realize what a despicable folk hero he had become in her mind. All of this shattered her cocooned world of integrity and triggered a disdain for both her father and Anna Torrealba. It erupted months of discomfort over an unwanted sister in the de Melo's home. In the end, it forced Anna to move on from Miriam's Delight when Rafa returned her to her maternal family. Unsettled, she spent periods of her life in various missions in the region with close and distant relatives and did anything to survive. From there on, an opaque cloud separated the two sisters, and they never met again.

Madeline never heard of the passing of her sister, Anna, when she succumbed to malaria later and often wondered what had become of her. Her life was quietly haunted by gradually realizing her selfishness and never openly welcoming and accepting her. She lived with an undesirable torment of conscience. Now she was confronted with an important piece of her family mosaic. It appeared to her that out of some rare adjustment in the universe, her sister's child had come back to her father's legacy, and deep inside, she had acknowledged this even while on the outside she refrained to express that acceptance. Denis Atkins and his wife, Anita, merely remained farmhands of the de Melo family plantation. This arrangement suited Madeline's construct of living with family yet simultaneously living a lie regarding the true essence of one of the last true relics of her father's legacy. She never ceased to admit in her mind that Miriam's Delight was as much her own inheritance, as it was Anna's and, therefore, Anita's in Anna's absence. However, she never formally took measures to ratify such realities she stored in her mind.

* * *

As if a flash of lighting had swooped across her vision, Madeline's eyes opened to see the large flotilla of motorboats ready to accompany her own boat, carrying the coffin with Anita's body. Another funeral procession on the Pomeroon River had begun as mourning family and friends escorted this loved one on this beloved ageless river. Madeline seemed brusquely awakened by this heart-rending spectacle not only of the loss of her niece but more so of the curtailment of a true family company in her life at Miriam's Delight. The vacuum being made by Anita's leaving was too grave to handle at this time of bereavement. She slumped into exasperation and pain and had to be led by the women with her into her house as the boats pulled away.

Denis and his son sat next to Anita's coffin as the procession slowly drew alongside the wharf at Charity. The canter truck that brought Anita's body from the hospital was loaded once more for the short road trip to the Charity Catholic Mission Church. The priest greeted Anita and her family, specifically welcoming Denis and Vernon, and proceeded with a short requiem service. The service was solemnly serene and quiet, decorated with only one hymn.

The priest declared that from dust did Anita come, and unto dust, she will return. He blessed the body of Anita sprinkling it with holy water and invited anyone to remember this daughter of the Pomeroon community. No one was brave enough to come forward, and the unbroken silence and serenity continued as the pallbearers were beckoned to take her from the church and lay her to rest at the place prepared for her at the burial ground on the edge of the settlement of Charity.

Denis became emotional, and for a second time, Vernon could see the tears streaming down his cheeks. Denis said nothing and held his son close to his side, and as if he was injected with a charge of burning electricity, Vernon's emotions exploded and he burst into a loud cry for his mother. His hurt was so infectious that the moaning in the church immediately spread into every corner of the congregation as the priest led the procession out of the church. Another road trip on the canter truck took the body back to the boat cortege, which began Anita's final ride on the Pomeroon.

Vernon stood by the empty hole as the priest said the final blessings and dreaded that his mother would be placed in that dark hole covered up with cubic yards of cold earth and left in isolation. The thoughts ravaging his young mind seemed to have instilled a mute effect on his person and blinded him to the rest of the proceedings. For a while, he heard and said nothing and stared into an empty distant portal in which his smiling mother appeared. He could feel her soft lips against his forehead and her warm palms on his cheeks as she funneled her love into him. He was overjoyed and in ecstasy. Then suddenly, he felt his father's hand pulling at his and saw only the two of them peering at a mound of earth in the cemetery. Most of those who had come to the cemetery were now at the river landing embarking their boats to leave.

Denis tried to lead Vernon to the landing, but his son pleaded with him, "Let us stay a little while longer, Daddy. Mommy was here just now, and I would like to see her again. Maybe she will come home with us. I have been waiting on this so long since she left us. Let us not leave without her, Daddy."

Denis's reply was heart-rending for his son. "She will not come home to us anymore, son. She has now gone to join our family in another place, your grandmother and her family and all my family who have left us. Let us go home, son. Let her enjoy her new life with the family she always longed to get to know. They will wait for us, and we will join them sometime. That's all we can hope for."

Denis could not control his tears that had welled up for the last weeks and his distress at this unexpected parting from his wife, which shattered the very equilibrium of their contented family. A new challenge with new chapters to be unfolded lay before Vernon and Denis, and they left that cemetery to face the challenges ahead with the serenity and patience they needed to borrow from Anita Torrealba-Atkins, loving mother and wife.

In his young expectations, Vernon lived with the hope that he would see his mother as vividly as he saw her during her burial and resolved to search for her every day for the rest of his life. He was certain that her loving personality would watch out for him and guide him as she had promised, and that he would continue to feel those soothing lips on his forehead and those comforting palms on his cheeks. Even in her departure, he had found her as the new beacon in his life.

CHAPTER 6

A FATHER AND SON BEGIN A CONVERSATION

The months following his mother's funeral saw Vernon transformed into a compulsive introvert. He preferred to live in his own private space that housed the wonderful memories of his mother's love for her family. His threesome family had lived so happily in their humble setting, unreserved to express the joy of being together. His father adored his mother and forever referred to her as his Parakese Pearl. She in turn submitted to his reverence with the reticent and luring smile she always reserved for him. He grew up in the warmth of that Eden-like home that had dissipated too soon.

They continued to live at their thatched dwelling next to Mrs. de Castro's big house. His father did all he could to fill the gap in Vernon's life without his mother. But while he realized that this was impossible, Vernon never for a moment wanted his father to feel that he was failing. He loved him doubly as if his mom was still with them. He was fast growing up to be able to see that his father was making a lot of sacrifices to deflect the disruption in their lives.

Denis's day started early at six in the morning when he would report at the big house next door and distribute the day's work among the team of laborers. His workday in the fields began at seven, followed by a lunch and a siesta break from eleven to two in the afternoon when the sun was at its hottest. Work then continued until six when the tropical dusk had already begun. Such a workday reduced the exposure and debilitation by the strong middle-of-the-day sunshine. Rainy days were less worrying. Once workers were in the fields when the rain started, they would remain and work as if it was a hot sunny day. Yet if a shower of rain started prior to them entering the fields, for some reason, they would wait until the shower had passed and not dare to go out.

Knowing that he had left his son in bed as he turned out for the day, Denis made sure that he returned to get Vernon out of bed at eight, prepare his first meal of the day, pack his lunch, and boat him over the river to join the throngs of school children walking the river road to the Charity Mission School. Denis was punctually waiting at the koker mouth jetty at three-thirty in the afternoon to greet Vernon from school and bring him home for the snack Denis earlier prepared. They later had dinner together at eight, at the end of his day's work. This routine continued for years until Vernon assumed more responsibilities in keeping the home even though his dad gave no indication that caring for him was a burden. He saw it as a duty of love and a promise to his Anita.

Denis used to be an ever-avid listener to Anita's stories to their son each night as she cradled him to sleep against her bosom. He wondered how much of it was her own recanting of the stories she was told by her family as she grew up. Now he was recognizing that Anita's storytelling to her son was indeed a handing down of the oral tradition in the Torrealba family. She knew her grandmother, Sonya, for only a shorth while but was too young to really understand and appreciate the overflowing love she had and her close bond with her family. Anna communicated that well to her daughter, and while Anita was not anxious to delve into her past with her husband, in turn, she found it necessary to hand down what she knew of her family to her offspring.

There was no surprise when Denis began to carry on a nightly conversation with his son as they lay in bed together. Such a conversation ended when one or both of them fell fast asleep. He seemed to be consciously continuing the tradition Vernon's mother began with their son. Because of this, Vernon not only grew closer to his father but also learned a lot about his family, their reservation life, and, more heartfelt, the meeting of two similar souls and the short journey they embarked on together in this life.

Often, Denis would remark that Vernon was becoming the picture of his mother and that each year he was looking more like her—and usually that would trigger his storytelling.

"Yours is so much like the face of that pearl I met at the Moruka mouth landing many years ago," Denis Atkinson reminisced, and his conversation between them began on one of those occasions. He spoke as if he wanted his son to know the secrets underlining his love for his mother.

"My father and I would paddle our larger canoe through the Akawini Creek and head to that landing where many Moruka folks on their way to Charity would stop for rest, socializing, and replenishing food supplies for the rest of the journey across the Atlantic stretch, and up the Pomeroon River if their stocks were not sold out earlier. We frequently did this to acquire reasonably priced cassava bread, casareep and other commodities, like fruits of turo, cocorite and awarra palms, dried fish, smoked wild meat, and bundles of troolie palm leaves for thatching roofs. We would retail most of it at the Akawini mission, but if there was a surplus, we would sell it to hucksters at the Charity market on visits there," Denis Atkins explained.

* * *

It was on one of those trips that they ran into Nathan Torrealba and his family who were buying rations to return to Parakese. A casually dressed young woman was helping them pack their corial for the trip back the following day. She was struggling to fetch heavy carton boxes to the edge of the stelling and handing them to Nathan, who meticulously made use of every bit of space in their canoe. Only bench space was left at three points in the vessel for the three paddlers—Nathan, his wife, Margie, and his niece—to manage the heavily laden motor-powered corial when the engine was not operating.

Denis's father offered to assist the young lady and said, "Let me do this, my daughter, don't strain yourself." But before he could begin to do so, Denis was already in the process of lifting the closest box and handing it to Nathan. Anita merely stared as if in awe at him and smiled that luring smile she possessed. It melted any manliness Denis thought a healthy young man had and sent a stream of cold shiver down his spine. It was love and infatuation at first sight, as her thin cotton dress revealed a silhouette of her firm bra-less nipples. An intoxicating passion overcame Denis, and he dreamed of wanting to know this woman forever.

As twilight on the Moruka drew nearer, the few remaining canoes and their owners had started to tie up their boats securely for the night and prepare to depart at first light in the morning for their Moruka River or Pomeroon River journeys, some heading home, others continuing their commercial venture to Charity. This ensured that the Moruka mouth landing remained a busy venue of chatter, laughter, and the odd guitar, mandolin, and banjo strumming. The trade store enjoyed a night of good business, especially in the sale of pak-pak, D'Aguiar and Russian Bear rum, and Banks beer. The lively cheer and friend-making persisted in the dim light of two kerosene lanterns and open bottle flambeaus until they exhausted their fuel.

Denis left his father with his friends and explored the wharf, hoping that the family they helped earlier had not left already before nightfall. Often various Moruka folks would make a short trip even at night to the Waramuri mission where there were always traces of extended Moruka families. Denis was hoping that this did not occur.

At the far end of the wharf, he spotted Nathan Torrealba's laden corial still moored, tied at the stern to bamboo poles planted in the bed of the creek and with lashings at the bow against the stelling. The occupants of this boat were sitting at the edge of the stelling, huddled as a group with a skimpy blanket covering them from the chilly night air.

"It feels a bit cold tonight," Denis said to the threesome.

To this, an instant response came from Nathan Torrealba, "We are quite accustomed to this. We do this all the time, almost every fortnight. We are tough and cope easily. We have had far colder nights than this. Usually, the early morning hours are the worst, but we manage. You and your father were very kind today to help me with loading my boat. Where are you from?"

"We are from the Akawini mission, and helping strangers is something we gladly do without being asked," Denis assured him. "I was sad to see your daughter struggling with those heavy boxes."

"She is my niece, or grand-niece to be exact. My two children have their own families in the Waini, and I have grandchildren in the Barama area. I have never left our home area of Parakese to live elsewhere. It has a magnetic force on me. I love the place. My elder brother, Augu, brought me up, and it is only right for me to care and protect his granddaughter."

Denis suspected that there was a deep and intricate story beginning to unfold, and this stranger was easy to converse with, in a pleasant yet thought-provoking way. There was a taint of sadness in the story, and he could hear the jabbing noise in the silence of the two women with Nathan as they lowered their heads in silence. Reluctantly though, Denis felt compelled to investigate with no intention of baring badly healed scars. "What happened? Where are your brother and your niece's mother, pardon me for asking?"

"It's alright, son. We have lived with this for a few years now and life must go on. The memories at Parakese were good. The boat accident was devastating. I lost the dearest souls I ever knew, and she lost her grandmother." Nathan nodded at Anita, whose eyes were heavy with sadness and tears. "Her mother, Anna, was spared that tragedy only because she wanted to stay back with my children, her cousins. From that time, Anna became my daughter, whom I loved as I did my own children. I became a grandfather for her daughter when, at nineteen years old, she gave birth to Anita, and as fate would have it, she has remained with my family until now. I am an old man who has outlived both my niece, Sonya, and her daughter, Anna. But I have this beautiful young lady in my family to remember them by." He pointed to Anita.

"Sorry, sir, for taking you back there. I was simply curious and meant no harm. I am sad for your niece and feel for your loss and the hurt. Sorry, my name is Denis, Denis Atkins."

Nathan was glad to have the discourse with Denis and quickly responded, "I am Nathan Torrealba, this is my wife, Margie, and my niece, Anita. You are a fine young man, son, not like those ones drowning themselves in alcohol in the trade store. I hope you keep to these ways. Someday you will make a good husband for a lucky woman."

"Thank you, Mr. Torrealba. I wish you all would come and stay with us at the mission on your trips to Charity. You could take the Manwarin route slowly and not bother to face the Atlantic. It's an invitation I know my father will agree to."

To which, Nathan replied, "Who knows? Maybe one of these days we may do just that. My brother was always a wanderer, roving all the missions in the Moruka and the Pomeroon. He was fond of Akawini and Wakapao and had lots of tales about Cabacburi, St. Deny's, and St. Monica. He was a frequent visitor to Waramuri and Santa Rosa and even traveled to the Orinoco Delta a few times and spent time with distant relatives in Tucopita. I miss Augu and Verna and their beautiful Sonya. Also, now I miss their granddaughter Anna, Sonya's child."

"Is Anita's mother back somewhere in the Northwest District?" Denis innocently inquired, eager to gather every information on this flamboyant individual sitting in their midst.

He looked at Denis with some degree of disorientation and perplexity, then lowered his head and muttered, "Anita also has had her share of our family's tragic past. She lost her mother, my niece, Anna, when she succumbed to a strong bout of malaria and suffered an unbearable fever and cold sweat, without adequate medication and healthcare, until her time ran out. In a way, they are all still in this region. Their substance and spirits feed us to live on until it's time to reunite. We feel and talk with them every day and that keeps us modest in this mortal life."

Denis's guilt for broaching this topic and engendering this discussion was having the better of him. The only escape he could think on the spur of the moment was to wander off into the trade store and gradually return to his father's corial. But a new urge in his soul drove Denis to find some reason to return to the Torrealbas.

"Kindly let me have two of the cheese sandwiches, and please cut them each in two," Denis instructed the salesperson behind the counter, cleaning out his pocket to find the right amount of change to pay for the food. Walking back to the Torrealbas, he just hoped that his gift clothed in his covert ulterior motive, to spend more time with the young woman who had captured his heart at first sight, would be accepted. The Torrealbas were happy to have something to eat, and Denis was relieved of his unashamed, brazen imposition of himself into their company again.

Nathan pointed out, "You truly read my mind, son. I was just about to go and buy something to eat as we did not eat since mid-morning and creek water, and some dry cassava bread is hardly enough to sustain us till tomorrow morning."

Denis's father approached them in the dim light and laughed as he spoke to Denis, "You deserted your ol' man, Denis. I was wondering where you were, but now I can see you've found some good company and a beautiful person your own age." He was referring to Anita, who blushed with embarrassment.

Denis abruptly stuttered an introduction of the Torrealbas: Mr. Nathan, his wife, and their niece, Anita. "So nice to talk with friendly Moruka people like them."

The affability of the elder Atkins won the friendship of the Torrealbas, who engaged him in an engrossing broad-spectrum discourse of the northwest region, hunting and fishing, escapades and travels to the

Barima, Waini, and Orinoco Delta. That gave Denis somewhat of an opening to come up with an idea to meet Anita alone. "I am going into the shop to get an aerated drink. Can I get something for anyone?"

He was quite relieved when everyone politely refused his offer because he only had enough money to buy about two bottles of drink. But he persisted and sheepishly asked for Anita to come and have a drink, and surprisingly, this had the approval of Nathan and his wife. "You two young people go and get a drink. Give us a chance to catch up on the things that make this part of Guyana the special place to live in. We are true-blood Essequibians, who share the wonders of this dear land we cherish and protect it from those Demerarians and Berbicians, who look down on us as the Cinderella County. One day Cinderella Essequibo will become queen over Demerara and Berbice. Just wait."

Anita joined Denis hesitantly. In the shop, however, he was overwhelmed by her smile and the few sentences she uttered in their exchange. They sat on stools at the far end of the counter out of clear visibility of their elder folks. She sipped very slowly from a straw inserted into a bottle of Juicee cream soda drink as Denis registered every movement of her flexible tongue on the straw. For him, that was teasingly erotic. Every bit of her in front of him was electric, and tentatively, Denis took her sweating hands in his. Her reciprocal squeeze and a kiss of the back of his hand erupted in him an emission of bliss and delight at having this angel's consent of his company.

From that moment on, their conversation was wordless. They stared at each other endlessly and vibrantly exchanged their souls as their eyes magnetically peered into each other's. Then Denis's frozen spirit melted when he saw Anita's erotic smile and felt her soft lips on his cheek. Her shy kiss awakened a new lease of vigor, and his heart, and his body, began to show a sudden conversion from paralysis to strength and desire. Denis pulled her close and kissed her on her lips, which was greeted with a most sensual discovery between them. He longed for this to be a categoric sealing of love and the beginning of a wondrous journey together. Denis prayed for this to continue after they would have to part the next morning, and onward forever. He began to dream of how this could materialize.

As the night grew darker and the boat owners dozed off on the stelling waiting for the dawn, Anita and Denis slowly trekked back to their elder folks, who were still active in laughter and conversation. A friendship was struck and that was so encouraging for the couple. As they parted for the night, there was hope and reason to meet again at an invitation from either side.

When the crowing cocks at dawn started to herald the light of day, a stir of movement also began among the hazy-eyed overnighters. The mullets and catfish playing in the placid river water showed that they, too, were up and about. One by one the corials and ballahoos, those paddled and those motor-propelled, left the jetty and began their journey some downriver towards the Atlantic and the Pomeroon and the others up the Moruka to the Manwarin creek and the Moruka missions. The Torrealbas had boarded their corial and paddled it alongside the Atkinses'. Denis and his father were in no hurry to leave since their journey to Akawini could be done in a short time. Nathan shared a pot of coffee from his boat with Atkinses, and after a cup and a chat, both their boats moved off in the same direction. Puzzled, Denis asked his father where they were heading, knowing that a trip to Parakese was too far and they were least prepared for it at this time.

"We are going to take the Manwarin route to the Pomeroon and the Akawini mission. It would be a nice, casual trip today, and on the way, we could stop at a fishing place and catch some haimara fish. It would be nice to share something with our Akawini folks when we return," Denis's father explained.

The two boats traveling together told Denis that a bond had formed between these two families, and he was delighted. Both corials were powered by small outboard engines, the Atkinses' by a three-and-a half horse-power Seagull, and the Torrealbas' by a five horse-power Penta. Their faster boat operated at the half throttle, as the Atkinses traveled to the Manwarin mouth, was intentional so as to stretch the time of the families together. How Denis wished their journey to be unending!

The families veered into the Manwarin and halted for a few minutes to share pleasantries and thanks for becoming friends and mutually bidding farewell and a safe journey home. As the gunwales of the boats touched, Denis leaned over and shook hands with the Torrealbas, giving an additional kiss on the hand for Anita Torrealba. He longed for a heartier farewell, but this had to suffice for now. Then the two boats parted with the assurance from both captains that they would meet soon again.

* * *

Such stories helped Denis Atkins develop a close relationship with his son, Vernon, and dissipated any fear to discuss anything freely. They lived as father and son who were fast-growing to be brothers. Each was eager to collaborate in anything the other was doing and discussed every decision they made as to the continuation of a once whole family. Vernon was fast becoming a handsome and humble teenager, exhibiting all the quality traits of his mother. At fifteen, he was physically fit, strong, with wavy flowing hair as Anita's, and bigger than his age suggested. He possessed a resilience to face any task and challenge. Denis recognized every trait of Anita in his son and, in a hush, idolized him as an angel, as he did his late wife.

CHAPTER 7

A TEENAGER'S DISCERNMENT; A WIDOW'S REMORSE

Denis Atkins found it disruptive to leave his farm work at three every day to wait for his son's return from school and to settle him in for his afternoon snack and homework. He wondered if this routine was acceptable to Mrs. de Castro, or if she was merely enduring and tolerating it. He raised the issue with his employer as a request for Vernon to stay at the big house with her until he finished work late in the evening. He would get Valerie's mother to pick him up when Valerie was picked up.

"That's a great idea, Denis. I would love the lad to keep me company. Without Anita, I am feeling lost and alone. I know Anita, too, would love this. What I should have offered my niece, I can now give to her son. In fact, what I should have shared with his grandmother, I can now deliver to my sister's grandson."

Denis Atkins replied, "I am not asking anything more than a place to stay after school and some supervision until I come home to give him his dinner and put him to bed. In this way, I would be able to concentrate on every priority on the farm without too much distraction. I owe this to you and Miriam's Delight for giving me a permanent home and a fulfilling life away from the reservation. What more can a poor buckman ask for?" he said with unashamed humility.

Mrs. de Castro was taken aback by this comment and cautioned him never again to describe himself in such derogatory terms. "You are a hardworking and honest man, and your being part of the indigenous races has not diluted any of this. You married a mixed Amerindian woman, whose mother was my own sister from the same Portuguese father, Rafa de Melo. Perhaps in the old days, I had a disdain for his Amerindian loving ways and his faithful allegiance to Sonya, Anita's amazing grandmother. But now I have processed that journey my father made and realized that his heart was overflowing with love and that overflow has produced a line of an amazing family. Vernon has a right to be where his great grandparents established his roots, at Grant Miriam's Delight, and from where, I have to admit, his grandmother was forced out by my nagging disapproval. My stupidity had a strong sway over my immaturity, prejudice, envy, and desired recompense for my father's infidelity to my mother. I am to be blamed for returning her to Parakese, and I cannot repair the damage. It seems that some cosmic forces had a hand in the separation of two sisters. But in the end, it was me," she regurgitated. "Don't I have another chance as those cosmic forces lean this time towards me?"

Madeline de Castro continued her confession, as if seeking absolution from Denis Atkins, who listened quietly and provided ample room for her to drain her pent-up guilt and express remorse for the strange distance she kept between Anita and herself. It provided a lot of answers for the peculiar relationship they had, which Denis Atkins vaguely understood, nor pried into, nor questioned. Up until now, he considered it the behavior of an eccentric widow, who liked her privacy and aloneness. His attitude to her was to let her be and simply undertake the tasks of his employment at Miriam's Delight in a manner that did not displease his employer. He was aware of how his ethnic origin had been classified amidst the authoritative influence of the Portuguese community and the growing new settlers in the Pomeroon.

She continued: "My father had brought Anna to Miriam's Delight under the guise that he was adopting an unfortunate orphan, you know. For that, the church community reiterated the high humane status he enjoyed all his life," she recalled. "Today I will assume responsibility for Vernon at Miriam's Delight, not as a humane guise towards an unfortunate orphan, but as a cause for true bonding with my lost bloodline. Vernon has every right to be here, and I have a duty of love to support him now more than ever. I am overjoyed. He is family, and by extension, his father is also. I need no thanks and acknowledgment for this."

A boat pulled up at the jetty, and someone yelled for Mrs. de Castro. It was Valerie's mom delivering Vernon. The sprightly lad leaped out of the boat and greeted the older lady, who opened her arms and requested Vernon to come to her: "Come and give your old granny a nice hug. There is a snack ready for you inside." She turned to Valerie and her mom and said, "Come and join us, you two. There is plenty for everyone."

Valerie's mom excused herself and promised to stop by another time when she was not in a rush to prepare her family's dinner. They paddled off to their farm at the end of the range, drifting swiftly with the falling tide.

Inside the big house, Madeline de Castro led the young teenager into an empty room near the kitchen-dining room and told Vernon to leave his bag and books there. "You will do your homework here when you have had your food at the dining table. This is where you will work and rest every day after school until your father returns from the fields."

This time, the big house was less unfamiliar to Vernon. On several occasions during his mother's illness and hospitalization he had spent time at Mrs. de Castro's. Yet he could not change the underlying feeling of non-belonging he had there. The thatched house next door was more comfortable and inviting in its unpretentious bareness.

In any case, he began to question in his mind why he was not considered big and mature enough to stay by himself there. He, nevertheless, conceded to the arrangements made by his father, and before long, he was rather enjoying the company of the old lady. He could have done with less pampering but enjoyed the many stories Madeline related about Rafa and Mona de Melo and about the beginnings of Miriam's Delight from Amazon rainforest to a productive and valuable riverfront farm. She told him of the coming of the Jesuit priests to Charity and the building of the church and school there, and one by one, the building of church and school at Martindale, Marlborough, St. John's, and Siriki, and she told him of the early productive sugar, coffee, and tobacco estates owned by the first settlers to the Pomeroon, the Dutch.

She proudly emphasized that the Dutch first settled in South America right here in the Pomeroon, with the military post and fort, Nova Zealandia, at the junction of the Atlantic Ocean and the mouth of the river. Many of the old Dutch plantations were abandoned after the emancipation of slavery, and the early Portuguese, who were brought to the colony to replace African slave labor, instead took occupation of large segments of reforested estates and developed coffee, citrus, coconut, and indigenous food and fruit farms. That pattern prevailed to the present time, with the various newcomer ethnic groups, who all melded into the unique microcosm of the country in that one district. Madeline's pride of the Pomeroon exuded a tacit claim of the strong original inputs of her Portuguese heritage to the formation of the character of the region and its people.

Then when she realized that the teenager she chatted so pleasantly with was noticeably less Portuguese, she highlighted something she felt she had missed. "But you know, my son, if the Amerindian people did not let others use their land, none of us would have been here. All of us owe you and your father's people."

* * *

As the annual church and school fair drew near, Madeline was busy preparing a variety of savory foods to be sold. She reminded Vernon that parishioners from other churches along the river would all converge on Charity for the gala of the year. Vernon was anxiously anticipating the day when his friends would gather for fun and excitement. Some of them whose family settled away from Charity at the other mission areas may very well attend the fair. He was hoping that he would have another opportunity again to meet Kayla from St. John's, whom he thought of often since the day he and his father traveled with Kayla and her mother from the Suddie Hospital when his mother was hospitalized. He was too broken and dazed by his mother's illness to even renew the friendship they once had as young school children at the Charity Mission School. He remembered how beautiful she looked that day and earlier as a young fellow student at Charity. He was lucky to meet her on a few occasions since then and wished there was less distance between their homes that restricted their ready interaction.

He was looking forward to meeting up also with Albert, Lloyd, Barbara, Verna, Isri, Nona, Adele, Desmond, Sirini, Valerie, Abel, Esar, and Savitri, to name a few of his school and family friends. Together they could have an enjoyable day while their parents worked the stalls and food courts. His favorites among these friends were Valerie, Abel, and Adele. He thought that Adele liked him in the early days, but he was too shy to reciprocate, always thinking that the van Sertimas were very wealthy, and he was just the son of a farmhand. It was awkward for him to invite her to their thatched cabin.

He met most of these friends daily and enjoyed their company but felt it would be more enjoyable if he met the few other friends he had—Kayla for sure, from downriver, and Carol, from upriver, both of whom his discerning eyes were beginning to distinguish as different, having something in them that was intriguing. The occasional weekend meetings with them when Charity was transformed with the crowded convergence of the river people for trade and commerce, for religious and social gatherings, and for the replenishing of survival stocks always aroused a desire for more frequency. This was unquestionably out of his control, and something he wished he could change as he grew older and more independent.

The jukebox was blasting country and western music, ballads, rock and roll songs, and old-time calypso music. A crowd was quickly building up at the Charity Mission School grounds on a bright sunny day. The food and game stalls attracted a seemingly unending line of patrons. Valerie, Isri, Albert, and Lloyd were the first of Vernon's friends to turn up. He was pleased as punch, and in no time, they were attacking cans with tennis balls for attractive prizes and playing various games. Valerie stayed close to him while the others dispersed among the crowd and reappeared every so often to brag about their achievements and show-off their winnings.

Denis had given his son some pocket money, and this was supplemented by Mrs. de Castro, unknowing to Denis. He played a few of the games but restricted himself seeing that Valerie was not keen to participate in the challenges that attracted the young teenagers. He invited her to join him at the ice cream stall Mrs. de Castro operated. It was well patronized, with a long queue lining to buy cones. On spotting him, Mrs. de Castro beckoned him by hand and requested him to help with cranking the churner to hasten the production of the next batch of vanilla ice cream. The supplies she was serving from was running out, "You have come at the right time, Vernon. You are godsent. I badly need a hand this very moment."

Valerie smiled and led Vernon to the churning bucket. Inserting the ice and salt in the outer cavity indicated that she was familiar with making ice cream from a churner. Mrs. de Castro loaded the inner bucket with the cream ingredients. Working together, the two teenagers efficiently collaborated, chatting and laughing. They were enjoying each other's company and did not mind that they had lost the rest of the group. The noon sun was taking its toll on frolickers, and the few coconut and cassia trees at the edge of the trench running alongside the main road became a cool breezy haven and a pleasant dining area where friends and strangers alike were having a delightful time. At the other end of the fairgrounds, next to the church, another gathering had assembled in the shade of the mango and rubber trees. However, there was still a buzz of activities at the stalls throughout the day.

Valerie connected with her mother and was assisting her in monitoring the pots of food she was preparing and serving without a break. Vernon explored the various stalls, looking closely at every group and individual before him, instinctively or more consciously looking for both Kayla, Bernice, and Carol. He felt that any or all of them would be the highlight of his fair. However, as only the last two hours of the festivities remained before the evening darkness began to envelop everything, he was giving up on this wish with a degree of depression. As he walked back to Mrs. de Castro's stall, he could see the profile of a face he thought he recognized. Kayla was desperately trying to find him.

"Hey, Vernon!" she shouted from a distance, and the two young people sprinted to each other, suddenly braking to stop for an embrace.

"I was beginning to concede that you would not come to the fair," said Vernon.

"I could not miss it. A boatload of St. John's people came here since early in the day. My mom and I left them to see her sister and some of her folks at Jacklow. I had to wait a good while for a ride to Charity, and that's why I am late," Kayla explained with a gleam in her eyes. "You are not sad today as the way you have been the last years. I like you this way," she continued as Vernon took her hand in his and led her in a stroll across the fairgrounds.

He responded with a shy smile. "And you are more beautiful than any time before. I wish you were still at school at Charity. We would be best friends."

Her reply sealed his joy for the day when she said, "We would be friends even twenty miles away. Distance does stop people from being friends."

He said with satisfaction, "Then you must visit me whenever your folks come to Charity. I will look forward to this, promise me."

"I would love to meet up with you more often if it is fine with your father that I stop by at Mrs. de Castro's place," Kayla unapologetically replied.

Vernon assured her that his father would not object. "Come, you hear! I will wait for you. I will tell my father."

The volume of the jukebox music was markedly lowered, and revelers knew that that was the cue for the day's proceedings to wrap up. Purchases at the stalls were reducing, and some stallholders were already dismantling theirs. The main road to the wharf, with the numerous boats tied up there, had become a busy escape. People were accustomed to departing for home at dusk to avoid the fast fall of night that rapidly covered everything like a thick blanket of darkness. Most of those returning to dispersed areas up or downriver had either left already or had arrangements to stay with relatives or friends. Kayla grasped the hand of Vernon so tightly that it left no doubt in his mind that something creative between them was forming. Their teenage hormones were beginning to betray their restrained timidity. A polite and discreet embrace developed into two youthful bodies holding firm against each other, and she kissed him on his cheek. He, in turn, smooched her on her lips as they parted, hearts full of emotions and desire. She blew a kiss to him as they moved in opposite directions.

Denis Atkins had left the fair in good time to collect a motorboat from Miriam's Delight to fetch Mrs. de Castro to her home. He was soon back at the fairground gathering his employer's belongings and carrying them to the boat. At six-thirty, when only a glimmer of light remained, they turned into Miriam's Delight.

Mrs. Castro beckoned them. "Come in and have dinner with me before you go to sleep, you two young men. I have something prepared, and it would only take a minute or two to heat up."

Denis replied with a grateful acceptance, "Thank you, Missy. That would save me from going now to prepare dinner for Vernon. He looks tired and needs to wash and rest soon."

* * *

The next day, early Monday morning, as Denis was apportioning work for the farmhands, Mrs. de Castro called him and asked him to come in after he dropped Vernon over the river for school. "There is something I need to discuss with you and do not want to put it off any further," she said in a toned-down voice.

"Alright, Missy," he replied, wondering why the somber tone. Did he mess up in his tasks in some way or another? He was worried because he never ever wanted to displease her. He enjoyed being at Miriam's Delight and had nothing to complain about. Mrs. de Castro had always treated him with respect, albeit keeping a dispassionate and somewhat formal distance between them. He recalled that she was fond of Anita in a weird kind of way, the reasons for which he only began to understand in Anita's last days. "Now what?" he was thinking.

Denis wrapped at the door of the big house at the ground floor entrance as soon as he returned. He was too nervous to delay hearing what might ruin his day.

"Come in, the door is not locked," Madeline blurted out as Denis uneasily entered. "Sit at the table while I heat this coffee and food for you."

She was preparing a breakfast of 'bake" and salted fish cooked in tomatoes and thinly sliced white potatoes. Denis was totally confused. This was one of the few times he was invited to have a meal with Madeline. This, though, was at a time he thought he was in for a scolding. It did not make sense.

"I don't think you had your breakfast yet," the elder woman articulated. "Am I right?"

Denis confessed that he rarely ate until eleven each day when he came in for his midday break. He would feed his son and get him to school on time and proceeded, without losing time, straight to the fields to join the other laborers, partly to conscientiously put in his full share of work and to carry out his encouraging supervision. This way, he was able to evoke a positive attitude among workers having to endure the drudgery of coffee and citrus farm work. Coffee berries were picked one by one and toted around their necks in bags called *joras* as they balanced precariously on locally made wooden three-legged ladders. They climbed the same ladders to prune the tall Valencia orange trees and to pick ripened fruits at harvest time, evading as much as possible being pricked by sharp thorns. These thorn-filled sprouts were gathered by ungloved hands and heaped in piles about a hundred feet apart where they rotted and broke down over the months. It meant that they were susceptible to painful scratches and punctures of their skin when they least expected. Theirs was hard and treacherous work, and Denis was aware of and empathetic to it.

"That doesn't seem to be a good habit, Denis. You work hard, I know this, and you need to take care of yourself, especially without our dear Anita around to fuss over you and your boy. I will have to see that you do this for her sake. So, sit and have a meal. I need to talk with you seriously," Madeline reiterated. She began by focusing on the food in front of him. "Is the bake and saltfish, okay? This was my dad's favorite for breakfast, and I continue to remember him every time I make it. Rafa de Melo was a good father. He loved me and my mother without question. He had a lot of love to give and gave it in so many ways to so many people, those he knew closely and even strangers in need. I may have judged him negatively at one time in my life and retaliated when he seemed to have betrayed my mother. But he really did not, you know."

She continued, repeating a story Denis thought he heard before, "It was only my anger and disdain. I am sorry for that and for the embarrassment and hurt I put him through when he simply acknowledged his responsibility for his decision when he brought a young girl as an adoptee after my mother died. He genuinely wanted me to treat her as a sister, which I was not prepared to. That period of Anna and me together at Miriam's Delight with my father was rough and tumultuous and resulted in my father's unannounced trip to the Moruka with Anna, whom I never again saw. I have lived with this guilt all my life, and I do not want to die with it before I make amends.

"I have called you here today to take the first steps to erase that black stain in my heart. I have enjoyed keeping Vernon after school each day, and I can sense he is becoming more comfortable with me and that is good. He is my grandson, and I want him to know and accept this. He is Anna's grandson, and with her not around, that truly makes me his grandmother. It is the least I can do for Anna. I really need her to smile with me when she sees her grandson and the way I love him, and more than anything, I need Anita to feel happy that her son is well looked after by a close family and you, of course. I am proposing to you that you let him stay with me in this house that has always been too big for me alone anyway. Please consider this positively. I am not coveting your son. I just want to support you to give him a good life with all the essentials."

Denis was taken aback by the request and instinctively imagined what a vacuum would be left in his thatched cabin without his son there. His countenance drooped in anguish under the weight of that suggestion. He stuttered, "But-but-but, Missy," then he took a long silent pause before saying, "Okay, Missy, it will be good for the boy as he is growing up. But-but-but how would I make out without him? An important part of me will be gone, Mrs. de Castro, and I worry that this could disrupt his wellbeing, too, not so long after we lost his mother."

Mrs. de Castro took the time to ascertain that. "Vernon has heard me regularly tell the story of his grandmother and is quite comfortable to know that he does have a caring grandmother in me, his grandmother's only sister. And he would not be separated from you at all, Denis, because I have an important project for you to work on. Your current cabin is required for two additional hands to work here. I am asking you to give that house up as soon as possible."

"I don't understand, Missy," he reacted. "What happens to me? Are you laying me off from Miriam's Delight? I haven't done anything wrong, have I? I am sorry if I did. I worked here beyond the call of duty to stay here and serve you effectively. This will break me forever. I could not recover from this. Please, Missy."

Her dry laugh taunted him like a kiskadee bird plucking her sharp beak into a ripened banana. She hurried to straighten out his warped assumption regarding her proposal. "What are you thinking, Denis? You have done a great job at maintaining Grant Miriam's Delight, just like my father did before. Every bit of work you do, every decision you take at this grant reflects what Rafa de Melo projected in his plans. You are irreplaceable, Denis. You belong here as much as Vernon and his mother were. I think of you as a family, and I cannot repay you for your loyalty and hard work at Miriam's Delight. You, too, must stay in this big house as soon as you make the necessary renovations."

Denis was relieved and had to pinch himself to come out of what he thought was a nightmare evolved into a wondrous dream. "What, Missy?" he asked incredulously. "What renovations are you looking at?"

Madeline de Castro outlined a plan to convert the whole of the ground floor of the plantation villa into a self-contained apartment. The changes to accomplish this would not be major. "First, we would stop using the inner stairs from the ground floor to the upper floor of the house. You would attach a deadbolt on either side of the door at the top of the stairs. In this way, no one can use it, coming down or going up. It will remain there mainly for emergency purposes. The small kitchen on the upper floor would be improved to become my regular kitchen, and you would remove the wall separating it from the dining room, making a large open concept room. That would make a self-contained living space for me, incorporating the three bedrooms, kitchen-dinette, pantry, and drawing room. But I would need my own entrance to the outside, and for this, you would need to build a balcony with stairs leading into the upper floor from the flower garden in front. That would make my life restful and serene, watching the old untiring Pomeroon traveling back and forth to the Atlantic every day and give me a chance to linger among the roses below when they beckon me as they often do.

"The lower floor already has three bedrooms, the current main kitchen, a living room, my father's small office, and a storeroom. This should be somewhat comfortable for you and the boy. I want this for him because I need him close to me the rest of my years if this is possible." She paused with a sigh of relief, feeling that her outline of the arrangement was clear. "Does it make sense, Denis? Or are there things I am overlooking? Please tell me that you are in favor, and you will begin work immediately."

There was a feeling of disbelief and joy interwoven in his floating mind. "I will be doubly indebted to you, Missy. It would be the best thing that has happened to me since Anita and I came here from the reservation to look for work several years ago. We had chosen to come here only because Anita had remembered her mother telling her of how she lived with this family, the de Melo family, for a short while in her young days and how kind the owner, Mr. Rafa, was. And that was confirmed in minutes after we met his daughter. She hired us and gave us a place to live in, and I have had no regrets since. Anita's parting has shed new light on the roots and life of Vernon, and I am pleased with your accepting him. It will give us a deep sense of belonging, one that we have lost since we journeyed away from the reservation at Akawini. I am ready to work on your plans, Missy."

CHAPTER 8

THE SPORTSMAN

Vernon enjoyed his new home as if it was his from birth. The years passed unnoticeably by, and at fifteen, he was energetic, handsome, and gifted, but going to school and doing his best was something both Denis and Mrs. deCastro had to remind him of frequently. His days at school were long until he returned often after five every day. But he was not studying books or engaging with teachers. He spent every free minute he had each day on the cricket ground, bowling or batting a hard cork ball or a ragged tennis ball. He was gifted in a special way as he sped in and catapulted a ball past a batsman or spun it with a wide turn, missing an outstretched bat.

When he batted Coach Alonzo would commend him for the straight angling of his drive. "This straight bat is what we would conquer the Siriki School team with. We are going to beat them for the first time this season—watch and see!" he remarked, overlooking the fact that the Charity team must first beat St. John's in the upcoming match. A loss could allow Marlborough to take the Lower Pomeroon Championship on points and the right to play Siriki in the finals.

The Pomeroon School Cricket Competition was a crowd-puller in a county where cricket was merely a growing sport in its early years.

The Essequibo senior team, which was a disorganized collection of players who pitted their raw and untrained skills against well-drilled teams from Berbice and Demerara, were easily overrun. They became openly a laughingstock, a team that merely presented full points to one of the other two teams and an easy advantage in the inter-county championship. At the school level, however, the sport was a great generator of civic participation, revelry, and rivalry. An inter-school cricket match was well attended by the parents from the schools, men and women alike. There was always a noisy crowd of spectators at the matches, commentating, coaching, arguing, applauding, and gasping—both in laughter and pain—as each inning unfolded. On match day, the host school was virtually on an unofficial holiday. Both teachers and pupils had little interest for a day of academic schoolwork and spent most of the day watching the match, which started at nine in the morning and ended as darkness set in in the late afternoon.

The last match of the downriver competition was in two weeks' time. The Charity School cricket team had been victorious in all its matches against Martindale, Liberty, Akawini, Hackney, and Marlborough. St. John's was the last hurdle left before going on to play the upriver champion, Siriki School. St. John's had also beaten all the other downriver teams, except Charity and Marlborough. This was a clash that was discussed in the rum shops and every gathering with some inclination to sports. A large crowd was anticipated at Charity on the last Friday of July, just weeks before the summer vacation. Boatloads of revelers were expected from the St. John's area, and farm work on the farms around Charity would definitely be put on hold for the day. That weekend promised to be a busy one at Charity, with its pubs gearing up for bright business and food sellers preparing their usual array of food and fruits.

The Charity cricket team was named, a fourteen-man squad of the best players in the school. Vernon stood out among his teammates because he was one of the tallest, gifted, fit, and, as the girls would say, the most good-looking on the team. He was aware of his popularity, especially among the female supporters of the team. He knew that Valerie, Adele, and Nona would be cheerleading from the sidelines for the team and for him more than anyone. He, therefore, convinced himself that his performance could not be less than magnificent for the team and his school but, more importantly, for these girls he admired. He knew he had not yet intimated to any of them how he actually felt about them. He was torn by the push and pull of hormonal forces in his teenage years to the extent that he could hardly choose one over the other even though at least two of his everyday female friends stood out in his mind. Valerie was a friend of his family. Without a father around, she implicitly accepted Denis Atkins as her surrogate father; Adele was secretly someone he wished he was more open to. Kayla, however, was the one he yearned for despite the distance that kept them apart. He wondered if she and her family would be coming to Charity for the day. He wanted so much to see her again because in the last few months, they met each other only a few times.

The last of the practice sessions for the team was in progress Thursday afternoon, the day before the match. The coach's brother, one of the three brothers who played for the senior Charity team, and Jim Patterson, another player from that team, turned up to drill some last-minute tips and techniques into the players.

"Are you going to bowl pace tomorrow? Or will you just spin?" Patterson joked with Vernon, aware that he was capable of both.

Vernon looked to the team captain, shrugged his shoulder, and replied, "It depends on what Suresh Misra wants of me. I am ready for anything, anything to secure a win."

Misra was the newly appointed captain after disgruntled feelings among parents that preferential treatment had been given to certain families for too long. He knew he would be on trial before his critics and joined in with, "I will use all the talents we have on the team whenever they are necessary. Let us make those decisions on the field tomorrow."

Once the stumps were removed, the two senior cricketers stayed and worked with the boys to put the final touches to the wicket. The dust was swept off, and a heavy roller was tugged by two people, back and forth, to make the pitch as level as could be achieved. Water was sprinkled at various times during this process, and a final soaking of the turf was administered before they left the ground.

Early the next morning, as Vernon and his father were making their way to the school ground, two boatloads of noisy St. John's supporters led a three-boat convoy towards the Charity Stelling. The third boat carried the team, whose arrival was greeted by the Charity coach and match organizer and a throng of inquisitive young students eager for the headteacher to announce a relief from classes and permission to watch the cricket. This was at the mere discretion of the headteacher since that match day was not a designated school holiday.

The two competing teams made their dugout at the opposite ends of the school building where enough school benches were laid out, about twenty seats for each team. The St. John's team arranged their communal gear, whitewashed batting and wicket-keeping pads, gloves, stumps, and bats. The playing eleven and the stand-by players from both teams were donned in stiffly ironed white clothing, cotton shirts, and drill fabric trousers, exuding an air of formality to the day's proceedings.

The two umpires for the day, a teacher from each school, proceeded to the middle of the ground in the middle of the wicket and were soon followed by the opposing captains, Suresh Misra and Reynolds Garraway. The St. John's captain won the toss, calling "Heads" at the spin of the coin. He decided that his team would bat first. He signaled to his opening batsmen to put on their pads and get ready to start the inning. Misra led the Charity players out to the middle and meticulously set them at strategic points in the field. He threw the brand-new hard red cork ball to Reginald Alonzo, the previous captain, who opened the bowling with his quick left-arm deliveries. His pace and accuracy subdued the St. John's batsmen. The next two bowlers continued this trend, and after some ten overs, St. John's had trudged to a dismal score of only twenty-three runs. But they did not lose a wicket and were prepared to play a careful rather than an aggressive and attractive game.

At the end of the tenth over, Misra, Alonzo, and Joe Carter met for a quick discussion and called Vernon in to join the circle of strategists. Misra handed Vernon the ball and said, "I am not asking you to bowl pace at this time. Throw down some slow leg-spin and the googly in between, and let's try and make some inroads into their batting."

Vernon was pleased and scared at the same time but always enjoyed a challenge on the playground. This time, he was certain that some beautiful eyes would now focus on just one person of the team and not on the whole band of white-clad youngsters. He was eager to put his ability on show. He bowled his first delivery, and any mediocre batsman should have hit it out of the ground, a slow full-length full toss the batsman missed completely in his eagerness to blast it as hard as he could. It twisted his middle stump, and their first wicket fell. A tsunami of blood rushed to his head as he heard the joyous frenzy of the Charity supporters. He could see Valerie and Adele leading the chorus of applause at the edge of the ground. They were screaming his name, and he was so surprised to see Adele, who was normally of a subdued nature, joining the rapturous ovation. He bowled another four overs without success, and Misra took the ball back from him. It made him feel for a moment that his one wicket success might have been a fluke, and the pleasure of it quickly vanished.

Carter and Alonzo then removed five wickets between them. An additional two bowlers could not stem the flow of runs, and with seven wickets down, St. John's had scored ninety-eight runs and was threatening to amass a large total. A total of one hundred and fifty runs would be a strong total for any school team in the competition, and one that would pose a tricky challenge for the host team. Misra called Vernon in for another spell of bowling and instructed him to continue bowling slow leg breaks. At one hundred and thirteen runs of the board, he was saluted by the partisan crowd again. He had got his second wicket. This time, his head was cleared, and with a renewed vigor and a sense of duty to his school, he bowled with deep concentration and penetration. The team was bowled out for one hundred and twenty-eight, and he had taken the last four wickets.

Mr. Patterson, a teacher and a key cricketer in the senior Charity team, threw an arm around Vernon's neck as the team entered their dugout and said in jest, "You have earned your lunch; you have done us proud. But the job is not done That's not a bad total. However, it is one that the Charity players could overrun easily if they do not get too carefree."

Vernon could not help but recall the first match they played two years before when Martindale, of all teams, one of the weaker ones, bundled them out for a meager total of seventy-six and humiliated them. They must put that defeat behind them and positively attack that total to win. Valerie, Adele, and a bevy of their friends surrounded the last of their players to walk into the dugout and cheerfully hauled Vernon out of reliving that gloomy moment at Martindale. An early lunch was taken at eleven-thirty; the hot midday sun was coming down in all its fury.

At twelve-thirty, Carter and Misra walked out to face the talent of the St. John's bowlers. They were an accomplished pair of opening batsmen and had made easy work of many a total for the team. Today, though, they were struggling, convincing many spectators to blame the turf wicket for being slow with many deliveries suddenly deviating. At sixty on the board, four wickets had already fallen, and Vernon's knees were shaking as he walked out to the crease. In the heat of the midday sun, he was literally shivering out of a debilitating fear and a tugging rush of adrenalin to do something spectacular. His batting performance was intense that day. He had very slowly accumulated a painful twenty-eight runs without much fluency. At ninety-four runs for eight wickets, the Charity team was on the verge of going down— another thirty runs to win and only two tail-enders to bat. At a drink break at the edge of the field, his father scampered to his son's side and softly uttered in his ear, "Let my Anita lead you, my son. I really feel she is here with us today. Do your best for your mom."

Vernon was still not out and someone the whole Charity community was looking to for a miracle. He gritted his teeth and was ready for the challenge. He felt a new energy taking him over. They lost their ninth wicket at one hundred and seventeen and needed some twelve runs more to get over the line. The total crept up one run by one run and caused anguish and horror when a near-miss could have run out the last wicket. It was not to be.

Then a carnival broke out with most of the spectators celebrating on the field with the Charity players. Vernon had hit the last boundary to seal the win. He had become a hero. Everybody was patting his back and head. Teacher Gloria ran up to him, hugged him, and kissed him on the cheek, something he never dreamt of before. There was a widespread joy for having been plucked out of the jaws of defeat by an unapparent hero. When the victory sank into the young lad, he could not figure out how he had accomplished this. He was noticeably on the brink of despair at one stage and was just waiting to bow out and submit.

Denis assured him, "Your mom, the Parakese Pearl, has led you triumphantly to this championship, my son." That moment was a vivid reminder of his mother's gentle encouragement, like whenever she saw he was unsure about something, she would run her tender fingers through his hair and plant a soft loving kiss on his cheek. Vernon was overcome by joy and her promise to be with him always. He felt she was with him undoubtedly.

Denis was proud as punch for the achievement of his son. He stayed close to him as the two teams mingled together at the post-match gathering, along with their parents and the management. Teachers from both schools participated in friendly camaraderie. This was a restricted gathering, and even the close supporters from both schools were not allowed to come to the closing ceremony.

The Charity headteacher called the two captains to the stage and introduced Suresh Misra from Charity. But instead of Reynolds Garraway, someone else was at the stage. As vice-captain of the St. John's team, Adrian da Silva was substituting for his captain, who had to leave earlier with a side strain. The headteacher congratulated both captains for their good example in leading their teams in a friendly rivalry and a nail-biting finish. "I think both teams have won today: one, the Lower Pomeroon Championship, the other, the hearts of all the cricket lovers here today," he said. "This St. John's side, which not many people gave a chance to topple Charity, came so close to defying the odds. They have accepted defeat with grace. We wish them a safe trip back to the river mouth and wish them better luck next year."

Denis and Vernon were heading downstairs back to the ground to see friends who were still waiting around. Denis queried, "Wonder if that St. John's captain, da Silva, was Gwendolyn's son. He looked like a mixed-race person like his parents."

Gwendolyn, who was a family friend of many years, was a so-called "boviander" and an Afro-Amerindian woman who was married to Eugene da Silva a coconut plantation owner. His darker complexion and curly black hair betrayed his Portuguese name. The da Silva's had intermarried freely among the ethnic groups in the Pomeroon. Eugene da Silva's Portuguese, East Indian, and Amerindian ancestry added to the good looks of their uniquely hybridized children.

Vernon's mind flashed and triggered his own silent query. "If the St. John's captain was Gwendolyn's son, he has to be Kayla's brother." He had met him once or twice in passing and in actual fact did not remember him. But Kayla was nowhere to be seen that day, and that saddened him.

Denis moved closer to Adrian da Silva and politely asked if he was Gwendolyn's son. The young da Silva smiled and responded in the affirmative. "Why did your family not come to the match? They missed seeing how well you performed today. And it would have been nice to see them," he added.

Adrian quickly corrected that assumption. "They did bring me to Charity this morning and went on to Jacklow to be with relatives. My family is not a big fan of cricket in any case. They should be back here soon to get me."

"Okay, we would wait a while and say hi to them," Denis continued.

The Atkinses and the da Silvas caught up minutes later, and the appearance of Kayla with them drove a flash of wonderful joy into the heart of Vernon. They walked together from the school towards the Charity Stelling, Kayla and Vernon close to each other and volubly exchanging the delight of being together. At an invitation from Denis, the group proceeded to Miriam's Delight "for a drink." This visit was warmly greeted by Madeline de Castro, with whom Gwendolyn and Eugene, plantation owners alike, were long and lasting friends. Denis's friendship with the da Silvas grew out of the interaction between them and Madeline over the years. They shared seasonal laborers, which was what originally initiated the friendship between the two families. In the past, Rafa de Melo would tie up his launch, *Esperanza*, at the da Silva's landing while he waited for the rising of the tide when he was traveling to the Moruka.

While the Atkinses' presence under her roof at Miriam's Delight had eased some of the effects of the loss of Anita, which too often rekindled a state of guilt and remorse, the visit provided an interval of pure satisfaction amidst a recent period of melancholy and loneliness for Mrs. de Castro. She busied herself with lavishing the guests with refreshments and conversation and amidst exchange between the adults; Vernon and Kayla unobtrusively slipped out and ended at the bench on the jetty.

Locked arm in arm, they cherished the bliss of being together, just at a time when he questioned if their friendship was petering out. There was a strong bond between them, which he acknowledged verbally, "You are the person I am always dreaming to see, Kayla. If only you were living close by."

She laid her head on his shoulder and massaged and petted his thigh. This drove his heart into a frenzy. He tried to kiss her on the cheek, and as she turned towards him, his lips touched the corner of her mouth, turning on a fire of desire in both of them. She pressed her lips against his, and Vernon had his first erotic kiss. Little did he know that it was also the first for Kayla. He wanted more as their sweaty hands clasped so firmly, as if they were glued together. She looked at him with eyes struggling to hold back a tear and the news that she would be leaving at the end of August for Georgetown to attend St. Rose's High School. There was a deafening silence that followed.

The stirring at the big house turned out to be the guests taking their leave. Denis and Mrs. de Castro escorted them to their boat at the jetty. A visible space of about six inches was exhibited by the two teenagers, trying to create a semblance of just an ordinary meeting up of friends.

"Okay, Kayla, it's time to leave. I hope the two of you had a nice time meeting up. Come on, let's go," Gwendolyn said. "Say goodbye to Vernon. We have a long trip before us." She smacked a soft kiss on Vernon's cheek and looked away immediately to her family. Adrian de Silva shook Vernon's hand and told him he did well for his team and stole the victory they had hoped for. The boat reversed and once away from the shallow of the riverbank sped off downriver. The Miriam's Delight occupants watched them until they were out of sight and then slowly trekked back to the house.

* * *

That night, Denis spared no candor to chat with his son in a grown-up and mature manner. He commended him for his sportsman skills and his patience when things looked bleak on the field at the climax of the match. "You have done well today, Vern, and I saw how popular you were. I wondered why you did not spend more time with Valerie and Adele, who cheered you on throughout," he rhetorically asked.

"They are my friends, and I like them very much. All the boys love them, too, and they play up to all of them. I see them every day. But today, I was badly missing Kayla, whom I always seem to be thinking of these days. It made my day for her and her family to come here today," he replied. "I am glad you invited them, Dad." Vernon uneasily admitted, "Kayla is different from all my friends. She is polite, shy, beautiful, and comfortable to be with. Her smile awakens a hankering in me to want her to be around. But she lives too far away. Today, she said that she will leave the Pomeroon at the end of August to go to school in town. That left my spirit shattered. She is going to be farther away than St. John's and out of reach for me. Adele also will be moving in the next days to the Rupununi to live with her grandmother on their cattle ranch. So, only one of my three best friends will remain at Charity—Valerie. I am somewhat bewildered but glad that Valerie will still be around."

Denis's mind sailed back in time to his younger days when he had several girlfriends, but once he had met Anita that momentous night at the Moruka River mouth landing, no other girl mattered in his life. He began to remind Vernon of the special affection he had with that

Parakese girl. "So many times, I paddled or used our small engine to travel through the Manwarin to the Moruka River mouth stelling under the guise of buying commodities to retail, but the ulterior motive was to meet with the girl of my dreams."

The Moruka mouth landing was a special place for Denis because it was the place he courted and wooed his wife to be. Vernon was curious and asked his dad if he ever brought Anita to his Akawini mission during that time, and was he allowed to do so. Denis giggled and told him that his family had to have Anita and the Torrealbas over at the reservation for him to get close to his wife. "It worked," he declared.

That process impressed Vernon, who brazenly posed a question to his father, "Could I invite Kayla here, Dad? May I have your permission to invite her when her family visits relatives at Jacklow? Her mother visits her sister there regularly. I could see if Kayla would come out with her."

"I can't see why not, Vern. We have an extra room in our apartment. It would not have been possible at the small, thatched cabin. But would she or her mom come or allow her on her own here? Let's see if you could win them, son. You love her, don't you? You are a chip off the old block, with a deep romantic streak." The encouragement from Denis inundated Vernon's heart with the support he had looked forward to winning. Denis, however, drifted back to their discussion on livelihood building; he reminded his son that finding love is an important facet of life, but it has to rest on a sound and contented livelihood.

For Denis, love and work were two peas in the same pod. He reminded his son that preparing for a productive livelihood required the appropriate training and education. "It is good for Kayla to have the opportunity for secondary education in Georgetown. Her parents can afford it, and she likes studying, and that would serve to prepare her well for work and building a family one day. I am happy for her. You will have to keep your friendship through letters and enjoy her company when she returns to the Pomeroon during her vacation." Vernon shook his head in the affirmative.

"And Vern, you need to be seriously thinking of what you want to do for a living. Preparing for a job is important so that you do not end up doing fieldwork on the farm with me. I have managed, but it's hard work in rain and in shine. Every job has its ordeals. But I wish you would choose something that entailed less of the drudgery of coffee and citrus production," Denis paternally suggested.

Vernon appreciated the advice from his father and thought that delving into carving out a livelihood to maintain a family in the future was indeed imperative. It would also divert him from his grueling anguish of losing Kayla to school in Georgetown. He was always fascinated at how Joe Adonis and his father fashioned wonderful wooden boats at their workshop at the first river bend from Charity. They would frame the vessels from what seemed like unpliable timbers and long lengths of boards. They would neatly weave them together into vessels that did not leak, looked inexplicably sturdy, and magnificent, and they seldom painted them in any one color but in a combination of various horizontal bands of colors. They stood out among the many boats that plied the river. He wondered if his skills could be honed in that direction and how he would ever get to learning that special art of boatbuilding. Or was there another profession he could choose?

CHAPTER 9

KAYLA'S DEPARTURE— A VACUUM TO BE FILLED

Kayla and her family visited Grant Miriam's Delight three times before she left for Georgetown. Gwendolyn da Silva might have realized that Kayla needed to be cheered up from a state of silent lonesomeness on the verge of leaving home for a long period for the first time. She gave in to her daughter's poignant plea to see Vernon. The da Silvas delivered her at Miriam's Delight late morning on each visit and proceeded to Charity and Jacklow. She was entrusted to the Atkinses and Mrs. de Castro for the rest of the day. The school holidays afforded Vernon and Kayla time away from the classroom and the freedom to weld their friendship in a special way. However, Denis's work on the farm persisted without change. He was in and out during the day to ensure that his son and his guest were comfortable and had enough to eat and drink.

The two teenagers, though, were more drawn towards sharing the nourishment of Venus's nectar. Their close adjacency during those visits provoked the impulse to take advantage of being alone. The holding of hands and an innocent kiss were enough to trigger two bodies to cling to each other, imploring a total fusion of the two individuals. Sensuality took over, and in flights of eroticism, their exploring tongues led them towards the discovery of their whole person—body, mind, and spirit. There was harmony; there was unison, especially as she gladly opened herself and helped his hardened body to enter the cavity of her soul. She gyrated and grimaced as he forced his way as deeply as he could, not finding it easy to penetrate into her innermost secrets. Then she tugged him to herself relaxed and stifled a cry of relief. She was bleeding and that warranted a time-out from the sensual oneness and a thorough cleanup. They were both cautious about leaving any trace of blood to betray the truth of their interaction. This was the first time either of them came to such a climax in their relationship with anyone. They were no more virgins. This encounter uncovered for them what was behind the fierce urge to consensually invade each other's most secret and private yearnings. They calmly felt they knew each other in a new and fulfilling way, and they wanted more of it.

Denis came in and was amazed to see the two teenagers sitting innocently on the couch, chatting and having a friendly time. He offered them lunch, which they slightly picked at while reassuring him of not being hungry. He was back on the job, returning to the lower coffee fields where laborers were picking berries. He needed to be there to measure each person's harvest and place it in the collecting pile for transportation to the coffee factory late in the day. He recalled that in his own young days, any time alone with Anita would have been fully utilized to love every part of her body. He had made love to her many times before, concealing any traces of it. After it all, they married at Santa Rosa in a small ceremony of just about twenty relatives, mostly Anita's. The two families opted for this ceremony to avoid having them live together outside of wedlock, which was what they were moving towards.

That day, he felt the old priest was in a hurry to send them off, and he quite appreciated it, knowing that they would no longer be hiding to express their mutual love. As husband and wife, they would turn in to bed early that night and become one in a real way, as the priest said in the ceremony, no more fornication that he warned the young congregation about, but true married bliss. He remembered he asked Anita derisively what that fornication the priest talked about was, and

131

she jeeringly explained that it was what they were doing every time they had sex before their marriage day. He jovially responded, "So that was fornication you and I did for so long?"

She kissed his forehead and said, not at all embarrassed, "Yes, it was fornication."

Denis replied cheerfully, "That was really good fornication. I loved it. I hope this fornication continues between you and me."

As Denis went through the door, the two lovers embraced again, and another spate of lovemaking ensued. His ravenous energy pushed him to lick and suck her firm breasts and cover her legs and pubic area with countless kisses. He licked her vulva and penetrated her with his tongue, rubbing it against her firm and sensitively enticing clitoris. It sent a wild convulsion through her sweaty body as he arose and immersed his hard penis into her lubricated cavity. A strong ejaculation pulled them so closely together and wrapped them in a union they wanted to never end.

Kayla's mother collected her at about four in the afternoon, and when Denis finished work that day, he returned to find Vernon alone. He was surprised that his friend had left already. Vernon explained that Kayla's mother had picked her up early to return to St. John's before nightfall. He forewarned his father that Kayla would visit again the following weekend and maybe the weekend before she leaves for Georgetown for good. Denis approved of this and encouraged his son to make the most of her next visits and her company. "I think you love her, Vern. Do you, or is she just one of the girls you are friends with?"

Vernon nodded an affirmative reply. "She is special, Dad. I don't know what I will do without her in the Pomeroon when she is gone to town."

Denis was fast realizing that his son was evolving rapidly into a handsome eligible bachelor, whom his Anita would have adored in a different way from how she did all through his years of growing up. But sadly, she left too early. He thought of how easily Nathan Torrealba had approved of his grandniece's ties with the Akawini family they met many years before at the Moruka mouth landing; how he encouraged them to get married to halt the rumors of "her promiscuous behavior just like her mother's," and to seal what he from the first moment discerned as two people madly in love.

Mrs. de Castro had contacted the boatbuilding Correa brothers at Jacklow. They had a reputation for building the strongest and neatest workboats in the river. Grant Miriam's Delight needed to replace the old workboat left by Rafa de Melo. It had been repaired several times but was becoming more and more water-logged and heavy. Denis felt that if it was docked for a few months and allowed to dry out, it could still serve as a back-up vessel to a new boat until it was condemned somewhere down the line. Rod Correa was coming to meet Mrs. de Castro and Denis to agree on dimensions and style for carrying a large payload with efficient propulsion by an inboard Kelvin diesel engine. They needed to agree on what the capital outlay would be and the frugal Mrs. de Castro would need to give the go-ahead for beginning the project. Rod Correia arrived in a fast speedboat powered by a sixty horsepower Evinrude. Vernon was at the jetty when the boat pulled up and was fascinated by what he saw, a small wide flat-bottomed craft with a huge engine at the stern. It was built for speed and would only manage three passengers. He dreamt of building and running one of those one day and perhaps enroll for the Aripiaco Regatta. What a grand spectacle that would be for his admirers to behold. He daydreamed of people like Kayla and Adele making the trip to see him perform in his self-made speedboat and screaming out their delight at his winning.

As a powerful boat raced past from the jetty, he awoke from his dreaming and agreed that a lot needed to happen for that dream to become a reality. He must first go into learning the trade of boatbuilding and master the techniques and art of designing and building championship-winning crafts. This was what he now felt he was cut out to do. He would ask his father to search for an apprenticeship placement for him from any of the various workshops around the Charity area. He was intent on learning this trade. He wondered if Joe Adonis could be his workmate. They were great friends at school before the elder Adonis took him out of school to pursue something of more significance in his life. Joe liked school for only one thing, his love of cricket. He generally hated school and was absent often. His father thought he was wasting his time and was better off learning the trade. He never looked back and soon mastered the skill. Vernon felt he would get along better there than at other workshops where he would not have a handicap like Joe.

Rob Correa was leaving. He did not exhibit any elation at having signed a contract with Mrs. de Castro. He was not escorted out of the big house to his boat at the jetty. Vernon noticed an air of resentment and a rapid effort to take his leave from Miriam's Delight. Denis slowly made his way to the jetty when Rob had left. He complained with a sigh of relief, "What a difficult person to do business with, over-priced, aggressive and basically impolite to Missy. Good, he is not in the reckoning for the job. There are other builders we would have to get some quotes from. Missy has asked me to explore the possibilities and find the best recommendation. She has assigned me this task, and I need your help to think it through, Vern."

Before retiring to bed each evening, the two Atkinses spent quality time discussing a variety of topics. Denis loved reminiscing about growing up on the reservation. Often, he would relapse to recalling his adventures chasing after his Anita to win her final approval above any challengers. The awareness of liberal sexual activity among youths was an evident phenomenon growing up, and young couples were generally unsure whether a promise was real until marriage. He exhorted his son to learn to know his friends well before he made promises and commitments. He bragged that the promises between Anita and him were solid as a rock since they first met in the Moruka. Neither wavered for a moment because something beautiful connected them steadfastly. "If you find someone, Vern, with whom you are bound so profoundly and uniquely, you will know that you have reached a momentous junction in your life. Take your time and figure it out, son," he advised the young Atkins. "And don't be remiss to let your dad help you with your decision. Remember, I was well taught about relationships by the one both you and I trusted and adored, your mom."

That was enough to soften up Vernon to be more open to his father even though he did not feel uncomfortable with Denis's tactful prying into his love life. He took it to mean that his father was looking out for him.

Vernon thought that this was the right moment to raise the topic of building a career. He said with some degree of caution, "Soon I will finish school at Charity. I wished I was good enough to go to school in Georgetown, like Kayla will be doing. But I have never been bright and clever. I prefer to find a job where I can use my hands. I am better at practical tasks. I like building and fixing things, and your suggestion of learning to build boats is buzzing in my mind. I would like to try this soon after my school leaving certificate exam. I could use the time after the exam to join a workshop instead of wasting the last months of the school year, only attending to finish the year. I have talked with Joe Adonis, and he tells me that you and I should see his father and talk about it as a prospective plan."

Denis listened without interrupting. He wanted to hear from Vernon's own mouth and not give the impression that he was pushing him in that direction. Vernon insisted that he was thinking seriously about building boats and tried to explain to his father why he wanted this. What Vernon did not tell him was his fascination with fast boats and his dream of competing in the regattas in the future, at Aripiaco, Mainstay Lake, and even far away as Bartica up the Essequibo River. Unable to make an argument of why a boatbuilding career would make him a good speedboat racer, he chose not to venture there.

After a long pause left a vacuum in Vernon's request, Denis replied, "You decide, Vern, what you think you are capable of learning. There are various career choices before you, like tailoring, furniture making, mechanics, and building construction, in addition to boat building, and of course, you can go into farming, but without owning our own land, it would be like merely working as a farm laborer. There is a possibility, though, that we could ask Missy de Castro to let us use one of the several pieces of land her father, Mr. de Melo, left along the river. He was a big landowner but only developed and worked Miriam's Delight. Starting from the virgin jungle like he did would have its challenges but is still something to think about. Take your time and choose, and let's talk about your final choice later. There is no rush. You are still young, and I personally think you are smart. You could do well in anything you choose. Give it some further thought, and let's see, Vern."

* * *

The following day, Vernon asked his father if they could visit his friend Joe Adonis and talk with the senior Charlie Adonis. He was a reputable boatbuilder. He had his eldest and youngest sons, Billy and Joe, as his partners. His small family business sustained a good life for his family of six, two young daughters and four sons, who lost their mother to uterus cancer four years ago. Two of his boys worked the ten-acre plot of land they lived on and produced a regular supply of plantains, cassava, and other ground vegetables, as well of avocadoes and a wide variety of fruits. Their pineapples were in high demand locally, and the hucksters from the coast were always ready to buy off their produce. Their spacious house stood out to passers-by as they sped past the first bend in the river. It was a landmark for those heading to Charity, which they saw and greeted as they turned to the visibility of the Charity Wharf in the distance.

Denis agreed to visit the Adonises on the weekend, thinking that it would be a good opportunity to broach Miriam's Delight boat project with Charlie Adonis. Rafa de Melo had never used the services of the Adonises to maintain his boats. He relied on the Correa family, who were now seeking to bully his daughter. It was probably a sensible option to look for a new provider. What he did not want was for Charlie to think that he was proposing the boat project as a quid pro quo for an apprenticeship for his son. So, he had to address the issues with caution and prudence. He decided that securing an economical quote for building a solid workboat for Grant Miriam's Delight would be his primary reason for visiting Charlie and that exploring an apprentice placement for his son would be delayed and brought up at a later meeting.

The meeting with Charlie Adonis went better than Denis expected. He went to see the boatbuilder alone since Vernon was busy hosting and entertaining Kayla on her last weekend before she left for Georgetown. Denis was pleased with the outcome of his meeting and thought he had obtained a very competitive quote. He would need to present and get the go-ahead from Mrs. de Castro. She, in turn relying on her trusted farm supervisor, had no objection to what he had achieved. It was time for him to return to the Adonises and initiate the project with a contract and a down payment. Vernon was to accompany his father this time. It would be a learning experience in undertaking business in a more formal manner.

The river was overridden with fog that misty Saturday morning, and Denis did not want to risk an early start in the low visibility, where the sound of engines could be heard but the proceeding boats not seen until they were as close as about twenty feet away. Mrs. de Castro called the Atkinses to her upstairs apartment in the big house and had a full breakfast of fried eggs, bread, plantain chips, and aromatic steaming coffee freshly ground and brewed. This had become a frequent practice since the Atkinses were welcomed to live at the big house. This time, though, Mrs. de Castro was eager to hear the details of the quote one last time before Denis committed her and Miriam's Delight to a contract.

At mid-morning, as the warm Pomeroon sun enveloped everything, the fog had almost cleared completely, and the Atkinses were on their way downriver. They pulled their boat alongside Adonises' jetty. Charlie Adonis greeted them with a broad ear-to-ear smile and ushered them in under one of his work sheds where a large passenger boat was more than fifty percent completed. The guests were very impressed and inspected every aspect of the craft, amazed at how neat and close every joint and seam was. It was a good specimen for the Atkinses to observe since the size of the boat Miriam's Delight was looking for was similar. The major difference was that theirs was to be structured as a workboat without the trappings of a tent and rows of seats and backrests against the gunwales. They came to order an open boat with a front deck, a few removable seats, and a covered engine room. Space for cargo and good balance were the most important features.

For Vernon, he thought that a boat laden with cargo should also be fast and exquisitely shaped. His young and untrained mind had already begun to envisage boats of different shapes from the boring Pomeroon "bateau" styled structures. A sharp bow splitting the waters rather than a raised flat front end would reduce the strain of the engine to propel the craft, just like the larger sloops and schooners that plied the coastal areas to and from Georgetown and the Caribbean Islands. His suggestion won instant approval from both Billy and Joe Adonis and, after a delayed thought, from their father. The senior Adonis looked at Vernon and asked, "What are you up to these days, son? Are you still at school?"

"Yes, I have a few more months at school," he replied.

"Then what next? Are you going to join your dad working at de Castro's farm?" Charlie asked.

"Don't think so, Mr. Adonis. I want to do something different like learning a trade," he nervously replied.

Charlie looked at Vernon and paused, then continued, "I could do with some more hands in this shop, as new orders for fast boats are streaming in with all the new outboards engines now being bought in the river. But boatbuilding is a job people have to like, and they would have to accept the techniques and work hard with limited hand tools. Maybe one day we would have better tools and techniques, but it is how it is at the moment. Have you given any thought to this as a career?"

"I have indeed and wondered how I could even get the training to do it," Vernon answered.

Charlie continued as if offering a place to the young Atkins, "All you have to do is to get the permission from your father to join us and become a trainee. My two boys here started that way, and today, they have mastered the art better than I have. I wish you would think about it."

Denis then interjected that Vernon had earlier asked him about becoming an apprentice and would much appreciate it if there was an opening for him. "He could start soon after he wrote his school leaving certificate exam. That would be a marvelous opportunity for him."

Charlie agreed. "So we have a deal, Vernon?"

He tensely replied, "Yes, Mr. Adonis. I would love to join Joe, my friend, here."

Back at Miriam's Delight, Denis was quietly overjoyed at what unfurled that day—a contract for the new boat and an offer for Vernon to start training for a career. "That was not difficult at all," he assured.

Mrs. de Castro was very pleased and remarked, "My niece would be smiling at her son this moment. She is still around looking out for him, I bet."

* * *

Kayla was soon to leave for Georgetown. Her parents were going to travel with her. Together, they would join the "overland" bus at two in the morning, early on the coming Friday. The route was called the "overland route" because it was the beginning of a long journey over a few land areas even though the journey also involved crossing two major Guyana rivers. The trip entailed a bumpy and slow ride by bus from Charity to the Supenaam River mouth, then a rough boat ride across the choppy Essequibo River mouth, stopping at two of the large islands on this river before ending at Parika, a fast-growing township. Passengers then joined a packed so-called hired car traveling by land along the twenty-five-mile West Coast Demerara Highway to Vreedenhoop, the township on the opposite side of the Demerara River across from Georgetown. This last stint usually required rushing into a government ferry that crossed that river every half an hour. The overland route was so named because it was the alternative to traveling to and from Georgetown by the fortnightly Georgetown-Pomeroon steamer that primarily transported farm produce and timber. It also catered for passengers who were not intimidated by the rough coastal Atlantic waters en route to the capital. Vernon was planning to be at Charity to see his Kayla off. It would be the last time he would touch and hold her until she returned for vacation.

Denis decided to accompany his son that early morning to the Charity bus terminal. Some four buses were parked at the end of the public road at Charity, with their conductors sleeping inside, awaiting their respective trips at various times that morning. The overland bus was parked closest to the wharf, right next to the police station, which was lit up and staffed by two officers. They kept a close eye on any overloading of the bus. But the bus conductor reduced the threat of the police by having passengers walk up the road to the first bend and wait. All the excess passengers in an overload agreed to this arrangement to ensure that they were not left behind. Those who wanted to secure seats arrived at their earliest, occupied their seats in darkness, and waited patiently for the departure.

Kayla sat at a window seat next to her mother and father. Her brother Adrian waited under the market shed with produce buyers who were guarding their goods. He had bid them farewell already and was waiting on them to leave before he started back to their coconut estate at the Pomeroon mouth. When Vernon spotted Kayla, he left his father and entered the bus to greet her and her parents and soon after came down the bus steps, followed by his heartthrob. They seated themselves on the bench at the foot of the main koker, and there they sullenly hugged and caressed each other in the cool morning darkness. Their passionate embrace and kiss ended when the lights on the bus were lit up, a sign that they were soon to depart. The young couple walked towards the bus only to see Denis disembarking after spending time with the da Silvas. Adrian da Silva joined Vernon and his father at the side of the bus under the window against which Kayla was sitting. The bus's engine revved up and slowly it rolled from its perch under the close eyes of a policeman doing his duty but quietly allowing an overload he knew was soon to happen down the road. The police officers were cognizant of the limited transportation afforded to the public and the necessity for people to travel when required. Kayla waved a frantic goodbye, her whole arm stretching out to touch Vernon's. Then only two fading brake lights were seen as the bus sped off on its way.

Letters were exchanged regularly between Vernon and Kayla in the three months that followed. The two lovers poured their love for each other in the hand-written pages of letters that were posted without delay. There was the receipt of a letter each week. They both waited impatiently for the next. Vernon began writing his next letter the next day after he posted the last. There was too much in his anxious heart to release in order to diffuse an explosion of the despondency he felt building up. Then for some reason, Kayla's letters were less frequent until there was a gap of three weeks before a seemingly rushed half-page letter arrived from her. It said that she appreciated all the letters she had received from him and wondered why he was writing less. Yet she reminded him that letters were not the same as arms embracing her and all those words of love were hardly from lips pressing against her cheeks.

Vernon did not know how to translate her seeming retort into what trend of thought was actually troubling her mind and their relationship. Then when her next letter arrived after a lapse of more than a month and four letters from him, he was thoroughly disheartened and somewhat suspicious. He replied and begged her to explain why her growing silence. There was no answer and no more letters from her. He was devastated and wondered if he had said something wrong. He was helpless and could do nothing more to revive the friendship and the wonderful time they had together.

Denis saw a change in his son's temperament and wellbeing. He missed meals and spent much time alone cloistered in his room. But he laid off from saying anything about it and allowed him time to come around on his own. His friends at school also sensed something unhappy in his demeanor. Their initiative to cheer him up and get him back to that point where he was agreeable and the center of camaraderie among his peers again failed. They attributed it to dread about wrapping up his last months at school and guessed that he did not want to stay in the circle of school children anymore.

Months later, Vernon was indeed glad to be finished with school. He felt he was free to become a self-made man and to build up his personal defense and coping mechanisms against the hurt he was secretly enduring. Valerie was one of the few who did not give up on him but stopped at Miriam's Delight whenever she could to spend time with him. She had the last year at school, and her visits often reminded him of what he was missing as a senior schoolboy. He was missing all the cricket he played, and after their last recent defeat by Siriki School cricket team, he regretted that he would not have the chance to avenge that defeat and win the Pomeroon River Championship. Valerie's visits became more often and longer each time. She was never in a hurry to go home, and on occasions, her mother or brother had to come and get her. She was feeling a strange fondness for a friend that seemed not to respond to her caring in any enthusiastic way. She was intent upon changing this.

At their next meeting, she sat with him in his room and started petting his hand. He was reluctant to provide a similar response. She took his hand and kissed it ostentatiously and waited for his reaction only to be surprised by his arm being flung around her neck, drawing her to his body. He whimpered and asked her to pardon him for largely ignoring her in his last year at school. He did not try to explain why. He felt that his relationship with Kayla might have been known by several of his friends, except they had no idea how deep it was.

The Jameses and the folks at Miriam's Delight were close family friends and that explained the camaraderie of Valerie with Vernon and to his group of friends at school. He wanted that to remain their position, and especially that of Valerie's, in order to dispel any conclusion that Kayla was his preferred girlfriend.

He uttered to Valerie, "You have been a true friend to me, Val. You never judged me for my humble background and for my insensitivity towards those who tried to accept me. I was too conscious of my family's position as laborers and of my poor thatched home where I felt terribly embarrassed to invite my friends. I never felt I was in the same status and category as my friends at school. I really had a complex regarding my inferior status. But you never presented a hint of this nor rubbed any of it into our friendship at any time. I remember how you and your family stood by my father and me when I lost my mother. You were kind and compassionate. I cannot forget."

And she replied serenely, "You are a wonderful person, Vern, and one of very few of our peer group that is sincere about who you are. I always knew that what I saw in you was what you really were. No showoff! No pretense! And I felt if I were to cherish friends, you had to be at the top of the list. I mean this. I never knew how to tell you about the crush I have always had on you. Maybe you have now grown out of the teenage shyness that kept us close but yet apart." She squeezed his hand and pulled it against her breast. He reacted by cupping that breast in his hand and fondling the other with his face. It was a first for both of them to express such personal emotions towards each other.

Valerie's advances on him did appease some of the hurt he was feeling over the silence of Kayla. They lit up his carnal drives again for a moment. Valerie James was indeed a seductive human being and very charismatic and liberally inclined. But it was not enough to heal a wound that was festering. He could not bring himself to believing that what he and Kayla shared was not substantive enough to last not even four months after her separation for school in the city. Vernon wanted so much for the infatuated person in front of him to be his Kayla. This, however, was not the case. He had to measure his always strong desire for sharing with the other sex, against his deep commitment to Kayla whose heart he thought he had already won and who did not have to prove her sexual prowess. She had it all. Valerie, however, was revealing her true feelings for him, and this was equally awakening the secret spark within him for her which he now realized he did not allow to grow. He was now, for a moment, truly torn between two beautiful women.

He released Valerie with the excuse that his father would soon be coming in from the fields and requested help to prepare him something to eat. They both moved to the kitchen area, still holding hands and peering into each other's eyes in silence. Valerie left a little while after Denis retired home for the day. "Will see you soon again, Vern, maybe after school," she exclaimed as she walked through the door.

Denis had noticed that his son seemed to be struggling with some kind of depression. He kept to himself frequently to the point that he appeared antisocial. His answers to question and conversation with his father or Mrs. de Castro was unusually curt. He himself knew that feeling very well. During his obsession to win the hand of Anita, he panicked that it was not happening fast enough. Later, in the prime of enjoying her beauty and love, she left him dejected and broken. But she, nevertheless, left a part of herself in Vernon, which he promised to cherish and protect. Denis sincerely wanted to turn Vernon's downcast spirit to cheer. "Maybe you are missing Kayla, son?" he rhetorically remarked. "But you are writing letters to each other. That has to be enough until she comes home on vacation. Just stay patient and in love. And you have other friends to keep you company. There are Valerie, Bernice, and others. Enjoy their friendship while you wait on Kayla. Try not to sink into grief because she is not around. Her schooling is important, you know. I can see how you miss her, but you have to be a strong man as you mature."

"Dad, how I miss Kayla so badly and don't feel like talking about it," Vernon replied.

"Do talk about it, Vern. That will keep you in love. I am here to listen and support you until she comes home in a few months," the older Atkins reassured. "It is called lovesick, Vern. That's what grown-ups suffer when their love is not around. I understand."

Vernon then moaned despairingly, "But she has not replied to my letters, so many in the last month. Why? I don't know. That is distressing me. I just don't want to lose her."

Denis was glad that his son was opening up about what was bothering him but had no recommendations to resolve the gripe he was enduring. He was cautious about suggesting a reason for the silence from Kayla and did not feel he had any viable solution to his son's predicament. "Let's just wait and see, Vern. Maybe there is a good reason for her not writing."

CHAPTER 10

A MASTER BOATBUILDER IN THE MAKING

Vernon had already spent three months at the Adonis boatbuilding workshop. He was enjoying the experience and kindness shown him by the owner and his family, especially Joe Adonis. Although more than three years older than Vernon, the two young men found a brotherly bond. Both of them had lost their mothers and struggled with filling the vacuum that created. They both looked forward to settling down with the love of their lives. Joe Adonis was engaged to Marilyn Evans and was impatient and miserable that their marriage was not happening fast enough. He was puzzled why the Evans family had doubts about him and, consequently, lived and worked to change that. Vernon was the only friend he dared to share his deepest anguish with. Similarly, Vernon felt secure to divulge his turmoil of the break with Kayla. They both provided each other a hope that the light at the end of the tunnel will appear and stay in their lives.

The Miriam's Delight workboat was in the finishing stages before the launch. Denis had arrived at the workshop to inspect the status of the contract and ensure that all the details were adhered to. The two Adonis siblings and Vernon were busy with the caulking of the hull of the vessel from the inside. The major caulking from the outside had already been carried out. Once this was completed, the boat would be laid on each side to perform the sealing and painting of the outside. It would then be laid back on its keel and stabilized for the major task of embedding the Kelvin diesel engine. It had newly arrived by the Pomeroon steamer from Georgetown. It would require every bit of the ingenious skills of the Adonis craftsmen to winch it into the boat and onto the well-anchored base, and permanently pin it into place. Then the engine cover in the form of the small cabin would be constructed, and the inside of the vessel would be finally painted. That would complete a great project.

Charlie Adonis greeted Denis and walked him to the boat. He was so proud to see his son confidently holding his own alongside the two more experienced boatbuilders. He smiled and commended Vernon to his father, "You have a master boatbuilder in the making here, Denis. He learns fast and works hard. His heart is in this trade."

Denis smiled in dispassionate reply and nodded slightly. "You have been generous to him, Charlie, and we all have a lot to thank you for. I am personally grateful because you drew him away from the lingering pain and void of losing his mother. He will soon have a career to build a life on. Young men nowadays tend to marry young, and soon he would be looking to settle down with a wife. I know he is thinking and worrying about this these days. Working here has drawn him out idle daydreaming and focused him to concretely work for his future, thanks to you and your family."

Charlie Adonis responded, "Well, I think Vernon could build a boat on his own from scratch right now. He has all it takes. He has been a great addition to my team, and I hope he stays here and not move to another workshop. To this effect, I want to tell you that as of the next month, he will formally be paid a full salary as part of this outfit. In conscience, I cannot continue to just pay him that pittance of a stipend a trainee gets. He deserves more. And better yet, he and my boys would get a nice bonus once Mrs. Castro pays the last installment."

Denis was heartened by the progress his son had made in a short time and quietly ascribed it to his Anita's guidance from wherever she was. He sensed that his Parakese Pearl was always in their midst. He thought that she must be proud of him.

Denis reported to Mrs. de Castro that the Adonises had done a splendid job on the boat and that it should be launched in a matter of weeks to which she commented, "The old workboat of my father can now have a rest. It has served us very well. You know, Denis, I would like to remember my father through this new boat, and so I want to name it *Esperanza*, the boat on which he traveled the nook and cranny of the Pomeroon and the Moruka. That boat was the one that we shared as a family and made excursions on to so many places. It was a compact living space on the waters, and we looked forward to living in it away from home. There are good memories. At one stage, I also thought that there were terrible memories because *Esperanza* took my father into the life of the Torrealbas, and I hated it for my mother's sake. Today, I see it as a blessing in disguise and regret not welcoming your mother-in-law into our lives. I was too young and bitter to understand the implications. Now, all I do have of my immediate family is my sister's grandson. Vernon should know of Rafa de Melo's journey and the boat that carried him to places and into lives. *Esperanza* is its name. It has brought hope into the future of Miriam's Delight. It is all becoming clear just as the light breaks through the morning fog on the Pomeroon."

Charlie Adonis was surprised to see Denis Atkins the next morning. Worried, he asked, "Is Mrs. de Castro not happy with something? We can make whatever adjustments she wants. That is not a problem."

"Well, yes," Denis replied. "There is a major addition she would like, a name for the boat. We did not discuss this before."

Charlie Adonis was relieved and laughed. He grinned and said, "That's a minor thing, man, a piece o' cake. We would put the name on both sides of the bow and also against the stern. What name is she thinking of?"

Denis replied, "*Esperanza*, that was her father's launch."

Charlie remembered that boat and the gentleman Rafa de Melo was but was quick to quip. "He was also a woman's man, and that was the reason why there were so many rumors of his escapades in that boat. I never believed them. He was a good churchman. But those rumors did swirl around. They are now in the past with nothing to prove any of it." He called out to Vernon and asked him to create a template with the name, *Esperanza*. "You take the lead in this, Vern, and once it is agreed on, we will bless this boat with a name to be later christened at the launch."

He shook hands with Denis and invited him to bring Mrs. de Castro. "Bring her next week to see for herself what she is buying before she breaks a bottle of grog on her deck and takes her away."

* * *

At the launch of the *Esperanza*, there was a large crowd and a carnival atmosphere. A few bottles of rum had been consumed, and spirits were high. A throng of half-drunk and sober workers placed themselves at strategic positions on the launching ramp. Some had sturdy ropes to pull on, and others had prizing poles at the stern of the vessel to join a combined effort to give the *Esperanza* its first taste of the Coca-Cola-colored Pomeroon water. The launch was easier than expected because there were many willing persons available to lend a hand. As the boat floated for the first time, the tentative boatbuilders breathed a sigh of achievement that her balance and elegance were outstanding. She was indeed a work of art, from her sharp bow to her wide berth and narrower stern. Charlie Adonis climbed onto the stern deck and inserted the rudder into the metal holders. He connected the rope from rudder to the steering wheel riveted at the gunwale alongside the Kelvin engine, behind which an operator could easily occupy the built-in seat and reach and manage gear-shifting and throttle, as well as maneuver the steering.

Denis and the helpers brought the boat alongside the Adonis jetty and tied her up. In the meantime, Mrs. de Castro was making her way to the bow. She dipped into her handbag and withdrew a sparkling bottle of red rum. The crowd sighed an "ahhh" as one said, "Get the glasses, chaps, we have the drink." Then, as if timed with that exclamation, there was the thump of the bottle on the sharp bow of *Esperanza*, followed by the words of Madeline de Castro, "We christen you for Rafa de Melo. *Esperanza* is alive again."

Denis started the heavy sounding engine, and its rhythmic repetitive beat soothed the hearts and energies of all the boatbuilders and the owner. The boat reversed, with Madeline occupying the front seat covered by an umbrella and Denis at the controls. They drove out of sight.

* * *

Vernon's attachment at the Adonises' boat workshop grew his self-confidence. Charlie Adonis could not help but admire how he listened attentively to clients' questions and instructions, accepted propositions, and provided alternative advice when necessary. He became popular, and most clients would see him first before they approached the owner. He was an asset to the team. The volume of business had noticeably increased, and Charlie quietly and openly admitted that Vernon's presence there had made a difference.

An order for a large, fast ballahoo had come in from the Parika area. John Bachew had heard of the work at this workshop and was looking for them to design a Pomeroon ballahoo boat for both speed and for carrying a payload of seventeen adults. He was transferring his slower passenger launch on the Parika-Bartica run to a faster open boat. It would be equipped with a lifejacket for each person on board, canvas sheets for ready use in rain or from splashing of waves, and space for adequate fuel storage. A seventy-five-horsepower outboard engine will provide ample speed on that run and entice passengers to opt for it. He was convinced that if this scheme proved successful, it would transform the nature of river passenger boats, especially with the widespread purchase and use of outboard instead of inboard engines across the country.

Bachew expected to have this boat delivered in two weeks' time, but because the lumber would need to be ordered from their "sawpit" of choice up the Siriki Sands, Charlie conceded to doing the job rather in three to four weeks. Vernon and the Adonis boys were told to come up with designs accommodating Bachew's suggested dimensions and be ready to discuss these in two days' time. A hybrid of Joe Adonis's design, with key elements from Vernon's, was settled for. It entailed a bow lifted a foot over the regular curve. Vernon believed that this would reduce the amount of front suction of the vessel while carrying a fairly large load of passengers. His plan was also to adjust the stern to be less of a vee and flatter than usual with a splashboard at the bottom floor. This would help the boat to better stay flat on the surface of the water and at rapid speed, like the smaller speedboats, mimicking the motion of a hovercraft. He was convinced that a bigger engine would more efficiently make the boat skim the water and generate a lot of speed. He vividly remembered the Correa's short stubby speedboat that came that time to Miriam's Delight and generated so much speed. The only drawback was that it could only carry three persons, or more safely, two. The design was agreed upon.

Charlie and Billy Adonis met with Carl Duncan from the Siriki Sands a few days later. As Charlie spoke, Duncan made a list of all the materials required for the project and left. A few days later, he was unloading the first batch of cut lumber, which was laid out to dry in the sun. Duncan's income depended solely on orders from house and boatbuilders. The competition was great among so many like himself at Siriki, Abram's Creek, Aripiaco, and Pickersgill, who manually sawed lumber from select mature trees they fell in their region. He had supplied materials on a regular basis to Adonis, and prompt delivery of the whole order was vital for keeping them as a client. He delivered the full order that week and enjoyed a decent payout for his and his family's labor.

The next few days saw the frame of the boat taking shape. "It's looking good, guys," Charlie said to his sons and Vernon. "I think we have to work overtime to get this job done in time. Please don't get upset about this. Bachew wanted his boat in two weeks, which was impossible, but we could give it to him in three weeks. That should be more satisfactory to him than four."

A finished product was soon to be churned out of the Adonis workshop. Bachew had arrived around midday to witness the launch. He did not bring the new seventy-five horsepower engine to have a trial run. That would have been too much of an inconvenience. Rather, he was able to borrow a forty horsepower Yamaha from his friend Ali at Charity. They came together in Ali's passenger boat, a small seven-seater ballahoo armed with the engine lying on the floor of the craft.

Charlie Adonis, his team and neighbors gathered and dragged the boat onto bamboo rollers on the launching ramp to the water's edge. As it touched the Pomeroon water and floated elegantly for the first time, there was a cry of excitement. Bachew was overjoyed and pleased with the job. He took out a small bottle of rum from his back-pocket and crashed it against the side of the large ballahoo, saying, "We give you your first drink and christen you."

They anchored Ali's engine on the fortified stern, the so-called tuck, and about eight persons embarked on it to have a trial run. Bachew was amazed to see how the elevated bow remained high over the water and was eager to see what difference this would make. To his satisfaction and astonishment, every one commended the finished product. One of them remarked, "If a 'forty horse' can be so fast, what an amazing boat this would be with a bigger engine!" That pleased Bachew, and his boat provided wide advertisement for the work of the Adonis boat workshop.

The new-styled ballahoo became a phenomenon. Several orders poured in, and while the team had no reason to complain of work shortage, they were, nevertheless, overworked and tired. Charlie agreed to give each a few days off one by one and a holiday bonus to have fun and to come back refreshed. Vernon was delighted.

CHAPTER 11

IN SEARCH OF KAYLA

Both Denis and Mrs. de Castro were astounded by the amount of money Vernon accumulated in such a short time. He worked hard, earned, spent little, and saved. He never stopped dreaming of having Kayla around again. He would lavish her with gifts, just like he did with love. But after all they did together, she had remained an enigma. He found it difficult to decipher why she would break up with him and not even tell him out of politeness and respect. If she had actually done that, he would be ripped to shreds, but there would be some tormented closure to a chapter in his life. It would be a categorical signal for him to move on. He would then be more open to other friends who wanted to get close with him on another level, something he stonewalled and blocked so far. He had a deep urge to go to Georgetown and look for his Kayla. If he found her and she turned her back on him, at least he would know where he stood despite his dread of this.

The elder Atkins was empathetic with his son's situation. But he worried about his wanting to go to Georgetown in search of Kayla. He had hoped that by now Vernon would have gotten over her departure and silence and resigned himself to cope without her. In addition, neither he nor Vernon had ever made a trip to the city. The farthest they ventured out of the Pomeroon was to the Suddie Hospital on the

Essequibo Coast, during the illness of Anita. They were aware of the overland route to Georgetown because they knew of the bus starting very early each morning from Charity and of friends recounting the thrills and challenges of that trip. The mid-morning trip from Charity to Adventure and then the large steamer trip to Parika would be more comfortable and less stressful. The only snag was that that trip arrived in Georgetown at night, and if new visitors were not sure of themselves, they were easily spotted by predators who had no mercy in, what was commonly known as, the "choke and rob." That was one characteristic of the capital that Essequibians detested. They stayed away and only visited if it was absolutely necessary. At the time, if in the Essequibo, the "choke and rob" was met with civic arrest and justice for the predators, who once caught would get a sound beating from a crowd and an everlasting stigma. The prevalence of this horrible activity was, therefore, far less in the county of Essequibo and other rural areas.

The other discouraging fact about Georgetown for the Atkinses was the lack of relatives and friends there who could accommodate Vernon if he did go. Denis asked of his son, "Where would you stay, Vern? Would you know how to find your way around?"

Vernon shook his head. "But I could learn quickly, Dad, and I can find cheap lodging at a guesthouse. I have some money to pay for this. People sometimes talk of boarding houses in Regent and Robb streets that have rooms to rent. Five nights are all I have to cater for. I think I could manage with some help and information from talking with people there. I am not afraid to ask for information," he responded pensively.

"And where would you look for Kayla?" Denis continued his query.

"She left here to attend St. Rose's High School. I could locate that school and ask for her. They should know where she stays," he responded with a degree of assurance.

There was an urgency for Vernon to put his dream into reality and begin that journey. He had a week off from work and would return to work on the day and time agreed upon with Charlie Adonis. He wanted to show that he could be trusted to keep his word and that he genuinely wanted to retain his work attachment with that workshop.

Denis suggested to Vernon that they could make a trip to St. John's and inquire of the da Silvas, Kayla's parents, of her whereabouts in Georgetown. But he also realized that that might open up a whole can of worms and questions as to why they were seeking information on their daughter. He concluded that it was inappropriate for that action in order to avoid suspicion and any embarrassment of having to explain a love relation between his son and their daughter. He, therefore, conceded to Vernon's plan to make the trip and deal with the complexities on the spot as they arise. Denis agreed with his son that he would not take the daytime trip because he would arrive too late at night and finding lodging then would be problematic. The overland trip would be better. He would arrive in Georgetown around seven in the morning and would have time to first find a place to stay and a base from where to start his search.

Mrs. de Castro reluctantly accepted Vernon's plan to travel to Georgetown. She repeatedly objected by asserting that there were many pretty girls around to choose from and there was no compelling need to look for a person who had already deserted the young man. She posited, "It's easier and smarter to break off a relationship with that kind of girl *now* than to have her run off and run away after marriage." She called on Vernon to give her up and try to cope, assuring him that he will get over it in time and find a better friend and partner. But when she saw how adamant Vernon was to go, she quietly said, "Go with caution, Vern, and do what it takes to find peace of mind." Madeline had firsthand experience of having someone run off on her. It starved her of peace of mind for decades. She knew what it felt like to be in those shoes. She hugged Vernon and handed him a small parcel.

The overland bus pulled off from Charity that morning with Vernon dozing off against a window and trying to stay awake to wave goodbye to his father. Denis, on the other hand, was fidgeting and anxious. In his mind, he said to Anita, *Take care of your son, my angel! Keep him safe and secure and help him to find answers and peace!*

As the bus turned the first bend and disappeared, Denis returned to Miriam's Delight. He paced in his room, and when he tried to sleep, he was jolted by nightmares. He left for work in the morning with heavy eyelids and a worry that clouded his mind. By the time he had fatigued himself with heavy work lifting bags of coffee berries, there seemed to appear a more positive hope in him for his son's adventure. He wanted to believe that the trip might not be a mere leap in the dark for one who knew nothing of long traveling to a place he had never visited before. Rather, he believed that it could be a positive and enriching discovery of learning about new places, meeting new friends, and clearing his turmoiled heart. He could also very well not find Kayla and further deepen his gushing wound, or find again his first love and return a new and stronger man. He trusted his son, who had matured in a manner he never encountered in his own growing up. He believed that he would be fine.

* * *

Five grueling days and nights disrupted by the anxiety of his son being away in unknown surroundings had nevertheless flown by rather fast. Mrs. de Castro was worrying as well, trying not to reveal it to Denis. The late afternoon bus bringing in passengers from Georgetown off the Adventure steamer was on its way. Mrs. de Castro came downstairs to remind Denis that Vernon should be coming home today. He was unaware of Mrs. de Castro's disquiet regarding his safe return and was taken aback by her concern and reminder.

"I am leaving in a few minutes for Charity to get him from the afternoon bus," he said to Madeline. He walked to the jetty and paddled a small boat across the river and walked the rest of the way to the bus terminal.

The first two buses arrived and there was no sign of the young Atkins. The later buses usually fetched passengers from all the villages on the Essequibo Coast, picking them up and dropping them off at any stop the passengers requested. By the time they drove into Charity, there were only a handful of passengers, unlike fully loaded ones that started from the Adventure Stelling with Georgetown passengers. Despite Denis's disappointment of not seeing his son on the first buses, he decided to stay on and wait for the other later buses. At five, when he was told that there were no more buses expected until the overland one at one early in the morning, he glumly returned to Miriam's Delight. Mrs. de Castro was disheartened also.

"I will go back to Charity from midnight and wait again. I believe he will come tonight," he assured Madeline.

He frantically jolted himself out of a catnap close to one in the morning and headed straight to the small boat he paddled this time to the Charity, landing close to the main wharf. A short walk and he was under the koker, waiting for his son. A half an hour later, the night bus pulled in. Surely enough, Vernon was on it and disembarked into the grasp of his father. He spoke very little, and Denis decided not to rush him for a report on his endeavor. He merely asked if he was feeling alright and told him that he should be hungry and sleepy. Vernon simply said, "Yes!"

Mrs. de Castro was out in the open on the jetty under a bright moonlight, waiting. This was definitely not what Denis ever saw from her before. She seldom came out on the jetty at night and turned into bed at nine-thirty each night after the death announcements on Radio Demerara. This time she broke her ritual. She was overjoyed when the boat pulled up with the two men in it. She embraced Vernon with the greeting, "Come here, my son, you're back, and I am happy for you." She offered them a meal upstairs, but both refused and told her sleep was what they wanted.

Before they fell asleep, Denis said, "Tomorrow you can tell me all about your trip to Georgetown. For now, you must catch up on some sleep."

A new workday had begun the next morning for both the Atkinses. In a jiffy, Vernon had sped off in his small engine-propelled ballahoo. He had a rousing welcome by the Adonises. They asked about his break in Georgetown, and he assured them that it was wonderful and that the city was a beautiful place to visit—huge buildings, crowded streets around the stores, and beautiful clothes and shoes to buy. "But here in the Pomeroon is the best place to live, where people are friendly and easy to talk with. People there are snobbish and arrogant, and I think selfish," he regretted. "I am glad to be back at work with you guys. You stand out over the Georgetown folks."

Charlie Adonis joked, "You have a heap of work to do now you are back. We have piled it up and left it for you. No breaks again for a long time."

Vernon grinned and said, "Bring it on. I am ready."

That evening, there was a poignant discussion between father and son. Vernon explained how he found a friendly family, a mother and her two daughters, who operated a cookshop in Regent Street and had a spare room to rent to him for a small fee. The main charge from her was the meals he ate there. He felt they tried to treat him like family when they learned that he was far away from family in the Essequibo. They thought he came to town to find work and suggested a few shops and large stores where he could inquire. Mrs. Silvie Persaud told him that he was free to make her home his home until he found another place to settle down into.

He told his father how he walked long distances each day looking for places where Kayla might be. He found St. Rose's High School after a long walk, seeking information and directions from several people. He said he was happy and for a while thought that his search had quickly ended. However, he was bombarded and interrogated by two nuns about his motives for looking for Kayla. They wanted to know every detail about him and who sent him, how he knew Kayla, and what he wanted from her. They made him feel like he was after the young woman for one thing and one thing only, which both embarrassed and unsettled him. In the end, they revealed that she suffered badly while a student at the school. She was always homesick and was on the verge of a nervous breakdown when they called in her parents and recommended she be hospitalized. She was taken to St. Joseph's Mercy Hospital for treatment. They were not sure if she was still there or if she was sent to the mental asylum in New Amsterdam, Berbice.

He told his dad, "I literally shook with fear that she was losing her mind and blamed myself and my letters for driving her to the brink of a mental breakdown. That day, I walked all the way to Kingston in Georgetown and found the St. Joseph's Hospital. She was not on their register. She was discharged about two weeks before, and her parents had taken her up the East Coast. I feared for the worst, that she might have been really consigned to that dreaded mental asylum. I did not find her, and it dawned on me that I may have lost the love of my life indeed. I am broken-hearted, Dad. But I am hopeful that I will be with her again sometime when her parents are ready to talk about her condition and reveal her whereabouts."

In Guyana, at that time, there was a terrible stigma related to mental and psychological problems. Families remained tight-lipped about any encounter with those disorders, fearing that they would be categorized negatively as mad or so inclined. People suffering from mental problems were tucked away in residential clinics called asylums and were treated with a degree of scorn by the uninformed. Vernon felt that the da Silvas had kept a secret of their daughter's illness and put a lid on the matter, covering it up from an outbreak of rumor. He did not blame them because they were trying to protect Kayla from the ravages of such rumors. He pleaded with his father not to divulge any of this to anyone, not even to Mrs. de Castro. Mrs. de Castro was simply told that Kayla was well and was staying with family recuperating from a medical problem she was hospitalized for. Madeline said nothing further to anyone, suspecting that Kayla may have had a pregnancy and abortion after a romping time with Vernon on her visits before going to Georgetown. Or, she thought, she was probably expecting a baby and kept by a family somewhere until delivery. She knew of a few families in the Pomeroon who took those protective measures to save their daughters and families such disdain and oftentimes derision. She did not care to worry anymore about the matter and possible outcomes and refrained from bringing up Kayla again in conversation.

Denis had finished selling a boatload of oranges, tangerines, lemons, and grapefruits at the Cooperative Depot when he ran into his friend, Romeo, a neighbor of Gwendolyn's sister at Jacklow. Tactfully, he asked about Kayla, essaying a rhetorical statement. "She must be doing well at school and soon to come home for the long school holidays. Funny how a year has already passed since she left? It would be nice to see her again soon."

Romeo was quick to reply, saying that he heard from his neighbor that Eugene and Gwendolyn da Silva would be going to spend the vacation with her at the Madray's plantation in Mahaica. The Madray's La Grange plantation was one of the largest copra producers in the country, and the two families had been close for many years, bonded by their mutual interest in coconut production, as well as holding leadership positions in the National Coconut Producers' Association.

When Denis related this news to Vernon, his son was skeptical and did not believe it. He reiterated in his mind that she was ill and was being treated somewhere. He hoped that she was not really in the mental asylum in New Amsterdam. But even that would not deter him and preempt his wanting her. Then he concluded vocally to this father, "So that would mean that she would not come home for another year. I am still prepared to wait that long on her and longer if necessary."

Valerie stopped by at Miriam's Delight to see Vernon after his Georgetown trip. She was not aware that he had gone there until two days after he left. She was told at the Adonises' workshop that he was on a break from work. Joe Adonis informed her that the three boys were all having breaks at different times, and that Vernon was lucky to have that trip to the capital. None of them had ever seen Georgetown. Valerie was not angry that Vernon had left without saying goodbye but found it strange after their close encounter a few days earlier. She still harbored an intention to become his only girlfriend when he was ready to get involved. She believed that boys liked to have fun with girls but were timid to build a lasting relationship, and that Vernon would grow into closeness with her if she continued patiently with him, without complaining about his lack of sexual advances and warmth toward her.

That Saturday afternoon, Denis was at the Charity depot, selling the produce he had harvested at Miriam's Delight. Valerie was aware of this and was happy to be with Vernon alone. Vernon welcomed her and sat in the drawing room. An initial silence broke when Vernon began relating the experience of traveling alone for the first time so far away.

He was thankful that he had adequate funds to cover the trip. The gift he got from Madeline de Castro turned out to be a small wad of dollars. It made him appreciate her care and her acknowledgment of him as someone belonging to Miriam's Delight. He was more convinced than ever that she was his grandmother, or great-aunt to be more precise.

"So, what did you do in Georgetown, Vern?" asked Valerie.

"I did a lot. I walked all over the town until I was too tired to continue. There were some interesting places I saw. The huge market as I got off the ferry on the Demerara was amazing. It had so many shops of all kinds there. I stopped there to eat something after a night of traveling and enjoyed a sardine roll with hot pepper sauce and a lemonade. I was then attracted by how it looked inside and strayed through all the maze of corridors. There were clothes shops, some that sold shoes, hardware, pots and pans, dishes and cutlery, gold and silver jewelry, fresh foods and groceries, everything. It's hard to believe, but you can find anything there from a needle to big machinery. It was a real discovery for me. They called the expansive metal-built structure 'Big Market.' I think its real name is 'Stabroek Market.' It blew my mind after being accustomed to the small shops at Charity."

Valerie agreed that it was an awesome place. "Sounds like an incredible place with so many shops under one roof."

"And there were other smaller ones like that, too, like Kitty and La Penitence," Vernon continued. "I didn't see those. They were too far away from where I stayed on Regent Street. But I went and saw one on Regent Street called 'Bourda Market.' The nice thing about that one was it was not far from the famous Bourda Cricket Ground, which I walked by but could not get in. I had always longed to see the actual ground where international matches are played since, here, we can only listen to the radio, glued to the commentaries. Oh, I enjoyed the sights in the city," he asserted, masking the tiredness and disappointment he endured in search of his Kayla.

Valerie's appetite for his story was whetted, and she wanted more, not only the story but also his company and his body's warmth, a feeling she was concealing under her attentiveness to all the details of the trip.

If the story was prolonged, she would be with him for hours and that would help to cultivate an affinity between them. She questioned again, "What about the world-famous St. George's Cathedral? Did you see it?"

"Yes, for sure," he continued. "I walked past it and was also lucky to see the St. Rose's School, a huge one many times bigger than the Charity School or any of those on the Essequibo Coast. This building reminded me a bit of the hospital at Suddie, and so I did not want to stay around there too long. Queen's College was not too far away from it. I also had a long walk on the seawall. I started from the Kingston area near the Mercy Hospital, and walked for miles to Vlissingen Road. The waves splashed fiercely against the massive concrete dykes and barricade of boulders, keeping the Atlantic away from the low-lying city. It was a wonderful sight. But when the tide was out and low, it exposed long and wide mudflats, which was not so nice. But the sea breeze made up for that. I sat on the seawall a few times and watched people go by. I spent time there thinking of my friends and family."

Valerie laughed, took hold of Vernon's hand, and asked. "Did you think of me while sitting on the seawall?" She started petting him.

"Of course, I did," lied Vernon. "I pictured you so vividly." But in his mind, he was speaking of Kayla.

"Wow, what a great trip you had," she replied, then inched closer, smooched him, and kissed his cheek.

Vernon was turned on by her sensuality. He was starved of interaction with Kayla and generally with any female. Valerie's body felt good against his. He kissed her on her lips and quickly ended it. She was worked-up in a manner she did not anticipate and wanted more of him. She started to caress his groin and a rush of blood hardened his penis that forced against his crotch. She circled it in her palm and pulled him toward her legs. His hand slipped under her dress and rested on her groin also. He felt the cavity between her legs and inserted his index finger and played with her moist clitoris as their kiss became wild, saturated, and passionate. They were both aching to engage in the hottest of sex, but neither would make a move to undress the other.

161

They were conscious that they were still on the living room couch. Vernon led her into his room and locked the room behind them. They lay in bed closely embraced, rubbing their bodies against each other but still fully clad. Vernon's mind drifted off to his childhood days.

Occasionally after school, a band of about eight to ten kids from the farms on their "main" would gather at spring tide, when the water level in the river was highest, on the Ramlall's jetty, which was the longest among those farms. It protruded to the edge of the mudflat to where the riverbed dipped into the deep channel. The depth was unfathomable. That jetty was built for accommodating larger workboats to avoid grounding at low tide.

For the young school friends, it was superb for sprinting off and diving safely into the deep water. A group of friends, which often included Lloyd Ramlall, Valerie, Jason Andrade, Kayla, (before she left to live at the river mouth), Verna, Cora, Isri, and Vernon, would gather there to dive and swim. At age ten, having stripped off all their clothing as they made for the water, no one appeared to care to notice the nakedness displayed. It was commonplace for the group of males and females to communally bathe in the river together those days and not focus on the immature and exposed hairless sex organs they bared without embarrassment. The carefree frolic of diving off the jetty in surprising bodily contortions and styles took precedence under the shade of the graceful courida tree grove, a type of mangrove with densely padded root base. The warm sunshine dispelled the chill from the water and encouraged the revelers to enjoy their stay together for hours. At the end of it, they dressed their wet bodies and dispersed to their homes.

Vernon marveled at how different his body was today and how enticing and captivating the grown bodies of those girls he knew then were at this later time, like the one with him that day. His Kayla's body he knew for certain felt as smooth as velvet and drew him like a magnet every time they came together, and this sensuous woman rubbing against him now had hypnotized him and left him wriggling with desire. Valerie stripped every piece of clothes off his frame and hurriedly undressed her own self. She lay on her back and pulled him over her legs. He was rearing to release a buildup of body fluids and his pent-up pining for lust and love from the one he had been looking for. He opened his eyes and realized that he was just dreaming. This woman outstretched under him waiting for a forceful penetration was not his Kayla. He was disappointed. He could not forsake the only woman he had really made a commitment to. "I can't do this," he sobbed in grief. "It is not right. I can't do this."

Valerie was taken aback and could not understand why Vernon had come so close to loving her but forsook her invitation. "Are you alright, Vernon?" she questioned irritatingly. "Did I not do something right or what? We were so close to sharing our naked secrets but blew it. I had no idea that you are one of those who object to sex before marriage. I thought otherwise all along. I am sorry for leading you up this path."

"You are a beautiful and smart young woman, Valerie. I do like you a lot. You know I have always cherished your friendship. I do not want to use you as a piece of property at my disposal. It's not fair. You need better than that, a person who would give you his whole person without reservation. I don't think I am at that stage. And who knows, we may or may not get there. I just need to wait. I just need to wait, just wait," Vernon explained and demanded of himself. Valerie did not understand Vernon's justification for the fiasco. She left quietly and made no personal contact with him for months, although they saw each other and waved from a distance.

CHAPTER 12

REGATTA SEASON AND NEW DESIGNS FOR SPEED

The Adonis brothers were successful competitors in the Pomeroon regatta for three consecutive years. They were familiar with the boat races at the junction of the Pomeroon and the Aripiaco River mouth. They once won the runner's up prize for speedboats in the twenty-five to forty horsepower engine category and third place twice the first years they competed. They were reputable as avid racers and were keen to cop the fastest boat prize in that category this year. In addition, their acquisition of a seventy-five horsepower Mercury engine and their enrolment in the bigger engine category was meant to spring a surprise at the upcoming regatta in August. Fewer boats raced in the higher category, and the majority of them were boats from the Essequibo River and occasionally from the North West District and as far away as the Courantyne River, bordering Suriname, the former Dutch colony.

Vernon was fascinated with the growing number of fast boats in the Pomeroon. One day he hoped to own his own and personally race as well. In the meantime, working with the Adonises to prepare for their participation was welcome. Their plan was to build two speedboats that would allow both the brothers to compete: one with their smaller engine and the other with the new Mercury. The older boat had still been active since the last Pomeroon regatta, running quick trips to and from Charity regularly and for cashing in on the occasional hire in the Pomeroon and Moruka Rivers. Vernon had undertaken a few hires for the Adonises since he joined that workshop and was thrilled to do so. He was bought over by the speed of that craft and proved to be a capable and dazzling speedboat driver. He was an upcoming legend because of the fast maneuvers rapid accelerations he managed, alongside the effortless mooring he accomplished.

He offered a suggestion to Billy and Joe Adonis. "I think the power of the engine at the stern of a speedboat is just half the job. If the boat is not meticulously built to maximize the power of the engine, winning races would be elusive."

Joe Adonis knew that his friend had made a good point but assured, "Our current racing boat is undoubtedly very fast. We lost the last time by inches, according to the referees. But we were not happy with that decision. I think they robbed us of the championship. We have to avenge that defeat this time."

Billy muttered a passive interjection, "That was the final decision, and we can do nothing about it at this time. What we have to do is to win by a boat length in August and leave no one the opportunity to fiddle with the results." He continued, "In any case, there are neutral judges this year—a businessman from Danielstown, and two others from Mainstay Lake and Moruka—no Pomeroon judges, like the Jacklow Bashar guy and the Abram's Creek Revero guy last year. They may have been corrupted by the Pickersgill group, whose boat narrowly won."

Charlie Adonis gave the go-ahead to his workshop team to do what it takes to win. He nonetheless added a condition. "Once the regular contracts are honored and fulfilled, you boys can spend all the time in the evening and weekends to get prepared for Aripiaco this year. We cannot relax on our bread-and-butter duties. More dedicated focus to racing would happen only if the prize was worth it. You can't live on a trophy and a few dollars one month in a year here. Fame is good, but it does not fill our belly. I will give a hand also. Four of us will do a lot in the next four months." The team accepted without contesting the elder man's wisdom.

On inspection of their speedboat, as they began refurbishing it, they were shocked to see how waterlogged the wooden boat was; the bottom was covered with stuck-on barnacles. There were signs of some early rotting also at the board ends where the paintwork had peeled. They were not discouraged and set about docking the boat in the sun, away from the cover of the workshop, and replacing a portion of the bottom at the stern. Once dried out, they would caulk it anew and paint it in attractive colors. They decided to change its name, too, from *Enterprise*, the name of their small estate, to simply *Adonis*, the workshop's and their family name.

They were astonished when Vernon, their newest hand, with only two years' experience at the workshop, offered a more radical recommendation. "Why don't you guys abandon this boat altogether and design two new ones with speed, balance, and maneuverability that outclass the other competing boats? In any case, we need to build a new boat to carry the Mercury."

The Adonis boys seemed partially interested but skeptical about whether there could be a superior design to what they had acquired in their racing craft.

Vernon didn't let up. "Didn't we come up with a great design for Mr. Bachew's passenger boat? It was acceptable to him, and we have heard no complaints or negative criticisms since."

Charlie Adonis heard the exchange about Bachew's passenger boat and had to express his satisfaction with that project. "I have heard that that boat is doing good business for Bachew on the Parika–Bartica run on the Essequibo River. Passengers are pleased with the time they save and the comfort that boat offers. I am told that it does three or four trips each day compared to the single trip his launch made before. Maybe you boys could try and think what features in that boat could be adapted for a smaller speedboat."

Billy agreed with his father and decided to work on a new prototype for two new racing boats. Vernon was buoyant that his suggestion was, after all, to be looked into. He pointed out that the current array of speedboats seemed to have a basic fault: They were prone to taking water and capsizing too easily in a sharp swerve. Swerving rapidly at nearly right-angle turns was critical to maintaining a lead or keeping abreast of other boats. The surfs, swells, and waves generated by several boats running side by side made it precariously dangerous when handling those turns. He expressed another observation. "The shallow depth and low gunwales of most of those speedboats look like a common flaw to me. I might be mistaken, but that's how I feel. They were built like wooden tubs that strangely generated enough speed. Imagine if they were shaped and built more creatively."

The whole team was focused on his remarks as if he was the brain behind the muscles and boatbuilding experience in the workshop. They silently welcomed his contribution and the interesting new ideas he brought to improving the styles and strength of the boats they produce. This time, they had begun to acknowledge it more openly. They all turned to Vernon and begged him to come up with changes on their current speedboat and find better design for new boats to be constructed in time for the August regatta. Vernon modestly apologized and said, "I think we all need to work on new designs. I have ideas and a few tips, and I am ready to offer these. We could learn from the design we used on Mr. Bachew's boat: a narrower bow and vee-shaped bottom at the front, a wider body, and a wide, flat stern area, but not as broad as the body. That would change the stubby flat-bottom style of speedboats. To me, they drag too much water and suction, which slow them down. The gunwales need to be higher for fast swerving that would not allow an intake of water; and a fast, viable craft needs to have a curved shape, bow up, and stern less high up but curved upwards also. Like Bachew's boat, the stern-half of the boat should be a nearly flat vee. The bow should be a pronounced vee to break the water easily and allow a hovercraft effect, with three-quarters of the boat skimming the water at high speed. Suction at both ends of the boat should be drastically reduced. That would be a fast boat, in my thinking."

They all nodded less inquisitively at Vernon's ideas. "Sounds good," Billy supported. "But how would you raise the gunwales without increasing the weight of the boat. Too heavy a boat would struggle against other lighter ones."

Vernon looked baffled and could not provide an instant solution. He, however, continued to complete the vision he had of a good-looking and efficient craft. "I see a new-styled speedboat almost covered by a lightweight low tent, sealing it from taking water as it leans at a fast turn. The gunwales would be raised to the roof of the tent, which would have something like a sunroof for easy exit in case of emergency. A low front windscreen would be built at the end of the front deck where the tent starts. There should be two side entrances or exit windows next to the driver's seat to be locked off for a race. The tent roof would taper down in an aerodynamic way to the level of a deck at the stern. I think such a boat would be built for a maximum of two persons on the front seat. The back next to the engine would literally be built like a box, which will compactly be loaded with polystyrene foam to render the boat unsinkable. The front deck would also be loaded with polystyrene foam."

Joe Adonis laughed supportively also. "You are talking about building a sports car for the water, man! I like the idea. But what about the weight?"

Vernon tried to assuage the fear of heaviness. "I think the tent should be built out of silverballi of half-in thickness. That should help to limit too much weight. But really, I think we should weigh every piece of wood used for the construction and that plus the weight of the engine should give us a good sense of what weight would be best to keep the boat afloat, buoyant, and made for speed. We should compare the current weight of the *Enterprise* together with the twenty-five horsepower Yamaha engine. That should be the guide for building the new boats. In addition, we would have to calculate the size of the boat to carry the seventy-five horsepower Mercury engine, regulating it against the *Enterprise*." There was a lull as the Adonises listened and absorbed Vernon's advice.

Billy showed a subtle belief in Vernon's discourse, as if he was beginning a new modus operandi of building boats in a more calculated and scientific manner rather than the mere traditional designs and fabrication they had practiced so far, albeit successful. He was enthusiastic to give it a try and see how it developed, especially after what he heard of Bachew's boat that largely followed Vernon's design ideas. He got together with the two younger men and started to measure boards lying on the boathouse floor. He suggested that they order wide-cut boards of a five-eighth-inch thickness and stay away from using marine plywood, whose use has grown in popularity among builders mainly because of the ease to work with it. Yet they carried their fair share of weight.

"I prefer regular silverballi boats. They don't retain water like plywood, and they take sanding and smoothing much better than marine ply," he stated. "Silverballi demands more work to bend and shape, but the finish is incomparable. I believe that we could try to add a thin fiberglass coating to reduce waterlogging. That would seal even the smallest gaps between the boards and joints."

The young men all agreed and felt very enthusiastic about this project. None of them had ever worked with fiberglass but would like to give it a try, if only they could get enough instructions on how to use it with the resin and hardener. They had heard friends talk about the strength of fiberglass, which they used to repair a few imported boats. Charlie Adonis half listened as he busied himself with working on a ballahoo to be launched in two days. He was curious about what he heard and stopped work for a while to discuss with the younger men. They were aware that it would cost a lot more and would have to be purchased in Georgetown. Charlie Adonis gave the go-ahead to his sons to spend some extra cash on fiberglassing their speedboats only on an exceptional basis if they thought they could learn in good time. Success on their own boats, for now, would open up a new avenue of innovation in the industry. He concluded that the use of fiberglass, though, on the outside of all the boats they built generally would not be economical.

"But perhaps, depending on the results at the upcoming regatta, who knows? An Adonis speedboat made out of that material may attract new business in the future," the senior boatbuilder predicted.

Charlie Adonis's message reached Carl Duncan at the Siriki Sands that evening, and early next day, he was finalizing a list of materials. Billy asked, "Would you kindly cut the boards about five-eighths of an inch thick rather than the usual inch thickness. We are trying to reduce the weight of the speedboats we are going to build. We would also like you to give us a third of the order of boards a foot wide if you can. We need an equal number of these for the sides of the crafts. We reckon that after planing and sanding, they would be a half-inch thick, and with ribs slightly closer together, our boats would be strong. You are part of our experiment, Carl. So, give us your best help."

Two weeks later, the frames of both boats were taking shape. The three young men worked each day until nightfall after their regular quota of work for Charlie Adonis. They saw it as a labor of love they were investing in. Every part added to the boats was scrutinized for accuracy to the blueprint they devised. Everyone was enthusiastic and put in a wholehearted effort each day. The new style, as outlined by Vernon, was gradually forming like a face on a wall, becoming more artistic and beautiful with every stroke of a painter's brush. There was a pleasing atmosphere among them in the workshop. Their only regret was that they could not get into learning and using fiberglassing on their new boat. Billy pointed out that they required more time to study the art and techniques well before they really put money into that skill.

"Let's start on that early next year and work towards that year's regatta. We could even try it at the Mainstay Lake Regatta first," he encouraged the others. The Mainstay Regatta was a more low-keyed event.

They carried out the construction of their racing boats out of the eye of the public, at the far back of the shed, and had a large canvas hung to block the view from the main part of the workshop where clients and customers freely strolled about. Surprise was the new name of their game until regatta day. The lumber sawed by Carl Duncan was of high quality; he had stuck exactly to the specifications requested by the Adonis.

* * *

Around mid-July, two new racing boats were completed. They were launched at dusk one weekday when there was little or no traffic in the river. The replacement of the *Enterprise*, *Adonis-I*, was first taken for a two-mile run, a mile up and a mile downriver, swerving and turning at nearly full speed. Joe Adonis held the throttle and spun the steering wheel as if he was an old pro in this boat. He stopped abruptly a few feet from the jetty and allowed the back swells to take him to the edge. Billy Adonis then hopped onto *Adonis II* and dazzled his coworkers and the rest of his family waiting to see the new Mercury engine and the new boat in action.

One of his young sisters cheered and screamed, "That's the champion at Aripiaco. My big brother and his boat are tops."

Both boats were hauled up and covered up at the back of the shed, and from time to time, they would be taken for a run at nightfall not to attract notice and trigger gossip of their innovative nature. Vernon had another idea.

"What is it you want to discuss, Vern?" Charlie Adonis asked.

"Nothing too important," he answered.

"Okay, let me hear," the elder man said.

Vernon quietly and awkwardly responded, "I am looking for a favor. But I would be fine with either a yes or no answer. I want to race the old *Enterprise*. I will use the Elto engine at Miriam's Delight. My dad is willing to have it refurbished and tuned up in time for the regatta. I can enter into the twenty-five-horsepower category, just like that boat did in the past. If you grant me this favor, I would make some changes to the boat after it is dried out enough."

Charlie Adonis smiled and pat Vernon on the back. "Go for it, boy. Make the best of an opportunity to race. I see you running hires in that boat when you did and think you are a natural with speedboats. Go for it, Vern,"

Vernon went to work the next days and made a visible difference to the shape of the boat. He lifted the height of the gunwales by about six inches and turned them outwards, making the width at the top of the boat noticeably wider than the bottom. He used a thin board as a splashboard to reduce the intake of water at fast turns. He also added a flange at the bottom vee of the stern on both sides. "I think those projections will help to keep the boat flat on the surface and reduce stern suction. I'll test it to see how fast I could turn at high throttle and fast speed without taking in water or capsizing. Let's see if there is a difference," Vernon cautiously remarked.

Vernon arrived at work a few days later with the Elto engine in his ballahoo. He unloaded it under the shed to keep it safe until later in the day when it was anchored at the stern of *Enterprise* and tied tautly to the rear seat. There were no remote controls. He, therefore, chose to operate it sitting in the middle of the short boat. This he thought would distribute his weight evenly between the bow and the stern and reduce the drag. He cranked the engine, started it, and kept it at very low throttle. He then took the middle seat and extended his left hand to operate the engine handle controls. In no time, he was moving at breakneck speed. He zig-zagged a few times and ran the boat for about a mile. The Adonises were amazed at the sharp turn he took without any incident. He sped back to the jetty to the commendations of his coworkers.

"You are now part of the Adonis Team, Vern. Together we are going to be a hard team to beat; can't wait now for regatta day. Aripiaco, here we come," Billy encouraged.

The last week of July saw the Adonis team practicing with their boats every late evening. On a few occasions, the *Enterprise* made the trip to Charity where onlookers gazed at the new shape of the boat. Many of them asked if it would race in the Aripiaco Regatta. Avid race fans thought it could pose a great challenge for Rickford Lane's boat that nipped it for the first place the last time. They were given an uncertain and cagey answer—"Maybe or maybe not."

* * *

August had arrived. The first Monday of August was customarily a public holiday. Charity, as usual, was overflowing with crowds, who had come from all over the district and the Essequibo Coast. Many of them had linked their Monday commercial activities at Charity with a trip up the Pomeroon to witness the regatta. Three sloops had made the journey to the Aripiaco/Pickersgill area with dozens of passengers. These vessels were anchored at three strategic points and tied in a triangular pattern against the mangrove bush. The referees were distributed two in each vessel to monitor the racing from different angles to ensure that rules and regulations were adhered to. By nine o'clock in the morning, there was already a relatively large set of spectators both young and older persons. The competitions would run from nine-thirty until five or six later in the day. More spectators were expected to attend this regatta, making it one of the best attended in the last five years.

The whole area was a colorful spectacle buzzing with excitement that echoed back and forth across from bank to bank of the Pomeroon River. The tee-shaped arena, stretching from the Pomeroon to the mouth opening of its tributary, the Aripiaco, presented a daunting course marked by lined buoys. Most of the racing boats were already tied up at Shohan's wharf and registered. The last boats could be seen in the distance speeding to the wharf. Vernon was the last one to arrive and register with *Enterprise*. The nearby grocery/rum shops in the vicinity were all doing successful business. Ballahoo boats with food and soft drinks were also cashing in on the opportunity to earn extra profits.

The races started off just after nine-thirty with the paddling competition. Single person *corials* (canoes) provided a beginning that augured well for the rest of the day. Submerged in water up to about a mere inch from the top of the open dugouts, these boats demanded balance and steady, timed paddling skills to stay afloat and generate speed. Two of them, unfortunately, went down soon after they pushed off at the start. There were laughter and sobs from the spectators, and by the time they bailed out the water and restarted, the others had left them far behind. The other paddling competition included ballahoos of various sizes with various numbers of paddlers. The competition that stood out was the one with eight-manned corials. These boats carried two other dedicated passengers, one at the bow drumming on the gunwale with his paddle keeping the paddler's rowing in rhythmic unison. The other one at the back was devoted only to steering, using his paddle as the rudder.

The speedboat racing drew the attention of everyone, and a hushed silence as the boats lined up each time for the start. Once they pulled off, there was deafening partisan noise. Spectators shouted out advice and encouragement to the competitors they were supporting. There were spills in almost every one of the speedboat competitions. Vernon was neck and neck in the twenty-five-horsepower category with a new boat and engine operated by someone that looked familiar as he glanced across his shoulder. It was Randolph Lane, who had controversially defeated Joe Adonis in the *Enterprise* in the last regatta. Next to Lane's boat was also someone he thought he knew, but his memory and the morning glare concealed who he was exactly. Spectators were convinced that the boats were faster at this regatta than before, probably due to the slow current in the rivers.

There was, however, a challenge at the crosscurrents where the two rivers joined, and the more daring racers tackled that obstacle without a reduction of speed. Those that could not lost about a boat's length at every lap. Three speedboats led the race, with only inches ahead between them. This prompted Charlie Adonis to despair for a quick moment as he blurted, "They're goin' to rob us again, man. It's too close."

Then, in an instant, Vernon swerved, hopping over the swells made by the Lane boat and took a short lead. As the racers throttled up for the last dash and tried to navigate a fast right-angle turn to the final ribbon, the Rickford Lane's boat took water and he slowed for a split second to revive balance. That allowed Vernon to finish with a flourish ahead of the third racer. It was a colossal win.

The three finalists drove alongside each other and shared congratulations. Rickford Lane could not fully accept that the Adonises' craft he defeated in the last regatta had beaten him this time. Vernon's skill did it; he had, in turn, avenged that questionable outcome.

"You ran a good race, Vernon, but you won by a fluke. You have to admit," Lane said.

Vernon smiled and conceded, "Maybe so, but a winner is a winner. You should know that better than anyone after your win last year. You still won this time, except in third place. It is still a win."

The third racer congratulated Vernon with a handshake and a slap on his back. "You have again deprived me of a championship, man." He smiled in resignation, remembering the cricket competition finals.

Vernon was dumbfounded. It was Adrian da Silva, Kayla's brother. He said, "Thanks. I have not seen you nor your family for a long time, over two years, I think. How are all of you doing?"

Adrian da Silva was pleased to see the winner again, if only with a taint of grudge. Vernon, though, was lapping up the applause for his win but giving the impression that he was ignoring it by diverting his attention to his fellow competitors. Vernon asked politely, "Is your family here?"

Adrian shook his head and explained that his parents were holidaying with his sister on the East Coast of Demerara and might not be back till September. That imparted a speck of hope in Vernon's mind that his Kayla may show up in a month's time. He pondered this in his heart and decided to quietly await her return, if only to verify whether or not she had broken off their relationship or if there were other reasons for her silence toward him.

He left and returned to the Adonis brothers, who were exuberant with joy at what the young Vernon had achieved, by racing with confidence for sure, but also by converting *Enterprise* to a weird looking but successful speedboat.

Charlie Adonis hugged Vernon and patted his head as Denis Atkins looked on with satisfaction. "Anita would have been thrilled at her son. Your mom is smiling for you my, son," Denis muttered. With his arm around Vernon's shoulder, he asked Vernon if he had seen Valerie, who had asked for him. He replied in the negative and wondered if she had overcome her anger at him. He had seen her off and on since their fateful parting, but they both kept their distance and merely waved at each other without engaging in any dialogue. He took it to mean that she was probably less angry at him for not satisfying the passion she showed towards him. He had no excuse for his action or non-action that day and was forced to stifle the real reason for it. The search for his Kayla had preoccupied him and blunted his natural impulse towards his other female friends.

The look of two new Adonis boats had attracted the curiosity of spectators, who argued among themselves about the need for changing from the traditional style of Pomeroon speedboats. Many believed that such a noticeable deviation from the normal would end in a "trashing" for them. A number of them shouted for their competitors to defeat them. "Teach them a harsh lesson. Show-off fancy boats don't win races."

Others eagerly awaited to see how a new version of speedboats would fare against their tried and proven counterparts. "They may have something to prove, I think," an elderly person observed. He turned to Charlie Adonis and offered his best wishes to his sons. "I like the look of those boats. They are different; they are neatly built and look like the Cadillac of speedboats in the Pomeroon. I hope they perform as good as they look."

The regatta day undoubtedly belonged to the Adonises' workshop. They had won every race they registered for and swept the competition with first-place wins in six of the twenty-four races, leaving the spectators amazed at their innovation and prowess on the water. It was the first time in the history of the races that a smaller boatbuilding workshop was able to capture the endorsement of such a wide spectrum of the region's boat-loving people. It was a huge advertisement, and Charlie Adonis was more than elated. He hugged Vernon and remarked, "What could we do without you, lad. You have been a godsend. All my family is proud of you and so they should be. You are like part of the family. I hope you continue to be."

As the evening darkness began to set in, the crowds were fast dispersing when Valerie showed up at Shohan's wharf where the Adonises and Vernon were packing up to leave. She was with an elegant young man, whom she introduced as Lennox Beharry, her fiancé from Somerset a few miles from Charity. The Beharrys were a well-off rice-growing family that was fast implementing mechanized rice production. "You have raced well, Vern, and captured the hearts of many people, especially the girls. I hope you find a good one among all of them," Valerie remarked with a somewhat facetious air.

Vernon laughed and replied, "I will find a special one when the time is right, you'll see."

The Adonis team untied their boats and were about to drive off together when Vernon spotted Denyse Validam returning to Cabacaburi with her family in their boat. With his father with him in *Enterprise*, he drove up against the Validam's boat and exchanged greetings with Denyse and her family. He reintroduced his father. Sitting next to Denyse was a male person of her age whom he had never met before and was sure that he was not one of her three brothers. As he pulled away and throttled up, he couldn't help musing that many of the close friends he had deliberately not mingled with since his awakening towards Kayla and her departure appeared to have found prospective partners. He had once endeared himself to Denyse and her family when they lived at Charity for a period in his young days. He once had a deep fondness for her. "She is one 'boviander' I could really fall for," he once boasted to his friends. His chances now seemed to have dried up, and he resigned himself to the end of that chapter in his life.

The Adonis family were having a drink at home as they relaxed and regurgitated the details of the race day when the Atkins men arrived. Their main reason for going straight to the Adonises' landing was to return *Enterprise*, offload Miriam's Delight Elto motor into their own ballahoo, and take it back with good news to Mrs. de Castro. Charlie

Adonis summoned them in for a drink and a short victory celebration. As they took their leave, Vernon said he that was going ahead to unbolt and remove the Elto from *Enterprise*.

Charlie Adonis stood up and whispered an order to the young Atkins, "Wait a minute, Vern. Why are you in such a haste to take off the engine?"

Both Vernon and his father stared at him somewhat baffled as Charlie Adonis made his announcement. "You have earned your two victories today, Vern, and you have also earned a reward from this workshop. *Enterprise* is rightfully yours now. It is our gift to you. You have taught us seasoned boatbuilders that new thinking can make a positive difference in our work and in our life. You are a smart and thinking lad, wiser than your age reveals. Your father must be proud of you."

Vernon was stunned by the announcement and gratefully and modestly accepted it, repeating several times, "Thank you, Uncle Charlie, I don't know how to thank you and your family enough."

Mrs. de Castro went out of her way that day and had dinner prepared for the Atkinses. She was thrilled by Vernon's achievements and pensively remarked, "It's in your blood, Vern. Rafa de Melo loved boats and speed. He loved this part of the country for the many rivers where he traversed. Your great-grandfather must be happy. Anita too must be proud of you as I am. The gift of that boat from Adonis is the right acknowledgment of how your life has evolved since Anita's passing. You are serious about work and balance it well with doing fun things. I wish more of the Pomeroon youths would emulate your example. You have a bright future ahead of you. I truly know that. You have become an eligible and prospective husband for someone who must match your temperament and attitude, though. I hope you do find that somebody."

CHAPTER 13

VALERIE'S BIG DAY

Wedding invitations were being distributed for the upcoming June wedding in less than three months. The news was widespread around Charity, in the Pomeroon, and on the Essequibo Coast. The talk swirling around was that this was going to be the wedding of the year at Charity. The wealthy Beharrys were sparing nothing to roll out a celebration to be remembered. Theirs was a family that started from modest means on a small acreage and incrementally built an outstanding rice production establishment and a name among the high echelons of Essequibo businessmen. Apart from their own large production of paddy, they also bought off the produce of small farmers and processed it to the last stage of polished white rice and by-products. In addition, chicken and animal feed was a large part of the output of Beharry's business outfit. Their large, flashy mansion in the vicinity of Charity, with multiple cars parked inside a large white-painted wrought iron barricaded concrete patio at the front, indicated the lucrative lifestyle they lived. Their daily existence was aloof of the common people and resulted in scarce social interaction with them, except for buying the fruits of their labor at prices they regulated for the small farmers. Isolation was a key characteristic of their daily life, which relied on the restrictive odd get-togethers of the small number of families in the upper ranks of the community.

Gossip was rife. Marjorie James's daughter, Valerie, would provide the Beharrys a vital link to the common folks, whom they had cut off and ignored, forgetting from where they started. This was affirmed as the motive behind the marriage. Conversely, there was tacit jealousy that the daughter of an ordinary person was chosen by the affluent Lennox Beharry. Their unspoken jealousy unashamedly accused her of marrying upwards like a so-called "gold-digger," derogatorily referring to her and her mother as blatant seekers of wealth. Those who genuinely meant well for her, however, were enthusiastic that the two young people were actively breaking down the divisive barriers that wealth creates. Their courting over many months convinced many that there was real love between a very good-looking couple. Their wedding would bring together in a ceremony all classes of the community and seal a harmony not only between two seemingly different people but among different groups. There was growing anticipation of the big day.

Marjorie James stopped in at Miriam's Delight one afternoon, bringing a gift of egg pudding for Mrs. de Castro. She was always proud of her prolific production of chicken and duck eggs, which earned a significant portion of their income and provided good food and gifts to share with neighbors from time to time.

"Your poultry farm seems to be doing well," Madeline rhetorically asked.

"I would hardly call it a farm, Maddie. It's a small project big enough for me and one of my nephews, who spends most of his time cultivating the five-acre plot opened up on the grant. It is enough to give us a living. I do most of the poultry work, mainly egg production and a few meat birds for home use. What is a new addition, is the half-a-dozen guinea fowls I bought some time ago. To my astonishment they 'churn' out eggs, it seems," she replied.

"That's wonderful," Madeline congratulated.

Marjorie continued less enthusiastically, "The trouble is people here are not accustomed to guinea fowl eggs. I have a problem selling them. We eat a lot of it at home, market some for a price far below value, and give away the rest. Have you tried those eggs, Maddie?" she asked.

"I have had them as a girl and liked them. I did not see a difference between them and chicken eggs fried or scrambled," Madeline replied.

"Then I know where to give some in future," Marjorie stated.

Madeline de Castro was very commending of Marjorie's industry and intent to be as self-sufficient as possible as a single mother. She never ceased to praise her for bringing up a beautiful and genteel daughter. She was one of the not too many young people who impressed Madeline and who won her admiration. "How is your daughter, these days, Marjorie? I haven't seen her a while. She used to pop in off and on but seldom these days," she commented.

"My visit today is actually regarding her, Madeline," Marjorie responded and handed her an envelope containing an invitation for the wedding. "She is getting married in June, right here at the Charity Mission Church. Your presence there and at the wedding party at the Greenheart Hotel would be most appreciated. I hope you would come."

Madeline smiled and looked agreeable at Valerie's progress as a terrific young person. "So, who is the lucky young man?" she questioned.

"He is Lennox Beharry, the son of Beharry from Somerset and Berks. He is a fine young man, who schooled at Queen's College in Georgetown. He has put off his plans to study law in Trinidad and has returned about a year ago to take over the rice farming operations from his father. My Valerie is head over heels about him and is looking forward to the wedding. I am pleased for both of them, and the thought of their wedding is already filling my head with ideas of grandchildren. I am so excited," Marjorie remarked. She took out a second envelope from her bag and asked if Denis was around. Madeline told her that he would not be home until near nightfall. She handed the invitation to Madeline and asked her to kindly deliver it to him. "Denis's and Vernon's presence at the wedding and party would be very special for Valerie and me," she assured Madeline. "She has invited several of her friends of over the years at school. Unfortunately, some are not living in the Pomeroon these days. It would be a nice surprise if some do show up," she added.

"But I have one more request. Valerie needs a father to walk her up to the altar and as you know." She paused and stared at the ceiling.

Madeline nodded her head somberly and said, "I do understand."

"I would be honored if Denis would be kind enough to do this. He and Anita have been our closest friends. I am kindly asking you to ask him to accept this responsibility. You would be the only one to ensure he does."

Marjorie James was a religious woman. She was a frequent churchgoer and a generous benefactor to the priest and the Catholic community, sharing her limited resources and her time. She was a key member of the management group in the church. She was always around preparing for Sunday Mass, weddings, baptisms, and funerals, cleaning the building, decorating the altar, and washing and ironing linen and vestments used in the services. Her daughter was sheltered growing up and was expected to participate in all the church activities Marjorie was involved in. She later was saddened by her daughter's estrangement from these activities and from religion in general. Valerie had only occasionally accompanied her mother to Mass and other religious celebrations. The exception was during the Christmas season. She loved the cheerful carols and hymns and attended church to hear the choir perform this music. Her mother insisted that her marriage must be solemnized in church.

The Beharry's were a non-religious family, although, in name alone, they were of the Hindu tradition. They lived through the last three decades practicing no religion. They knew very little of the beliefs and liturgies of Hinduism, Christianity, or Islam, the major religious communities surrounding them. Lennox Beharry said that he would have been content to be married in the courts in a small registrar ceremony accompanied by a lavish party and celebration. He, nevertheless, was open to a church ceremony if the Jameses could arrange it and if their church would allow it. His attitude to religion and now to celebrate their marriage reflected that of his parents and their family. Valerie was skeptical that the old priest at the church would discourage a mixed marriage. Or he might insist that Lennox become a Christian and be converted to Valerie's religion, a condition she could hardly demand.

A meeting with the priest was held at the church office in the presbytery with Lennox, Valerie, and Marjorie in attendance. The old European priest was more liberal and agreeable than both Valerie and her partner expected. He made it clear that he was not the one marrying the two people. He was just a formal witness for the church and an official registrar of the state. They were the ones marrying each other, and consequently, it was their commitment and responsibility to marry and live a strong spiritual relationship where the value of life, goodness, opting for what is right against what is wrong, and love without reservation between them was paramount. This then spoke the language and reflected the mindset of both Lennox and Valerie, and they bought into the church ceremony without objection. The banns of marriage were read out on three consecutive Sundays after Mass to proclaim that the two specified persons were planning to marry, as was customary in Christian parishes. The priest, as a rule, encouraged anyone with reasons why the two specified persons should not be married to come forward and declare it. This merely appeared, as a rule, the church felt it should maintain but one that parishioners never genuinely responded to. They felt they should not, and there had been no memory of a public declaration against a marriage. No one was about to object to this one.

Saturday, June 10, was the date fixed for the marriage ceremony at the church, followed by the celebration at the hotel. Marjorie, Valerie, and Mrs. Beharry made a timely visit to Young's Boutique in High Street, Georgetown, in advance of the big day to select and order a wedding dress. The visit entailed a car ride to the Adventure Stelling where the vehicle with passengers, driven by one of Beharry's chauffeurs, was loaded patiently and cautiously onto the vehicle deck of the steamer. It was offloaded at the long Parika Stelling and drove across the uneven greenheart wooden planks until it sped off on the West Coast Demerara Highway, rushing to get an early booking and crossing at the Vreedenhoop Stelling across to Georgetown. They were in the boutique by three in the afternoon, where the ladies settled on an elegant-looking gown, veil and matching shoes. They left the city at about five and traveled back in time to board the overland night steamer at Parika, heading back to the Essequibo Coast and onward to Charity. Their private vehicle ensured that they were back at Charity by ten at night, many hours before the overland bus was expected.

The purchasing of the bridal requirements in a joint group of their families, the classy manner of traveling, and the amity expressed on the trip was an experience Valerie and her mother were enthralled by. Never before had they been so relieved of the stress and fatigue of the strenuous journey to and from the city. The experience was a sign of things to come, which luck had thrown in their path. Marjorie prayed for her daughter's destiny to be blessed and guided by divine grace and love and that the easy access to material luxury would not sway her and her husband away from the spiritual qualities they should strive for. She wished that justice and fairness be the basis between them in their marriage and in their dealings with family, friends, and strangers. She hoped for lowliness and humility to be the beacon in their lives, like her religion taught, amidst the heights of financial security and opulence. She felt that love had brought them together, and that would build an intimacy to provide peace of mind that permeated their life.

There was a buzz around the church on the morning of June 10. The grass around the building was mowed neatly the day before. The smell of freshly cut grass pointed to the special nature of the occasion. The church and its altar were beautifully adorned with an abundance of flowers. The organist hired for the day was oozing out melodious music from the pedal pump organ. She seemed tireless and cheerful. A small choir sat prepared to choreograph the three songs they had rehearsed for weeks. Most of them were friends of Valerie. The bride was dressed and made up spectacularly by Marjorie and her sister, with help from Madeline de Castro and a beautician from a Charity salon. She would be transported in a convoy of decorated motorboats—one loaded with a jukebox bellowing out love songs—on the short trip from Marjorie's home to the Charity Wharf, from where the bride and her companions would board one of Beharry's luxurious cars in a motorcade for another short ride to the church. The four bridesmaids were all dressed in beautifully laced aquamarine long dresses.

Lennox Beharry was formally dressed. He looked spruce in a black tuxedo with waistband and a white shirt and dark blue bow tie. His cousin, the best man, was also in a tuxedo and white shirt but with an aquamarine bow tie matching the color of the bridesmaids' dresses. The groom and his family were already in the church, waiting in the front row pews, when the organ jubilantly began the "Here Comes the Bride" recital. The groom and his companions jumped to attention and waited in a staid posture as the bride was walked up the aisle on the arms of a handsome gentleman clad in a straight formal safari suit in matching black color as the groom. That was a big surprise for most of the packed church. Denis Atkins handed Valerie over to Lennox Beharry and moved to the bride's side of the church next to the mother of the bride, Marjorie James, causing a number of eyes to roll. A widower and a widow of sorts publicly sharing a daughter's big day was food for the rumor mongers.

Vernon was present in the back of the church dressed in a shirt and tie and a gray blazer, and out of easy sight of the bride and groom. He wanted to be oblivious in view of the gulf that grew between him and his childhood friend. He liked her sexiness as they grew up, and often desired her well-shaped body but was always torn between his intimacy with Kayla and Valerie's tempting sensuality. He knew so very well that she wanted him and probably for more than a one-night stand. He wondered if his seeming rejection of her that night when their hormonal impulses had lit them afire and sex was only an instance away had driven her to find someone new. There was no guilt in him for this but a possible regret that he might have forsaken an opportunity to settle down with a good human being, given his present predicament.

He was uncertain now more than any time before of his status with the one to whom he had given his heart. He worried if she had ended their togetherness and how he might cope with losing his two closest friends. He bowed his head and sat motionless throughout the marriage ritual. A thunderbolt hit him when she affirmed that she was taking Lennox Beharry as her husband to have and to hold until death separated them. Then a lightning flash zig-zagged before his eyes and shocked his heart when the bride and groom kissed in front of everyone in the church and a roar of applause filled the church. His vivid memory of her nectar sweet tongue plaiting sensuously with his and the firm breasts piercing his bosom ravaged his mind. He accepted that this chapter of love in his life had closed. Their mingling as friends and lovers had ended and a new affiliation as brother and sister might now have to begin.

The motorcade from the church to the hotel was magnificent. Ten decorated cars surrounded by throngs of guests and onlookers paraded like a carnival band to the beat of music from a blasting jukebox, which led off with the wedding march and then moved to Anne Murray's "Could I Have This Dance," followed by two or three other love songs that took them into the Greenheart Hotel. A crowded ballroom with tables surrounding a vacant dance floor was full. A bar was already busy, and spirits were being raised literally and metaphorically. Madeline, Denis, Vernon, four of Valerie's close friends, and two others were given a VIP reserved table next to the top table holding the bride, groom, and immediate family. It gave Vernon an easy view of Valerie with whom he exchanged a glimpse every now and then. He did not really think that he was a loser because an optimism consumed his person. His search for Kayla might have merely been on pause. But it was not at all terminated. He would continue to look for her and wait as long as it took. He now felt that she needed a break to recuperate in body, mind, and spirit and recommit to what is deep-seated between them, a base of embers waiting to be rekindled into the fire that was in their hearts.

After the meal, speeches, and toasts, the traditional dance of bride and groom and with members of opposite families was duly carried out and admired by all with loud applause. The floor was open to all, and a night-long dance and drinking party followed. Vernon was not in the mood for this and left early, hitching a ride back to Miriam's Delight. Denis stayed behind. He had not partied for real since he lost his Anita. This wedding party was a great means to help with his closure of that event. He was there also to serve as a dance partner for both Madeline and Marjorie James, which he did to their satisfaction and delight. They both commended him for being the best gentleman around. For the first time, he was more comfortable interacting with Mrs. de Castro, not as a plantation owner with her employee and her one-time laborer. There was a relaxed sharing as if they were of the same family. A noticeable evolution had continued in their relationship since the passing of Anita.

The wedding completed, Lennox took Valerie on honeymoon to the Caribbean Island of Martinique. They first stopped over for a night in Trinidad and, from there, boarded a flight to the peaceful and culturally rich country, where a Creole way of life vibrantly displayed a melting pot of Afro-Franco European people and their customs.

* * *

Relatively alone with Valerie not in her home anymore, Marjorie sought closer friendship with Mrs. de Castro. She became a frequent visitor sitting for hours at a time, sipping coffee or tea at Miriam's Delight. From time to time, Madeline invited Denis on his return from the fields to join them. She realized that Denis's rigid work life without the tenderness of a woman needed to be attenuated. It was as if she was cagily trying to be a matchmaker between a single father and a single mother.

She was also aware of Marjorie's long-standing friendship with Anita and her husband and the friendship of their children growing up. Denis was usually reticent to reveal his feelings. He was also discreet about broaching the topic of life without the physical and sexual comfort of another woman. What he was always vocal about was his forever love for the Parakese Pearl. He truly believed that she was present in another form or other forms sharing the life of her son with him. That pushed him onward from day to day.

Consequently, while she might have entertained innocent intentions for Marjorie and Denis, Madeline remained wary of Denis's independence regarding family matters and did not want to be seen as an intruder. Madeline liked Marjorie very much because her story and predicament were so similar to hers, regarding a runaway life partner early in their life and because she saw in her a stable and responsible person who worked hard and raised a fantastic daughter. She had seen the similar traits in the supervisor on her estate. There was a quiet wonder in her why the two similar personalities with the freedom to intertwine remained distant apart. She, however, saw a small fracture in this situation when Marjorie invited Denis to be the "father of the bride" and do the honors of giving Valerie away to her husband—and surprisingly, he gladly and willingly agreed. She had no qualms of being an enabler despite how the Pomeroon community took it.

CHAPTER 14

MADELINE DE CASTRO'S SUCCESSOR

Denis Atkins was up early as usual, ready to assign the day's work to the laborers at Miriam's Delight. It had become customary for Madeline de Castro to call her supervisor upstairs to her part of the big house and serve him a strong aromatic cup of coffee as he brought her up to date with progress on her plantation. That morning, there was no stir and movement on the top floor. Denis wondered why his cup of coffee was not forthcoming and worried for a moment if Mrs. de Castro was upset with him about something. But she was not the kind to mope about things that disturbed her. She would confront such things, and anyone she thought was erring, head-on. She was known to say it as she saw it from a position of superiority. Most Pomeroon folks knew her as that type of person.

Eliminating that cause for her no-show that morning, Denis grew somewhat frightened that she might be ill. He never looked ahead to that situation. She had no immediate family, except for an ailing cousin with her three children and five grandchildren. She met her cousin occasionally but was never close to her family. She preferred to keep her distance from her mother's, Mona de Melo's, family. Denis did not want to go out to the fields without contacting Mrs. de Castro.

He decided to go up the front stairs, through Mrs. de Castro's private entrance, and call for her. After banging on the door for a few seconds, a disheveled Madeline de Castro struggled to the door and opened it, holding on to it for balance. Denis took hold of her and sat her on the sofa. "You sure do not look well, Missy," he confirmed.

"My head started to swing last night before I went to bed, and I have had little sleep the whole night, twisting and tossing uncomfortably," she groaned with a grimace.

"I will take you immediately to see Dr. Jon at Charity, Missy." He led her to her bedroom and told her dress while he got the ballahoo and engine ready. But before he did that, he awoke Vernon and sent him off to Marjorie James and requested him to bring her as soon as possible to accompany Mrs. de Castro. The old woman needs a woman and friend to help her, not her employee, a man. He respected her privacy. Marjorie understood the urgency and was with Mrs. de Castro in a jiffy. Denis sped them to the Charity Wharf where a taxi car driver obliged to take her to Dr. Jon's clinic gratis, knowing that if she was referred to the Suddie Hospital, he would win the hire.

As he forecast, his taxi was hired for the Suddie trip after Dr. Jon stabilized her condition and referred her to the public hospital. Marjorie and Denis accompanied her to the Suddie Hospital where she was admitted. She had suffered a mild stroke in the night and was susceptible to another more severe one was the diagnosis given to Marjorie and Denis. He had made this trip a number of times and hoped that his prognosis was not like the tragedy he encountered then. He was ill-prepared to handle the operation of Miriam's Delight without her boss and mentor. He wondered what would happen with his life and his son's if she departed; their home, his job, his future and the future of the plantation could drastically be thrown under a shadow of succession demands from her few family members. Madeline's cousin and her family could very well step in and take over everything. He may have to return to the reservation. But what of Vernon? His peace of mind depended on his one parent's presence as he buried his chronic melancholy over Kayla's absence in his life. Denis was certain that Charlie Adonis and his family would give Denis a home without question. But a further breakup of his family was dreaded.

Marjorie decided to stay over at Suddie with friends and asked Denis to keep an eye on her home while she was at Suddie. She considered her nephew who worked her small farm a reliable person but felt that Denis's call on him would be a support for him alone. She sent a message to Valerie and her son-in-law, Lennox Beharry, and requested her daughter to bring her a bag of clothes and survival essentials. The couple were there that same day and offered to fetch her home on her return. They also offered to take Mrs. de Castro back to Charity on her discharge.

Denis visited Mrs. de Castro without miss every single day while she was treated in the hospital. He was overjoyed to see Mrs. de Castro up and about and cheerful on his fifth visit. She was looking forward to returning home the following day. She was eager to see Vernon, whom she said she utterly missed. She had given much thought to the future of her father's pride and joy, Miriam's Delight. She had also rejected any consideration of letting her family from her mother's side have a foothold in the estate of Rafa de Melo. His sweat, his hard work, his love, and his dreams have permeated life at Miriam's Delight up to the present time.

"Rafa de Melo's two daughters must inherit all he had," she confirmed in the presence of Denis and Marjorie. "Madeline de Melo-Castro is still alive and well," she whispered as she held the hand of Denis and Marjorie on both sides of her bed. "As for his second daughter, she had left her grandson with me, and I am the proudest sister at this time," she solemnly continued.

Marjorie James was confused. She never thought that Madeline de Castro had a sister. It reawakened in her memories of the vicious rumors a long time ago of the stately elder gentleman and her church's outstanding benefactor's secret philandering. She remembered how he was accused at the death of his wife, Mona, of harboring at Miriam's Delight his bastard daughter with a Moruka woman. She never believed it then, but now Madeline's revelation had overcome her. Her calculation told her that Vernon Atkins must be that grandson. That accounted for his handsome looks and the noticeable European mixture she saw in him. His ethnic mixture made him a heartthrob for the young women around him. He stood taller than his father and inherited the wavy dark brown hair of Anita and her forebears. She remembered how her own daughter, Valerie, was so infatuated with him and suffered for months before Lennox Beharry came into her life.

Valerie and Lennox arrived at the hospital. Hospital staff helped Mrs. de Castro to the exit door. Marjorie and Denis helped her into the car and packed her belongings in the booth. Denis was the only one standing outside as they were ready to leave for Charity. He said, "I will come in later with the next bus. Vernon will meet you at Charity and transport Mrs. Castro to her home. He is so anxious to see her to the extent that he has taken the day off from work."

He was about to walk off when Lennox spoke to him. "Jump in, man. There is enough space for three persons at the back or one more in front. These Holden cars are built in Australia to hold six persons. They are large. Just join us and let us all take Mrs.de Castro home. It's better that way."

Reluctantly, Denis accepted the offer. His lean and fit frame easily fitted next to Marjorie, leaving enough room for Madeline de Castro at the back.

Vernon was waiting on the front deck of Miriam's Delight big ballahoo when he saw Beharry's car pull up at the koker trench mouth, right next to the boat. He shyly waved at Valerie and her husband and saw them leave after offloading the passengers.

Madeline was extremely happy to be back in her own home and surroundings with a handful of people she treasured more and more as her days went by—Vernon, Denis, and Marjorie. "I am fit as a fiddle again," she blurted out, "and you all must remember not to leave me too much alone. I depend on the three of you like I never thought I would, and I realize how lucky I am to have you all. You are my family."

* * *

Denis's cup of coffee was ready every morning on her return, and each time, he was grateful that a recurrence of that scary morning recently did not happen. As he was sipping the enjoyable brew, Madeline told him that she wanted him home early that afternoon.

There were some urgent matters to put right at Miriam's Delight. She needed Denis to listen and discuss what she had in mind. "Come in early. There will be dinner for you and Vernon. We will all have dinner together at five when Vernon is home," she instructed. "I have got a nice young chicken from Marjorie and a dozen of Guinea fowl eggs. Let me prepare them in a nice Portuguese dish. So, have a good appetite tonight."

The dining table was nicely laid out when the two Atkins men arrived both cleaned up after their sweaty workday and casually dressed as for an evening of fun. "Sit down, boys, and let me tell you what the menu is tonight." She smiled like a waiter would, trying to impress her customers and secure a decent tip. "The chicken is a common casserole the Madeirans brought to Guyana. I have seared the chicken pieces until they are golden brown and added them to a tomato sauce rich with thyme and other spices. You will taste a strong hint of nutmeg and mace, which it is said was introduced into Portugal by their seafarers centuries ago. Usually, olives, potatoes, and other vegetables the farmers grew in Madeira were an integral part of the dish. But here in Guyana, my people used what was available. So, there are some Irish potatoes, carrots, and white yam mixed in with yard-long bora beans from my kitchen garden. The sauce, rich with garlic and onions, is what makes the dish so Portuguese. I have also prepared some guinea fowl eggs with salt fish, also fried with onions and garlic and lots of black pepper. Salted fish has always been popular among people of the Portuguese provinces. They cook it in many dishes; the most notable one was *bacalao*. Today in Guyana, everybody likes it because it is available in abundance, and Guyanese have created their own forms of bacalao even though they don't call those dishes by that name. I hope you like the mixture with Guinea fowl eggs."

"I have seen those birds at Mrs. James's place, but I have never tried the eggs. I am looking forward to tasting it," Vernon stated, then pointed to the round platter. "It looks mouthwatering."

"You boys have a choice of rice or bread, and there is a bowl of cooked greens, deer *callaloo*, to go with that," Madeline de Castro added.

The food was great. The atmosphere was relaxed, and the conversation flowed, with laughter interspersed with segments of sullen recounting. Vernon and his father were given a concise history lesson on the de Melo's family, and they listened to Madeline de Castro's regretful insinuation of no heirs to carry on their heritage. The meal completed, she asked her guests to sit with her in her drawing room. Her real motive for inviting Denis with his son was about to be disclosed. She handed each one a cup of coffee and began to explain to Denis what she wanted of him in the next weeks. "I am asking you to help me in the arrangements to create my will," she said somberly. "I am afraid to die without one," she said in almost a whisper. She then abruptly changed her expression to one of boastful joy. "I am not dying. Don't be so grim. Not yet for now." She laughed and assured them, "I still have some years to enjoy with my family, yes, with you, my family. I have an obligation to live out an apology to my only sister and a person Rafa de Melo adored, Anna Torrealba."

Vernon peered at Madeline and tried to finally make sense of what she was telling them. He recalled how his mother spoke to him when he was young to put the pieces together of his grandmother, Anna, and her family's Gypsy style of living and working in the Moruka and the Pomeroon. He was certain now that the Torrealbas whom Anita reminisced about were the other half of his heritage. He was proud of his line from Rafa de Melo's Portuguese roots and the intimate connection Rafa had with his Sonya, who turned out to be his Spanish Arawak-Warrao forebear. Vernon was proud of his undeniably hybrid background and felt that he was a true son of the New World. His outlook towards Madeline had changed considerably. She was indeed family and someone he should have less fear of inferiority about. He went up to her and hugged her. He said softly to her, "My grandmother!" as he kissed her on her cheek.

A stream of tears rolled down Madeline's face as she pulled the young man against her bosom and returned a similar kiss. "You are here to stay with me, Vern. Anita and your father stood supportively with me, a lone woman, in the rat-race of Pomeroon's macho growing farm reputation. I have survived while I understood the human feelings and weaknesses of a father who genuinely loved my mother and me."

Then she could not help but repeat, "His love overflowed because it was excessive. It is as if Rafa de Melo had a sixth sense and foresight to protect me and Miriam's Delight by defying the self-righteousness around him and the standing he had in this region, just to prepare for today. You are a true chip off that old block, Vern, and I see him in you," the elder woman related.

Denis listened to what was little less than a soliloquy and could firmly place the last jigsaw pieces his Anita told her son while rocking him to sleep in the old days. Her story was not as categoric as Madeline's reminiscences over the meal and throughout the evening. In his reckoning, he was still puzzled as to why she chose to have dinner with them to bare her mind and her conscience another time so soon after being discharged from the hospital.

Denis summed up his feelings about Madeline's narrative. "Your family's story has been an intimate journey of life in the Pomeroon that joined this river with the Moruka, just like the Atlantic Ocean does, and the Manwarin does. It has also connected me, a Pomeroon man, with a Moruka woman, a wonderful precious pearl whom I miss so much tonight. And yes, she is still recounting that story to her son, as she said shortly before leaving us, 'I will always be with you son' and 'ask your auntie Madeline to tell you of your grandmother and great grandfather.' Thank you, Missy, for opening this up to Vernon tonight. He must learn of his forbears. I have spoken with him at length of reservation life from where I came. Anita's side of the equation is clearer now to me, and I hope to her son. I am grateful to you for accepting us to work for you when we struggled to find work those many years ago—and for sharing the secrets with Anita." Her family secrets had been disclosed to Anita in morsels at a time, sometimes cryptically and enigmatically, enough for her to accept that that they shared a family connection. The details were never very clear and categorical as this evening.

Madeline looked at Denis with a degree of seriousness and said, "Before we close up tonight, I want to tell you my plans. My father's estate is equally mine as my sister's, whom I unashamedly forced out of her birthright, as you well know by now. The person who was the young Madeline de Melo is no more. She is a changed woman who has assumed the big heart of her father. He was always fair to everyone, and tonight I want to continue that fairness. I must inform you that this property equally belongs to Anna's grandson. Her share of the estate of Rafa de Melo will be passed on to Anna's immediate family in her absence.

"Vern, that means that you must assume the rights and responsibilities of a lawful property owner and my partner and shareholder. Half of all that my father owned must now go to his second daughter, your grandmother, Anna Torrealba. I know that if she was here tonight, she would be handing over her share to you. So, I am doing this now on her behalf," Madeline de Castro disclosed.

She instructed Denis to travel up the coast the next day to summon the lawyer, Dindayal Singh, to come to Miriam's Delight, as she was not able to make the trip to his office during her recuperation. She wanted him to draw up her will and to secure a power of attorney for Vernon. She told Denis that his trust had earned him the executive power of her will, and she looked to him to ensure that Anna's grandson was officially given his right.

Neither Denis nor Vernon really understood what it all meant and asked Madeline to explain what they had to do as a result of what she had just told them. Her reply was, "The lawyer will explain it all when he comes. I would also need to find two trusted witnesses to be present and to provide their signatures. It is my choice to ask Marjorie and her daughter, Valerie, to do me this honor. So, I am kindly asking you to stop by these two persons and get their agreement to be here when the will is written.

A meeting with the lawyer, Vernon, Denis, Marjorie, and the newly married Valerie Beharry went well. An agreement between Madeline de Castro and Vernon Atkins stipulated that both these parties were equal owners of Rafa de Melo's estate, with a fifty percent share each. Madeline also included a clause that was agreed upon that the whole estate would go to the survivor at the death of the other. To confirm her wishes in her last will and testament, she bequeathed all her possessions to Vernon Atkins, naming him the sole heir to Miriam's Delight and Rafa de Melo's estate at her death. Lawyer Singh's work was efficient and thorough. He billed Madeline de Castro amply for the extra work involved out his office and for submitting and registering the will with the courts.

When Denis returned Singh to Charity for his drive back to Reliance, Marjorie and Valerie stayed to converse with Madeline and Vernon. As the conversation centered solely between Madeline and Marjorie with younger two left out, Madeline noticing a hint of boredom stepping in and encouraged them to carry on their own chat as to not be forced to sit with them and listen. "Go in the verandah or downstairs and talk with each other. Marjorie and I have a lot to catch up on."

Vernon got up and went down the verandah stair, and Valerie followed. They instinctively went straight into Vernon's drawing room downstairs. The two had a lot to talk about since their heated encounter an uneasy separation more than a year before. Vernon wanted to know for sure that she had found the right person without coercion and not as a rebound from their parting. She admitted that she had missed Vernon's friendship but had independently found the best husband she ever could have found. She was very happy. She had found both Lennox and his family to be friendly and sensitive, just the opposite of the common perception people had of them in the region. She said that they were not good at casting their true character and did not see that as important. They were more interested in running a good business and quietly giving back to the community without seeking acknowledgment.

"Do you know, Vern, next month Lennox will be handing over a school boat and engine to the district council for use in the distant areas of the Lower Pomeroon River? He is now more aware of publicizing the same things his parents did in the past incognito. His family is pleased with the improvement he has brought to their business. Yes, I am a happy wife."

She disclosed her suspicion that he may have been close to someone else when she made advances to him. "I thought that we cared for each other and could have an intimate relationship and eventually marry. That was why the fire in my soul got out of control at that time. I was wrong. I only learned later that someone else was mad about you and you wanted her more than anyone else. Isn't that the truth, Vern?" She told Vernon that some of Kayla's friends had leaked out that news when she fell ill in Georgetown only months after she started at St. Rose's in Georgetown.

"Are you saying that she fell ill because of me?" Vernon asked in a perturbed manner. "I still love her and need her. She was everything for me. She still is. I never forgot her since she schooled in her younger years at Charity. People called it puppy love. She was my first love even when I was not sure of what love between a boy and a girl really meant. I just liked her vivacious, fun-loving nature, her strong will, and her different looks. Did she really fall ill because of me?" he asked guilt-ridden.

"Yes, because of you, and because her father forbade her to continue to hanker for 'losers like that laborer's son' as he put it. I guess referring to you."

Valerie told the sad-looking Vernon that Eugene da Silva had seen her love letters and destroyed every one of them. He had introduced her to his friend's family on the East Coast, whose only son had taken over their coconut estate and was in line to take over the overall management of their business. Eugene was keen to link up with that family in a substantive way and get involved in the joint establishment of an oil mill to compete with the Demerara oil and soap production factory on the East Bank of Demerara. It had a lucrative monopoly on a variety of coconut oil and by-products in the country. She explained that Eugene envisaged that marriage of his daughter with Aaron Madray would facilitate his business ambitions. He, therefore, did not hesitate to run down Kayla's "loser friends" and pressured her to consider marrying the young Madray after her General Certificate of Education exams.

Kayla was living in fear like she was all her life. That fear forced her to satisfy her father's wishes without questions and allowed him to get his way at all times. This time as an adult with a mind and heart that steered her in a direction she consciously chose, she struggled to defy her father. She fought to remain tied to the magnet that drew her to its core. Her father threatened to disown her for her disobedience to her family, and she eventually broke. She was on the verge of a nervous breakdown.

His wife, Gwendolyn, was more lenient and detested the tyrannical behavior of her husband towards their daughter, but failed to defend Kayla this time under a preference to smoothen out the frequent disruptions and quarrels in the family."

"Wow!" Vernon moaned.

Valerie stared at Vernon and continued, "Kayla had a long spate of psychological treatment at the St. Joseph's Mercy Hospital. They said she was diagnosed with signs of mental health problems. Mr. da Silva did not want her to come back to the Pomeroon. He feared that information on her mental and psychological problems could spread and reach the very family on the East Coast that he wanted to engage with through a marriage of convenience for his daughter. He, therefore, kept his daughter with one of his relatives at Ann's Grove on the East Coast to where Aaron Madray had easy access."

Valerie told Vernon that Kayla's frequent retaliation that she was not in love with Aaron was met by her father's assurance that she would learn to love him. He told her that time would heal all the wounds the losers had left her with and that she would find a bright and prosperous new beginning once they were married. Her hosts were told not to deliver letters to her so that she would be free of the mental strains they prolonged. Aaron made frequent visits to meet with Kayla, who treated him with respect but without any show of warmth. His attempts to embrace and kiss her were met with a cold response and a denial. Aaron Madray also felt like Eugene da Silva, hoping that Kayla would grow to love him in time and that patience and persistence would make the difference.

Valerie's mom was looking for her and ended up entering the Atkinses' home and joining the two friends on the couch. A few minutes later, Denis and Vernon were driving them back to their respective homes.

* * *

The Atkinses sat that night on their sofa overwhelmed by the happenings of the day in company with Madeline and the lawyer. They could not express their utter astonishment in words. Denis was pleased with what had befallen his son and joked, "Now I have another new employer," and then stared at Vernon.

"What are you talking about, Dad?" he exclaimed, knowing what his father meant. Denis smiled and continued, "But I guess 'she' is still the manager. That spares me taking orders from two bosses every morning."

Vernon was somewhat uncomfortable with the images of his father, Miriam's Delight employee, looking up to him as someone superior, the joint owner, even though Denis only spoke in jest. He confronted the thought by throwing his arm around his father's neck and squeezed him warmly. "As joint owner, whatever I own my father owns also. From today, you are no more the supervisor at Miriam's Delight. You are your son's representative and an essential part in securing our inheritance—my mother's, your wife's, and mine. Living in this big house now is not merely a favor given to us by your boss. It is the right of your son, who technically is now fifty percent owner of this property also," he softly and humbly whispered.

The light exchange with his father only masked the tormented thoughts inside him for a short while. Vernon soon fell into a somber silence.

"What's the matter, Vern? Are you not happy about the will and the acknowledgment by Missy? Or did Valerie's coming here today upset you?" Denis asked of his son and gave him time to ponder.

"Valerie has found the right person, a good man, and she is very happy. I am happy for her, too. And when she found out that Kayla was my real girlfriend, she was fine with that and went her own way. It worked out for her. But what she told me of Kayla's situation now is very upsetting," he intimated to his father. "Her father has forbidden her to contact me or continue her friendship with me. He calls me 'a loser' and 'the poor son of a laborer.' He does not think I have the class and the means he wants for his daughter. He has chosen a wealthy landowner for her and is forcing her to love him and marry him."

"What a thing, Vern. I don't know what to say. How can parents demand so much from their children? They forget that their children are born out of the uncontrolled passion they themselves choose to enjoy. Their children, too, should have the freedom to make their own decisions for their own passion and love, and that is the way it should be. They should not set conditions for their children's future in love and marriage. I am sad about this for you, son," said Denis, trying to offer some consolation.

Noisy bewilderment overpowered Vernon as silence prevailed for a minute between them. "I am not surrendering, Dad. There is a love and promise between Kayla and me that I feel positive about. I don't think it is over between us. But if it is, I will have to learn to cope and move on and heal the deep gash that would have been made in my heart and my spirit."

"You have grown so much in maturity, my son. I am here for you. You know that, and you can always turn to me for support and strength. I will listen. I will follow you with a father's vision, and I know for certain that your mom will look out for you also. Our family will continue to keep and grow together," Denis assured his son.

CHAPTER 15

KAYLA'S RETURN

The Christmas season was in full swing. The radio stations were piping out a plethora of Christmas songs. The atmosphere at Charity was festive. The market day on the weekends and Mondays was a tumultuous frenzy of activities. The Charity Mission Church bells rang out every morning at five to summon Catholics to come to the Novena Mass, which was held for nine consecutive days leading into the midnight nativity liturgical celebrations on Christmas Eve. This was the most attended celebration each year that provided a rough marker of the number of Catholic families at Charity and its surroundings. The Mass on New Year's Day was also well attended but showed definite signs of a drastic decline in church-going until again on Good Friday when the church building was overcrowded, matching and sometimes surpassing the crowds at Christmas. This trend was most typical in the rural areas of the country.

The news around the Pomeroon area was that Eugene da Silva's daughter, who was schooling in Georgetown, was returning with her parents in the new year after spending Christmas with family and friends on the East Coast of Demerara. Their return will usher in the beginning of preparations for her wedding to a wealthy East Coast coconut estate magnate, just like her father. Many felt that that was merely a match between the families, unlike another rumor that the couple was madly in love and she had agreed to the marriage.

Vernon was excited that her return to the Pomeroon was just a few weeks away. He was, however, shattered that his Kayla had chosen someone else besides him. He hoped he could meet her face to face again on her return and find out directly from her why she had abandoned him. He was prepared to accept whatever she told him and start to live anew amidst the damage of his heart and soul. It would be heart-breaking, but as Mrs. de Castro once admonished him, there were other good girls around to choose. He was feeling some regret that he had not taken the opportunity with Valerie when it arose, and he had not been brave or assertive enough to court people like Denyse Valydam, Adele Van Sertima, Carol Singh, and Bernadette Duncan. They had all found committed partners.

The Christmas celebrations at Miriam's Delight was fabulous, with Madeline de Castro assuming a duty to lavish the Atkinses with gifts and specially prepared meals. She made sure that the two men were her holiday guests for every big meal. The Christmas breakfast after midnight mass was memorable. The smell of garlic pork and the slow cooking casareep-saturated pepper-pot of venison exuded in the air. Freshly baked bread and boiled ham lay teasingly on her dining table. An array of chocolates and sweets were in good supply, as well as freshly made ginger beer, mauby, and sorrel drink. This was a celebration of a reunion with her grandson and his father. Madeline wanted to avert the possibility that Vernon would miss his mom at this time and Denis would grieve for his adorable wife once more. She wanted this Christmas to be festively joyous and not immersed in sadness and memory of their loss.

For Christmas dinner, Madeline invited over Marjorie James and her nephew, as well as Lennox and Valerie Beharry. She wanted to enable a reunion also of Marjorie with her family since she had had to live with a void in her home after the marriage of her daughter. Marjorie had also become a vital female support for Madeline since she fell ill earlier that year. Christmas was a great time to share the sentiments of joy and gratitude, and she felt she had a lot to be thankful for. She shrewdly thought also that inviting Valerie and her husband was one way of getting to know the Beharry family better, given the pejorative perception people had of them. She genuinely believed also that her overt mingling with a member of that family could help to breakdown the stigma attached to them. The meal was a great success. Vernon and his father enjoyed Madeline's cooking that they had become accustomed to, and so did Lennox Beharry and his in-laws.

She was impressed with the young Beharry and could not see why that kind of stigma was attached to his family. Lennox promised to invite everyone to his home at the next important occasion. He kept his promise, and New Year's Day was celebrated at his family's home with a fully laid table of Western and Eastern foods, like curries, dal puri, biriyani rice, payra, a milk sweet, and various Indian sweetmeats, which were enjoyed by the guests. Madeline felt that Lenox's parents were very affable people who had now become her friends.

Vernon learned that Kayla was coming home with her parents at the end of January. Friends of her aunt at Jacklow told Denis that the da Silvas would arrive at Charity on January 13 or 31. Their principal purpose is to initiate planning and preparations for her marriage with Aaron Madray. His family, who were staunch Evangelical Christians, were opposed to marrying in the Catholic church at Charity, as was proposed by Mr. da Silva. But after some coaxing, they reluctantly conceded to a very brief ceremony, a flashy party at the Greenheart Hotel, with a full reservation of the hotel for family and friends of the Madray family. They would then promptly return to the East Coast the day after for a gala ceremony at their Evangelical church, followed by a night-long party at their ranch-style mansion.

The young Atkins was overwhelmed by the news and the level of affluence they were showering on his Kayla. He had nothing near that kind of wealth. Even if he had, he would prefer to give her a heart full of love instead and seek reciprocity. He wondered if Kayla had fallen for this facade of material wealth. He never knew her as that kind of person. But if she did change, he believed that there was no place for him anymore. His modesty and unpretentious nature would rebel against it. The two of them would be so incompatible. Yet he found it difficult to believe that Kayla had evolved as such, even though her father's family are of that very ilk. He wanted not to believe that Kayla was merely putting on a show of simplicity and humbleness to hang out with him at the beginning and later just to have an affair. Vernon, nevertheless, left his mind open to that possibility. If that were really true, he would have little trouble in coping with the breakup. He would move on with his life in a different direction, maintaining his own simple lifestyle, where honest work is balanced with the pleasures of intimacy.

The private express hire cars were rolling into Charity from the Essequibo River steamer. It was an indication that passengers from Georgetown were arriving. Those who could afford a costly charter of such a taxi and were eager to save time, and the long dusty bus ride always opted for it. It showed off their class and their means and gave them status among onlookers at their destination. It also provided the opportunity for finding more comfortable seats on the passenger boats or to secure one of the special boats to charter on the Pomeroon River. The da Silva's did not require this status. They had the means to use the best services. At Charity, they would have one of their fast boats waiting on them.

Vernon deliberately waited not far away from the taxi terminal to monitor if Kayla and her parents arrived. He pressed against the counter of a small food kiosk, as if he was waiting to be served an order. He noticed Adrian Da Silva waiting in his boat and initially evaded his attention. But he later went across to him, shook his hands, and greeted him. "How is my cricketer doing, Adrian?"

"I am doing fine, and how about my regatta champion?" he replied in a similar vein of sarcasm.

"Great, man! Are you waiting on someone to arrive?" Vernon asked as if he had no knowledge of his sister's coming home.

"Oh yes, my family are coming in today. Soon I think." He untied his boat and drew it closer to the koker at the end of the Essequibo Coast road while Vernon moved closer to where the taxis pulled in.

The third car that arrived offloaded three persons he was very familiar with. Kayla walked sandwiched between Gwendolyn and

Eugene da Silva. She had lost weight but looked as ravishing as before. Vernon waved to her and her parents, and she waved back shyly and looked to the ground. Her mother instead said, "Hi, Vern," as they toted their bags to Adrian's waiting boat. Eugene was pleased for a fleeting moment as they passed Vernon that his daughter did not demonstrate any warmth toward the person with whom he forbade her to communicate. He felt at that moment that somehow Kayla seemed to have accepted his proposition regarding the Madray's after all her resistance. His decision for her to join that family seemed to be vindicated. Planning the wedding, then, should be smooth and exciting and properly finalized when Aaron Madray arrived two weeks later. Aaron would also have a firsthand look at the da Silva's plantation and large copra production. That should fortify the plans for end-product processing of what the two plantations produced through the establishment of a factory and the two-family business partnership.

Eugene da Silva wasted no time during his first week back to meet with the Greenheart Hotel management. He ordered the party area space, the whole ballroom, with no reducing partitions. Together, they mapped out all services required comprehensively itemized with optional prices to choose from. He affirmed that the two families concerned were looking for their premier package to be finalized in two weeks' time. He also indicated that, at that time, the groom's family would confirm reserving all the rooms for their family and guests. At his visit to the church, the priest was given a large donation. He agreed to solemnize the marriage with a stipend for the actual ceremony to follow. The priest waived the reading of the banns of marriage, as was his discretion to apply, and had the date fixed for April 3. Adrian was instructed to arrange the logistics for the convoy of boats for the twenty-mile ride to the da Silva's plantation at St. John's at the river mouth. Several boats would be hired and decorated. Each would have a crew to man them and assist with the boarding and offloading of guests in a methodic and safe manner, and the main vessel, to carry the bride and groom and their immediate family, would have to stand out with garlands and festive lighting. Eugene wanted to impress the Madray's to the extent that they would be comfortable with him as a solid business partner in their prospective coconut products factory.

Eugene was satisfied with the progress he made in the initial wedding arrangements. He expected Kayla and her mother to be excited as well. At home that evening, after explaining to his wife and daughter what had been agreed upon at Charity, he tried to start a dialogue with his daughter. "You must be looking forward to your fiancé coming to the Pomeroon in a matter of weeks, my dear?

She did not answer for a minute, then responded with a wry question. "Do you mean Aaron?"

"Well, who else, my dear Kayla? You know that he's due to come in two weeks' time. He did say that to us, you, your mom, and me. I thought you would be excited and overjoyed," Eugene replied, trying to generate some positive energy after the initial resistance from her, and recover what, in the last weeks on the East Coast, seemed to him like her acceptance and resignation to the match made between the two families. He continued, "You were so happy when we told you that we were coming back to the Pomeroon." He paused. "And you know, it was to make the arrangements for the wedding. What is going on now, Kayla? Are you getting nervous?"

She did not answer again, and another pause of heavy silence ensued.

"It is normal to be nervous close to your marriage. Your mom was, and I was also confused. But deep down, there was joyous anticipation. I am right behind you, Kayla, to support this serious decision you are making."

Kayla was upset and tempted to be rude to her father. She said nothing, exercising her self-control as to not show her frustration and rejection of all he said. She yawned and told him that she was tired and needed to have some rest before her trip with her mother to Jacklow to see her aunt, Gwendolyn's younger sister, the next morning. Eugene believed that she was probably tired after the trip from the East Coast of Demerara to the Pomeroon, especially after her spate of ill health the last months in Ann's Grove. He took it as a passing phase and felt that everything would be alright once Aaron was with them in person at St. John's.

Adrian clamped a twenty-five horsepower Johnson engine to the back of one of their boats, one small enough for mother and daughter and another two people if they needed to fetch anyone. The smaller boat would generate a lot of speed and eliminate a long slow journey back and forth with a bigger one. Either Kayla or her mom would be able to drive the smaller boat and engine more easily. Gwendolyn's sister was expecting them to spend two nights with her family. Her two girls, although younger than Kayla, had always been fond of her and she of them. Gwendolyn thought that the break away from her impatient, martinet husband would help her to settle her nerves and reinvigorate her once vivacious personality. Her composure had suffered badly since her illness at school, and it was further compounded by the suggestion of early marriage to a person she would have accepted more readily if there was a longer time to date and get close. That had not been the case. But she hoped with rather grave concerns that marriage would make them grow to love each other as her husband was convinced of.

Gwendolyn knew of Kayla's hankering for Vernon's company all through the years they were growing up. She even felt she had enabled and condoned her daughter's attachment to him, especially in the months before she started school at St. Rose's. But sensing the special friendship between them, one that changed Kayla's composure positively every time they met, she found it irrational to disrupt it or stop it. Unfortunately, her leaving for Georgetown brought about that disruption with dire consequences. She was convinced that Kayla would need to get over this before she could form another deep friendship with another person. Despite her husband's pressure on Kayla to get Vernon out of her system instantaneously and proceed into the new relationship he wanted for her, Gwendolyn felt in her inner self that Kayla needed time and space to assume any decision for a lifelong partnership without reservation and duress. She had been unable to express this to her husband, and her silence on the matter made him think that she was in full compliance with the match between the families. She now realized that he needed to be told this by someone he would have to listen to—herself.

As the two women were entering the boat for their trip to Jacklow, Gwendolyn asked her daughter to drive the engine, but she refused.

"You do, Mom, it is as if I have forgotten to do this. I so much wanted to come back to the Pomeroon to do the things I did as a younger person, which I missed, and now I feel uncomfortable to try again. I know I will come out of my mental troubles soon, and I will again love the things a Pomeroon girl does. You trust me, don't you, Mom?" Kayla pleaded.

"I will drive to go, and promise me you will drive on our way back," Gwendolyn said.

"For sure! It's a deal," Kayla replied.

Gwendolyn stopped at Charity to buy some snacks for her sister's family. On arriving, her sister hugged the mother and daughter one on each side and walked them into her home at Jacklow. Gwendolyn was surprised how quickly her daughter brightened up away from her husband's coercive demeanor towards her and realized that she had not done much to acknowledge the difficult period Kayla was going through. She had failed to stand up on the side of her daughter when her husband tried to use her as a pawn. She realized that leaving her at Ann's Grove with a second cousin who was not at all close to them did not make sense, except that she had become a bait for the fish he was trying to catch, his business ambition, that elusive factory in his mind. She had begun to muster the strength and courage to protect her daughter, as her mother and friend, from the dangers that she faced going forward.

Lunch was eaten, and Gwendolyn and the rest of the gang felt a siesta was the answer to their fullness and debility. Kayla leaned over her mother and whispered in her ear, seeking permission to go to Miriam's Delight. Gwendolyn stared at her daughter and saw the emotion in her request.

"You are going to meet?" she asked.

Kayla paused, then said, "Yes, Mom, my Vern."

Gwendolyn's stare continued in a stunned expression. She asked, "What would your father do if he heard of this, that you want to defy his order?"

"Well, he could throw me out of his home and disown me as he threatened. I can accept that. It would make me free again to choose my own captor, not his—and I know who that is," Kayla replied with a self-assurance.

Gwendolyn handed her daughter a wad of dollars and told her to buy him a gift at Charity. "You must not go empty handed," she said as her approval. "But let me drop you at Miriam's Delight and bring our boat back here. It should not be seen tied up at Madeline de Castro's jetty. You know how news spread fast in the river."

* * *

Sunday was a lazy day for Vernon Atkins after a full week of boatbuilding. His father, though, spent most of the day at Charity, selling the farm's goods to the government marketing depot and to traders.

Fortunately, Vernon was cleaning the waterfront of floating rubbish when the two women turned up. He greeted them with a broad smile and immediately gave up what he was doing. He lifted his Kayla up out of the boat and onto the jetty and walked her into their home as her mother drove off. Vernon Atkins was so dumbfounded he could not speak. He was shocked to see Kayla. The incessant kisses they shared as they sat in ecstasy together contradicted all the news about her breakup with him and his doubts about her radical change from the young woman he knew and loved. All of it was wrong and fabricated he realized.

She pulled Vernon towards her on the couch and in deep and sensuous passion wanted for them to make love. "Take me, Vernon, I am all yours. I missed you and thought I would lose you and be forced to marry someone I had not chosen but was pressured to hook up with. I have not, and now I'm back. Just let us love each other today, tomorrow, and forever. Take all of me and give me an offspring, a part of you to treasure. Together, our love could flourish and bear loveable fruits to share with this world. Together, we could make it a more beautiful place. I need you, my Vern."

Impassioned as well, Vernon lifted his Kayla and carried her over the threshold of his room and showed her the Garden of Eden he dreamt of sharing with her. They wrapped themselves together in a fusion of sensuality that exploded like a volcano shaking the foundations of their intimacy. She released a sweet flow of lava. No, a river of nectar that he bathed and flourished in, that drew him to explore the depths of that fountain of love. The passionate probe into the farthest depths he could reach then exploded with a series of aftershocks that cemented their bodies, minds, and spirits together. They were given paradise, not evicted from it. Together, they shared the heavenly bliss they had grown to love, all anew. He had not lost her. He had found a new grown and committed partner, and this time, they both would never let go of what they had. They would not allow anyone to take their love away.

Their lovemaking, interspersed by unending conversation and a reliving of the torments each endured when she left for school in Georgetown, continued until Denis returned home. They were fully dressed when he entered their home, and embracing his Kayla, Vernon smiled with contentment and said, "Here she is, Dad, my life, my joy, my strength. She has returned. I have found her again, and I have also found Vernon Atkins once more. I am my true self now, complete. We were two halves floating in a sky of dark clouds until today, when the sun shone on us again and connected us together once more."

Vernon went down on one knee as if proposing and kissing Kayla's left hand as his father looked on, he asked Kayla to be his love forever. "Just like this ring has no end, I promise to love you forever, my Kayla. Do you accept it."

"I accept your love, Vern, and this symbol of that unending circle of life and love. I do not want to lose you again," she confirmed.

He placed Anita's ring on her finger, and it fitted perfectly. "I have kept this gift from my mother just for you, Kayla, and I know that my father is delighted because it was he who had given this very special symbol to his Parakese Pearl many moons ago. She is looking down at you and smiling at us as her two children, myself and the one you replaced, the one that took her away that sad day. She remains an integral part of that unending circle of life in my family's intimate journey in the Pomeroon."

CHAPTER 16

FINALE

Gwendolyn da Silva pulled up alongside the jetty at Miriam's Delight, and Denis and the two young ones came out to meet her. Denis and Gwendolyn exchanged short pleasantries as Vernon led Kayla into the boat. The da Silvas disappeared in the distance and returned to Jacklow. Gwendolyn embraced her daughter and said nothing. Kayla offered her a sparkling smile. Her mother immediately received the message that she was happy and grateful. "I haven't seen you like this for over a year, my love. Isn't it he you really want?"

"Yes, Mom. Without him, I will sink into that madness and despair you and Dad were so worried about. I do not know how to convince Dad that Aaron is not for me. I never showed Aaron any emotion; I never let him kiss me. I kept insisting that I was a virgin and told him that I will only surrender that part of me on my wedding night to my husband, as my Catholic faith taught me. It was my white lie to keep him apart. He heard what I repeated to him every time and felt I was pointing also to his strict religious Evangelical Christian background, which he acknowledged. He praised me if only through lip-service and waited while I was secretly waiting to be freed of him. Today, I am strong and free again. I am no more a captive of his and Dad's aspirations. I have chosen my own captor again. His name is Vernon

Atkins. I was his captive since we lived at Charity many years ago. That never changed. The chains that bound me and the bars that secured us in our chosen prison just grew stronger," Kayla asserted to her mother, passionately sobbing for joy.

Gwendolyn repeated her questioning once more; this time more to herself than to her daughter. "What would your father do if he found out that you have defied him and went back to Vernon?" She provided the answer before her daughter could speak. "I will have to be truthful about it. He must know and he must accept his daughter's decision," she paused before adding, "with my support. I cannot let him foist his will on an adult daughter and starve her of her happiness—not anymore."

The next day, as agreed with Kayla, Vernon came to Jacklow to share lunch with them. He brought a basket of goodies Mrs. de Castro prepared for him when Vernon told her Kayla was back and he was happy again. Knowing that he was visiting her the next day, she surprised him with the basket of food and told him to bring her over some time and introduce her to his Auntie Madeline and, in jest and seriousness, reminded him that she was really his great aunt, an old woman with a young heart like her grandson.

Vernon's visit, where Gwendolyn and her sister and daughters were present, was endearing with a restraint on any lovers' erotic hormones. Gwendolyn's sister was won over by the charm of the young Atkins. "What a lucky girl Kayla is. She has a choice between two eligible bachelors, and my suggestion would be you know who," she teased. "I hope this does not disrupt Eugene's plans for that big upcoming wedding."

Gwendolyn interjected, "I think she has made her choice. Eugene will know, and he will accept it by hook or by crook. That is clear in my mind."

* * *

The next day, Gwendolyn and her daughter were on their way back to St. John's. Kayla gladly operated the engine, as promised, and arrived home as if with a renewed sense of optimism. She greeted her father with a broad smile and a warm hug. He immediately observed that his daughter was overbrimming with contentment and spark he had not seen for many months. He wanted to continue with the arrangements for her wedding. So, he asked her, "Are you ready to go with me to Anna Regina tomorrow to choose the wedding invitations and let us put in an order to print them?"

Kayla paused, and the silence surprised the elder da Silva. She asked him, "Which wedding? Not mine!" And she bluntly told him that *his* wedding was off and the date for hers was not yet fixed. "I will not be your Aaron's bride; you can find another one for him. I will choose whomever I really love, and I am ready to be disowned as you threatened me before. I am ready to leave your home. Just tell me to."

Gwendolyn sat and listened and did not intervene as Eugene angrily vented his feeling on her. "Why don't you say something to your daughter, lady? She is turning down a life of wealth and prosperity. I am certain she wants to go back to that loser son of a farm laborer. What a stupid girl she has become? What standard of life would she have from a boy with such low pedigree? Look at what Aaron and his family have to offer her and to us. We have to make her change her mind. Most of the arrangements at this end are in the final stages of planning, and I am sure the Madray's are far into theirs also. Say something to your daughter, Gwen!"

"I have nothing to say to her but a lot to talk to you about, Eugene. Hear me out. I know what she wants. True love. That's what she wants. She has found that long before you began to force her into the Madrays since you took her away from the Pomeroon for school in Georgetown. All along, you knew that was just a ploy to use your daughter for your collaboration with them. They do have a lot of money, but that is not what she wants. That is what you want, Eugene. You will have to find another way to get that from them, not by trading our precious daughter. She wants that boy you call a 'loser,' that son of a laborer. Why do despise the lowly laborers and the poor on whom your own prosperity was built and still depend? You could not do without them on this plantation. Marriage is not to raise your status and means in society. I know it is to build and live a just life based on honest work, love, and contentment. Kayla would get all of that from Vernon Atkins. He is a clever person with the kindest of heart; he is an accomplished designer and boatbuilder recognized beyond the Pomeroon. He has been a fine champion at the recent Aripiaco Regatta, he has only recently been selected to the Essequibo team for the Inter-County Cricket Championship, and most importantly, he loves our daughter. What more can she ask for?"

She paused and took a deep breath. "And if you are thinking that he has not got the wealth like your Aaron, you have a lot to learn. He is the inheritor of half of Madeline de Castro's estate left her by her father, Rafa de Melo. We know how rich and humble a man he was. It is public news now published in the Official Gazette, my sister told me. Madeline's estate and all their lands—the timber grant at the river head, the lands in the Dredge Creek and the Cojer Canal, the various pieces of riverfront lands along the Pomeroon, and his two gold claims in the Cuyuni River—are now in two names, your 'loser's' and his great aunt's, Madeline de Castro's. When she dies, he is her successor, and everything goes to him. Little did we know that Vernon's mom was Mrs. de Castro's only niece on her father's side. Her sister was Mr. de Melo's daughter with a Moruka girl. Madeline de Castro knew this and has now opened it up publicly by the actions she has taken recently in the deed polls and affidavits now registered in the courts."

"What are you talking about, Gwen?" Eugene asked, stunned. "Are you sure your sister is right?"

Gwendolyn replied, "The Gazette is right. But the main thing I want to tell you, and you can hate me for it, is that Kayla is an adult and can make her own decisions. She is a strong grown woman and does not need you to choose for her. Please respect her space. If you really are going to disown her and kick her out, you will do that to her mother also. What more can I say?" She paused. "That loser boy in your eyes, Eugene, is a winner with class and humility, just like the old de Melo."

Eugene da Silva struggled for words. "I am sorry. Every person has a story to tell, even the poor and the lowly. I now know that that Atkins boy is not what I branded him as. I am sorry. I am sorry also for sending our Kayla down a road of depression and despair. I am sorry. I am so happy to see her happy again today."

Kayla turned to her father and hugged him. "I beg you, Dad, to give Vernon a chance. He is my love and my dream since we were kids. I met him today against your wishes, and I recommitted my love for him. We have never stopped loving each other." Showing her hand to her father, she continued, "Today, he gave me this promise ring. It's his dead mother's ring, Mrs. de Castro's niece. Vernon's father gave it to him in her memory. He has given it now to me. Can't you see? He is the right one for me. That's the marriage I am ready and willing to plan with you."

Eugene da Silva lived with a lot of guilt and shame and was remorseful about his judgment of the hard workers on the Pomeroon plantations, including his own. He regretfully canceled the wedding arrangements he had initiated and called off Aaron Madray's visit to the Pomeroon. The old priest at the Charity Mission Church was told that the April 3 appointment had ceased to exist, but he was still given his stipend. Solemnly, the priest said, "It is good that this marriage has failed before it started rather than a few years down the line. The power of the true spirit of love is at work here."

Kayla's birthday was coming up on June 16. A huge party was arranged, gathering all her family and friends and Vernon's. It culminated in a magnificent nuptial birthday celebration. Denis Atkins was moved by what he saw before his eyes: a son he loved as an angel sent from the universal spirit of the universe and a new daughter in place of the one he awaited to arrive to cast new light in his life and his Anita's. That episode in his family's journey had triggered a brokenness he did not expect. But the couple before him somehow healed that brokenness and showed him a clear sign that his Parakese Pearl was very much still an integral part of the family. He handed a small neatly packaged gift to Kayla and told her to receive it on behalf of herself and Vernon from Anita and to open it when the two of them were alone at night and loving each other's company. It was a precious family heirloom he was asking them to safeguard and pass on to the next generation.

On opening that package, they were stunned by the beautiful pair of gold necklaces with heart-shaped lockets. The names on them, however, were not theirs. They peered at the engraved names—"Anna" on one and "Sonya" on the other.

Denis later explained that Anita had kept these possessions of her mother, Anna. They kept alive a history and memory and sustained her on the journey she, and now Vernon, was traveling. They were gifts from a benevolent plantation owner and his wife they labored for, to honor two lovable human beings. He refrained from mentioning his name.

For Vernon Atkins and his wife, Kayla, they were now embarking on a new chapter in that intimate Pomeroon journey.

THE END

GLOSSARY

Acouri/Agouti: A small rodent whose meat is a delicacy in the Pomeroon and other parts of the northwest area of Guyana. It looks like an overgrown bandicoot. It is known as agouti in the Caribbean Islands.

Adventure, Anna Regina, Suddie, Huist-e-Dieren: Key settlements on the Essequibo Coast and transfer points for passengers from Charity and Supenaam, the two end points of the Essequibo Coast road.

Akawini: A tributary of the Pomeroon River, close to the mouth of that river. An Anglican mission on this creek was a stopping point for canoes plying between the mission and the Manwarin Creek on the Moruka River. There was an affinity between the Akawini and Waramuri missions reserves.

Amazon Creek: A tributary of the Pomeroon River, serving as the border between the town of Charity and private farmlands.

Aquero: A settlement on the Moruca River close to Santa Rosa. It served as the administrative headquarters in the district.

Arawak: A First Nations tribe found on the coastal areas of Guyana, Suriname, and French Guyana.

Aripiaco: A large tributary of the upper Pomeroon that leads to several lakes at the head of the river close to the coastland settlements.

Atkinson Airport: The National Airport during colonial times was built at the Atkinson Base, which was formerly a US military base.

Awarra: A palm that produced large bunches of small orange red fruits with a unique sweet taste. The outer skin and inner layer over the stone are chewed to extract the orange juice. Then the husky remains are spat out. This fruit leaves a funny color in the mouth and on the teeth that requires a lot of washing, yet it is seen as a delicacy. The fruit is harvested only when they fall to the ground because climbing the tree is almost impossible with inch-long thorns covering the trunk.

Baboon: The noisy howler monkey.

Babricut: A platform or ramp made of cut green woods upon which fish and meat are cooked or smoked slowly over a wood fire in the outdoors, with coconut fronds or other vegetation covering it. The term is also used for a platform built in trees upon which hunters await a game, such as an acouri or labba, to come into the firing range of a gun or an arrow and bow.

Bacalao: A Portuguese dish of dried salted fish cooked with vegetables and special spices.

Ballahoo: A locally designed semi-flat bottom boat built from special wood planks.

Banga Mary: A brackish water fish caught at the estuaries of the rivers flowing into the Atlantic Ocean.

Barama: A river in the North West District of Guyana intersecting with the Moruka River.

Barima: A river that intersects both the Moruca and Waini Rivers in the Northwest District and runs into the Atlantic at the border between Guyana and Venezuela.

Bartica: A hinterland town some fifty miles up the Essequibo River at the confluence of the Essequibo, Mazuruni, and Cuyuni Rivers. The First Nations name is said to mean "red clay meeting the waters."

Beer parlor: A pub that specializes in serving beer but also sells other hard and soft drinks.

Dal puri: An Indian flatbread stuffed with seasoned cooked ground lentils and baked rapidly on an oiled pan.

Biriyani: An Indian rice dish cooked together with chicken and spicy condiments.

Blue sackie: A beautiful sky blue fast-flying Guyanese bird with a sweet chirp.

Boil and fry: A dish of local ground vegetables boiled to a soft texture and then fried altogether with onions and garlic and melding into a delicious mixture of taste and substance.

Bourda: A famous cricket ground built in a residential area of Georgetown in colonial times to support the English sport of cricket. It was once called the "Lords" of the Caribbean and hosted test and international cricket matches.

Buckman: The derogatory name used for First Nations peoples in the past. It is said that when Columbus arrived in the New World and from his ships saw these people hiding amid the rocks on the shore, his crew referred to them as hiding like "bucks" between the rocks. It is taboo to call someone a "buckman" today.

Boviander: A mixed race person of native and African blood so referred to in the Pomeroon.

Cabacaburi: An Anglican First Nations mission up the Pomeroon River, where peoples of Caribs, Arawaks and Warraos live. The cemetery on this mission is said to have graves and tombs of old Dutch families.

Calaloo: Green leafy vegetables cooked as a fried dish, or as a soup with meat, fish, or crabs.

Casareep: An edible sauce first made by the First Nations peoples from the juice of bitter cassava, a poisonous variety of yucca. The juice is boiled slowly on an open fire until it gets the color of soya sauce and the thickness of honey. The traces of cyanide in this precious edible sauce is said to deter bacteria from spoiling foods cooked in it. It is used for the special native and national dish, pepperpot. It is said to preserve meat and fish cooked in it for many days without refrigeration as long as the dish is heated every day.

Cassava: A staple root vegetable used for a variety of First Nations dishes, e.g., cassava bread, casereep, pepper-pot, and casiri.

Casiri: An alcoholic beverage made from fermented cassava juice.

Charity: A second-level port township on the Pomeroon River and a major point of departure and arrival for fast boats plying between Guyana and eastern Venezuela.

Choke and rob: The local reference to street mugging in which thieves assault a victim and rob him/her of their belongings.

Ciudad Guyana, San Feliz, Ciudad Bolivar, Tucopita: Large towns/cities on the Orinoco River in Venezuela and frequent ports of call for boats from the Pomeroon River.

Cocorite: A palm similar to awarra but oval in shape and whose thin edible layer under a hard skin is juicy and sweet.

Cojer Canal: The name of a large canal that may have originally been a small tributary of the river that was widened and deepened to provide drainage and irrigation for new farm settlements.

Compere: A godfather/mother was referred to as compere.

Cookshop: An economic homestyle restaurant that serves local dishes.

Corial: A dugout canoe.

Cuirass, gillbacker, queriman: Non-scaled sea fish commonly caught off the muddy flats of the coastlands created by the silt from the large rivers.

Cutty: A small bottle of rum that fits neatly in one's pockets.

Cuyuni: A tributary of the Essequibo River whose branches reach very close to the northwest areas of Guyana intersecting with various rivers. It is well known for its rich deposits of gold and diamonds on the river basin and within the river also.

Dasheen: A root vegetable whose young leaves are also used to prepare a delectable Guyanese dish called callaloo.

Delta Warraos: Native Peoples who peopled the Orinoco River Delta. The town of Tucopita was a central settlement for these people.

District commissioner: The official representing the governor and the government in Georgetown in the administrative districts during colonial times.

Dredge Creek: A tributary with supposedly fertile farms. Some believe it may have been named as such because of a dredge that sank and was abandoned in it.

Esperanza: The Spanish or Portuguese word meaning "hope."

Essequibo, Demerara, and Berbice: The three counties of Guyana which earlier were separate European colonies changing hands between the Dutch, French, and British. They are named after the large river that runs through each of them.

Fort Zealandia: The settlement at the mouth of the Pomeroon River on the Atlantic where the Dutch first settled in South America and established a military fort.

Garlic pork: A Portuguese dish in which pork is pickled in a solution of vinegar, garlic, and spices and fried days later. It is particularly popular at Christmas time.

Get-ball-bowl: A locally devised version of cricket with elements of rugby tackling to secure the ball and bowl it. If the given bowler dislodges the batter's stumps, he wins the chance to bat. Someone who takes a catch, stumps or runs out the batter also wins a chance to bat. Not a team spirited game, but one that emphasizes individual talent, aggression, or lure.

Georgetown: The capital city of Guyana on the Demerara River and the Atlantic Ocean.

Googly: This is a delivery by a bowler in cricket whereby the bowler spins the ball as if to bowl a leg break, turning from the legs of the batter to the stumps, except on this occasion it is delivered from the back of the hand and it turns from in front of the batter toward his legs and stumps. It is meant to deceive him to play a false stroke.

Grant: A term left over from the days when farmland was given out to pioneers who settled in the Pomeroon. Farms are still called grants at the present time.

Greenheart, Purpleheart, Cabacalli, Mora, Crabwood: Popular hardwoods among the many varieties in Guyana.

Guyana: An independent republic on the north coast of South America.

Haimara: A large game fish in the freshwater rivers.

Huist-e-Dieren: A village community on the Essequibo Coast. This Dutch name is one of various Dutch, French, English, Irish, Scottish, and others, reflecting the colonial heritage in the country alongside names from languages of First Nations peoples.

Jacklow: A cluster of farms in a settlement a few miles upriver from Charity.

Kamwatta: A settlement on the Moruca River in the North West District of Guyana.

Kayap: A communal First Nations work festival where families voluntarily team up with others to build or undertake work projects benefitting neighbors or the community. Food and drinks are brought by these families, which are shared during the day of work. Casiri, piwari, cassava bread, and other food and drinks are shared in a party-like work atmosphere.

Kisakdee: A yellow-breasted bird, pleasant to the eye, with a special call that sounds like its name, "Kiss-ka-dee."

Koker: A sluice or water gate introduced by the Dutch to manage the water levels on the Guyana coast, a large part of which lies below sea level.

Krakatoa-like: Explosive as the eruption of the Krakatoa Volcano of Indonesia.

Kumaka: A strategic settlement on the Moruca River adjacent to Santa Rosa.

Launch: This was the name used in the Pomeroon for a large wooden-covered boat with a cabin utilizing the whole berth. The cabin was divided close to the inboard engine room where the driver sat close to the throttle and gear levers and was perched elevated to look over the roof for ease of control and directions. The lengthwise seats were foldable to provide sleeping bunks. Some of these vessels also had a private cabin next to the engine room where important belongings were safeguarded, and which could provide privacy if an overnight stay in the boat was necessary.

Liberty: A settlement of several farms and coconut estates not far from the mouth of the Pomeroon River.

Logie: A basic lodging for laborers, which were originally utilized to house African slaves and later indentured Indian laborers. The term was later used for cabins to house workers.

Mahaica: A settlement on the East Coast of Demerara.

Mainstay Lake: A popular lake at the Pomeroon head inland from the villages of Mainstay and Anna Regina.

Manicole: A tall slender palm whose fruits attract flocks of parrots and parakeets. Its woody trunk was split into boards against which mud was plastered to create an adobe in the early logies.

Manwarin: A tributary of the Moruca River that joins with the Akawini Creek of the Pomeroon River.

Mari-mari: Songs, music, and dance that grew among the native peoples in the northwestern part of Guyana with some influence from their Spanish and Venezuelan origins.

Martindale: A settlement a short distance from Charity on the Pomeroon River. It is said that the property was a grant to the Martin family of Dutch connection, who gave it to the Catholic church to establish a school there.

Marudi: A large, wild gamebird like a turkey that makes a noisy call in the morning in the forest.

Mazaruni, Cuyuni: Two branches of the mighty Essequibo river, both joining the Essequibo at the junction of Bartica, a hinterland town fifty miles up the latter river.

Moruca: A narrow winding river in the North West District of Guyana, running into the Atlantic close to the estuary of the Pomeroon River.

Orinico: One of the largest rivers in South America in Venezuela. Some of its tributaries run into Guyana.

Ovaltine: A popular dry cocoa, egg, and malt mixture imported from the UK in tins and utilized as quick and nutritious drink for both old and young.

Pak-pak: A red Madeira wine imported into Guyana in wooden barrels and sold in the rum shops by the glass.

Parakese: A small hamlet on the upper Moruka River.

Parika: A major connection port on the east bank of the Essequibo River that serves as a hub to the towns of Bartica, Adventure, and settlements, such as Supenaam and Aurora, on its west bank and coast.

Pepperpot: One of the national dishes of Guyana inherited from its First Nations peoples, usually meat or fish cooked in a casareep sauce with whole hot cayenne peppers infused in it without being broken. Thus, the dish is not spicy hot but more of a sweetish salty flavor. It is said to last for days without refrigeration as long as it is heated daily, a food technology the first peoples mastered long before refrigeration was around.

Pirai: Also called piranha, a ravenous flesh-eating fish in freshwater rivers and creeks.

Piwari: An alcoholic beverage made from fermented sweet potatoes.

Pomeroon: A deep navigable, tidal river in the north western area of Guyana that flows into the Atlantic Ocean.

Quatro: A four-stringed musical instrument in the family of the guitar that was commonly used in mari-mari music to provide its energetic pulsating rhythm.

Rum shops: Pubs selling mainly a variety of Guyanese rum and hard spirits, as well as wines and other drinks and entertaining revelers on premises

Salara: A sweet bread made with reddened cooked coconut stuffing.

Santa Rosa: A Roman Catholic mission on the Moruca River that became a stronghold for Spanish-Arawak Peoples on arrival there from the Bolivar wars.

Scratcher: A musical percussion instrument made from a resonant piece of wood with a series of grooves against, which a piece of coconut shell, wood, or metal was dragged to render a squishy sound. It was commonly used in mari-mari and other string bands.

Shack-shack: A pair of percussion instruments made from dried gourds with seeds or pebbles within it and protruding handles. They were often used in mari-mari music bands.

Siriki: A community of farm owners on the Upper Pomeroon River, adjoining a sandy belt where much of the boat and house building materials are logged and lumbered.

Soesdyke: A settlement on the East Bank of Demerara that housed the national airport.

Spanish Arawak: Arawak First Nations peoples who came to Guyana from Venezuela starting from the Bolivar Revolution. Many have inherited a mixture of Spanish or Latino blood and surnames.

St. Deny's: Another Fist Nations settlement.

St. John's Night: It is said that the feast of St. John on June 24 has special significance for Arawak and Warrao Peoples in Guyana because they arrived in what is today the north west of Guyana on that day accompanied by their Christian priests. They were escaping the turmoil of the Bolivar revolution for Venezuelan independence.

St. Monica's: An Anglican First Nations mission in the hills of Upper Pomeroon River.

Stabroek: Originally the capital of the colony of Demerara, built by the Dutch when they settled that colony. It was later enlarged by the French and the British to form the capital, Georgetown, of the British Guiana in 1831.

Stabroek market: A large market built by the Dutch in what was their capital township of Demerara, Stabroek. It stands out with a large clock on its spire.

Stelling: A wharf or a jetty; a remnant of the Dutch settlement in the Pomeroon and Guyana.

Supenaam: A settlement at the junction of the Supenaam River and the west bank of the Essequibo River, a tributary of the latter. Located at the end of the Essequibo Public Road, it is a strategic port for the departure and arrival of fast passenger boats plying between Parika on the east bank of the Essequibo and the large islands of Wakenaam, Tiger Island, and Leguan.

Swank: Lemonade made from fresh lines or bitter lemons sweetened and pepped with vanilla or other essences.

Takouba: Old driftwood or submerged dead tree stumps and wood in the earth or in the waterways.

Tania: A root vegetable like dasheen.

Tapir: A wild game animal in the forests of Guyana, often referred to as "bush cow," but looks nothing like a cow and more like a huge oddly shaped pig.

Tibiciri: A long vine that climbs on the tall forest trees. It is harvested and prepared to make rattan-type furniture by skilled users.

Toshao: A tribal chieftain or captain at a reservation.

Trench: A drainage or irrigation canal.

Troolie: A palm whose fronds are very valuable for thatching roofs of houses and cabins.

Troupe: A card game very similar to whist.

Turu: The fruit of a palm tree also called by that name. There is a hard, large stone under a thin edible layer in this round bland tasting fruit.

Vlissengen Road: A key road in the Vlissengen area of Georgetown close to the Bourda Cricket Ground.

Vreedenhoop: A township at the mouth of the Demerara River on its west bank across the river from Georgetown, the capital.

Waini: One of the larger rivers in Guyana in the northwest at the head of which many gold and diamond seekers explore.

Wakapao: A tributary of the Pomeroon River and another of the First Nations reserves on this river.

Waramuri: An Anglican First Nations mission near the mouth of the Moruka River.

Warrao: A First Nations tribe found in the northwestern areas of Guyana. A large settlement of them reside in the Orinico Delta.

Whizz, Phensic: Commonly used medications in tablet form for pains and fevers.

www.ingramcontent.com/pod-product-compliance
Lightning Source LLC
Chambersburg PA
CBHW020442130626
46549CB00001B/262